Authors, Texts, Issues : Essays on Indian Literature

Authors, Texts, Issues : Essays on Indian Literature

Edwin Hudson

CYBER TECH PUBLICATIONS
4264/3, Ansari Road, Daryaganj, New Delhi-110002 (India)
Ph.: 011-23244078. Fax: 011-23280028
E-Mail: cyberpublicationsdelhi@yahoo.com

Authors, Texts, Issues : Essays on Indian Literature
Edwin Hudson

First Edition 2009

Published by :

G.S. Rawat for **Cyber Tech Publications**
4264/3, Ansari Road, Daryaganj, New Delhi-110002 (India)
Ph.: 011-23244078. Fax: 011-23280028
E-Mail: cyberpublicationsdelhi@yahoo.com

Printed at : **Asian Offset Printers**

Preface

As religion receded from politics and democratic capitalism developed, the West provided opportunities for the poor and temptations to the exploiter, thus making the American experiment a realistic testing ground for democracy. A chapter in history began to unfold, a chapter characterized by such materials as inspire myth-makers. Both marvelous and terrible, the development of the West came to be symbolized in the American mind by pioneering, Indian wars and cattle drives, by the talismanic figure of the cowboy a merging of Hispanic and Anglo traditions by the heroic yet shameful railroad story, by miners, farmers, and loggers.

The importance of western literature as a part of our national literature, however, has not been established. With professors and readers of history, the frontier has always been a respected topic. With professors and readers of literature, to mention frontier stories is to evoke automatic thoughts of popular stereotypes.

The contributing authors of have avoided the polemical trap of a special pleading and concentrated on presenting and analyzing their assigned topics. Yet one of the major underlying purposes of A Literary History is, by demonstration rather than defensiveness, to support the ongoing introduction of western literary riches to readers interested in American literature, culture, and history.

Admittedly, as always, there are problems in the court of literary evaluation. Those who study the literature of the India tend to believe there is an entrenched prejudice in favor of minor novels and mediocre poems written amidst the cultural prestige of India.

The undersigned is confident enough that this work of him would prove its worth and will be most informative to the readers.

—Author

CONTENTS

1

Cross-Cultural Essays on Anglo, American Indian Literature

ADVERTISEMENT

As the title suggests, the text is divided into three sections with a brief introduction to each section. The first and third sections have connections to the Southwest. The second section seems, therefore, out of "place" in that the Native American writers Gish chooses to discuss are not from the Southwest. His book would be more cohesive, and more useful to teachers, if he had discussed Leslie Marmon Silko or some other American Indian writers from that area. As is, his readers cross boundaries which may be political popular but which leave them feeling disoriented and puzzled by Gish's choices. He does tell us that "Earlier versions of some of these essays have appeared previously" in various listed publications; however, he does not give us dates of publication or specific journals for each essay.

Apparently, this text is loosely organized on the boundary theme because Gish is revising and republishing articles in book form and using the crossing boundaries metaphor to rationalize the disparate sections. This reader wishes he had spent more time on arguing and analyzing the rationalization; as is, the argument is weak and appears to be superficial.

In spite of these criticisms, interesting ideas appear in these essays.

"Part One: Anglo Visitors" is intriguing because the Anglo writers discussed--Charles F. Lummis, Erna Fergusson, Harvey Fergusson, and Witter Bynner--are often neglected and even unknown to many. This section will be of interest to teachers who want to bring into their classrooms views of the Southwest and its peoples by Anglos who visited or came to live there from the late nineteenth century to the mid-twentieth century. Gish is often forgiving of their cultural misreadings or what many would term "racist" views and allows them to speak often in their own voices so that we can understand their loving responses to the beauty of the land they encountered. He is particularly effective in defending these writers against the indictment of easterners such as Stanley Walker in the 1954 New Yorker and in convincing us that Walker's envisioning of these writers as victims of a landscape who end up with a style he calls "`New Mexico baroque'" is erroneous and unfair.

In "Part Two: Indian Voices," Gish presents essays on the works of Blackfeet/Gros Ventre poet and novelist James Welch and on the poet Ray A. Young Bear. The author's discussion of Welch's novels mentions numerous interpretations in passing, but with little documentation of where they came from.

If this text is to be valuable to generalists like himself, Gish owes us references to the many publications on Welch's texts. As is, his readings of Welch's novels are confusing. However, one area that is original and cogent is his reference to the names and possible genealogies of many of Welch's characters and their connections to Welch's own family history. Also, the most effective essay in the entire book is his comparison of James Welch's Indian Lawyer and the film Dances with Wolves which exposes the superficial elements of the film in contrast to the complex issues facing contemporary Native Americans found in Welch's novel.

Gish's claims for Chicano/a literature in "Part Three: Chicano Vistas" are extremely broad:

> *For Chicano vistas are the vistas not just of the U.S. and Mexico, but of North and South American and of all Spanish-speaking cultures, their settlement and their diaspora, literatures written in Spanish and English and indigenous and mestizo literatures.*

This passage is just one example of Gish's too general introduction that promises the reader much more than the specific analysis produces. Gish moves from this very broad introduction to concentrate with insight on two authors from New Mexico, Rudolfo A. Anaya and Jimmy Santiago Baca. The middle ground is missing.

"La Llorona, Magic Realism, And The Frontier" is more interesting and enlightening when it shows us how the various legends of this sometimes good, often evil, woman have influenced Chicano literature and popular culture than in revealing anything about magic realism or the frontier. Witchery, so prevalent in many Native American cultures of the Southwest not mentioned here, is explored in the fiction of Anaya. Also, in Gish's view, the mythic land of Aztlan in Chicano literature and history gives us a new view of the American West on a north / south axis rather than on the more traditional Anglo east/west view. Gish's essay, including analyses of Anaya's and Baca's works, is more cogently about the appearance of this magical place in the literature than proof of any new history theory. This entire section is most valuable in delineating how the myths and folklore beliefs inform Chicano literature and enrich the mythology and literature of the United States. To place too broad an interpretation on this valuable information and analysis is unnecessary and weakens Gish's argument.

There is no conclusion to bring these three sections together, to discuss the boundaries crossed in these essays. Also, while there are notes to each section, a bibliography for each section would be useful to scholars and teachers. The strength of this book is in the specific insights, often not sufficiently pursued, rather than in the too broad generalizations. Readers need more middle ground between the boundaries.

INDIAN WOMEN WRITERS

The Vedas cry aloud, the Puranas shout;

"No good may come to a woman." I was born with a woman's body How am I to attain truth? "They are foolish, seductive, deceptive - Any connection with a woman is disastrous." Bahina says, "If a woman's body is so harmful, How in the world will I reach truth?" [Bahinabai (1682-1700)]

Much of the world's literature has been dominated by a canon that nearly dismissed women's writing more than two centuries ago. The counter-canons that have emerged as the result of this exclusion have helped to establish women's writing in mainstream culture, but still in some ways fail to acknowledge women's literature coming from non-white countries. This essay is an attempt to highlight some of the works produced by women in India over the ages.

Although India has a history of ancient civilisations such as the Harappa and Mohenjodaro, and of matrilineal societies in the south, no written records of women's literary prowess exists predating the 6th century BC. The emergence of the first body of poetry by women in India could be attributed to the advent of Buddhism. Perhaps it was the freedom offered by the religion, the way of life it offered to women, and the principle of equality that it propagated which allowed women to pen their thoughts for the first time.

Buddhism offered women the opportunity to break away from the restrictions of home life, a major factor in the rise of Indian women's literature in the early 6th century BC. The earliest known anthology of women's literature in India has been identified as those belonging to the Therigatha nuns, the poets being contemporaries of the Buddha. One of these, Mutta, writes, So free am I, so gloriously free, free from three petty things - from mortar, from pestle and from my twisted lord.

Mutta's works, translated from Pali, offer an explanation through their interpretation. Religious escapism was the only way out for many women who were frustrated with a life inside the home. They chose to join the Buddhist sangha (religious communities) in their attempts to break away from the social world of tradition and marriage. Thus emerged poems and songs about what it meant to be free from household chores and sexual slavery.

Although the early forms of writing addressed the issue of personal freedom, the poetry that followed later was a celebration of womanhood and sexuality. The Sangam poets that dominated the era between ca. 100 BC-AD 250 wrote extensively about what it meant to have a female body. The translation of Venmanipputi Kuruntokai's 'What she said to her girlfriend' reads,

On the banks shaded by a punnai clustered with flowers, when we made love my eyes saw him and my ears heard him; my arms grow beautiful in the coupling and grow lean as they come away.

The content of the poem is bold for its time because it is expressing a woman's pleasure in sex. The poems written around this age echo a sense of sexual liberation.

S. S. Kalpana says that the 'commentaries that accompany these poems mention songs women used to sing while transplanting seedlings, drawing water and husking paddy.' Women apparently sang to keep vigil on the ripening grain and to ward off spirits. These songs took the form of poetry when written down.

According to A. K. Ramanujan, who translated most of the poems of the Sangam age, disparities in gender are evident in the way women have written about their experiences. Some of the poems echo the need for bodily love and passion, the foolishness of war and the 'spears' that men left with to wage wars. The ten anthologies and eight long poems of the Sangam age are the oldest and most prominent body of secular poetry extant in India. According to S. S. Kalpana, the absence of mythological references and Sanskrit words suggests the possibility that they were written before the Aryan take-over of northern India. This was also the time when the University of Nalanda was set up (c.a. 100 BC), which opened its doors on an equal basis to women. Most of the university records have been lost, but one can assume that the women scholars contributed to the expanding body of literature

Among the poets who wrote in the 12th century AD came the medieval Kannada poet, rebel and mystic, Akkamahadevi, whose life and writing challenged the patriarchal dominance of the world at large. She is supposed to have wandered naked in search of divinity.

The spread of Buddhism and the rapid acceptance of Islam forced Hinduism to rethink the caste system. As Hinduism underwent a revision of spirituality and basked in the new-found outlook of the Bhakti movement, so did the men and women associated with the religion. This is evident in Akkamahadevi's writing as she uses the image of her body to defy her critics when she says,

Brother, you've come drawn by the beauty of these billowing breasts, this brimming youth. I am no woman brother, no whore.

As a radical mystic it is no surprise that she uses the image of her genitals to convey her understanding of the Bhakti tradition and the Hindu idea of rebirth when she says,

Not one, not two, not three or four, but through eight four hundred thousand vaginas have I come. I have come through unlikely worlds guzzled on pleasure and pain.

Another poet of the Bhakti tradition was Sule Sankavva, who according to Vijaya Dabbe wrote poetry that could startle contemporary sensibility with its combination of the sacrosanct and the sacrilegious. Writing as a prostitute, her sentiments about the duplicity of society at large are strongly echoed in her only surviving poem, in which she says,

In my harlot's trade having taken one man's money, I daren't accept a second man's, sir. And if I do, they'll stand me naked and kill me, sir.

The poetry which followed a century later reflected the economic hardships of most women. It was still in the tradition of the earlier poets who used religion and god, and the discriminatory alignment of the oppressive caste system that worked against them, to define their writing.

Among the women who wrote was Janabai, the Varkari saint poet of the low caste Sudra community of Maharashtra, who in defence of her lower-caste status lowered the position of god to that of a fellow sweeper who aids her when she is tired and doesn't mind shovelling dirt for her. The same trend was observed with other lower-caste women who wrote to criticise the Hindu caste system which the Bhakti tradition had failed to eliminate.

This was also the period in India's history that witnessed invasion and gradual settlement by the Persian Empire. The rise of Islam, not only as a religion but also as the framework of the Mughal dynasty that ruled India for almost three centuries thereafter, brought a new set of experiences and influences to women's literature in India. Muslim women had to be literate to comply with the requirements of the Holy Koran which made it mandatory for every Muslim, male or female to pray.

Women made use of this rule of the religion to write about themselves and their experiences. One of the earliest to write was Princess Gul-Badan Begum who in 1587 completed the Humayun Nama which details the life and history of one of India's most powerful Mughal kings. She wrote so 'beautifully' in Persian that when translated into

English in 1898, her translator Annette Beveridge described it as the first novel-biography ever written by an Indian woman.

In ca. 1730, Muddupalini, a courtesan in the kingdom of the Nayaka kings of Tanjavur in the south of India, was born. Since the rulers of the Nayaka dynasty were scholars and poets, lovers of music and literature and patrons of the arts, they granted extensive patronage to women educated in the art of dance and music. There were other distinguished women poets and scholars in their courts who were recipients of this patronage. One of them, Ramabhadramba, writes about women in the Tanjavur courts who composed poetry in eight languages.

Maddhupalini's Radhika Santwanam consisted of five hundred and eighty four poems about the relationship between Krishna and Radha. In an unusual third section, Krishna complains that Radha insists on making love even though he doesn't want to. According to K. Lalita, no other Telgu poet, man or woman, has written about a woman taking the initiative in a sexual relationship. Her compositions created a stir in the literary world when they were published almost two centuries later. The erotic poems in her most reputed work, Radhika Santwanam, stunned even the most liberal of readers and critics.

Traditionally the only women who had access to scholarships and the arts of literature and dancing were courtesans. Their status in society was of high standing, and because of the wealth they accumulated due to patronage, their property endowed them with the ability to choose their lovers and friends.

Another courtesan who was raised within the Asaf Jahi Sultanate in the Mughal Empire was Mahlaqa Bai Chanda, who received an 'elaborate education and composed beautifully as a court poet and songwriter. Her poetry was collected and published after her death in 1824 as Gulzar-e-Mahlaqa (Mahlaqa's garden of flowers). According to Afeefa

Banu most of her poems are composed in the Ghazal form which originated in Iran.

Around the 18th century, however, a combination of factors led to the decline of women writing in India. The East India Company, established in 1600, whose initial purpose had been to trade, gradually took over as rulers and thereafter the British government established its rule in India. As a result of princes and kings losing their kingdoms, and being restricted by a small privy purse, there was loss of patronage to women in courts. Since these were women with education, the association of educated woman with 'bad' women became common. This led to the loss of education for women and the production of women's literature almost came to a standstill.

The trend of educating women began again in the late 19th century with the rise of the reformist movement in India which saw more women's participation in rebelling against British rule. This led to a new stage in the development of women's literature in India. The body of work produced was often related to the freedom struggle and the reform and nationalist movements. Although there were still women such as Bhabani and Jogeswari whose writings in the early 19th century questioned the patriarchal dominance of their husbands, the majority concentrated on the freedom struggle.

The earliest woman writing during the reformist period was Savitribai Phule, who along with her husband championed the cause of women's education. She was the first woman teacher in modern Maharashtra and together with her husband started the first school for girls. Her writing carries the mark of an activist and scholar who wholeheartedly believed in the cause of the untouchables.

Among the women writers who followed was Pandita Ramabai Saraswati who was educated both in English and in Sanskrit. In her The high caste Hindu woman she argues against the patriarchal reading of the Hindu scriptures and early scholarly works of learned Brahmins which encouraged a repressive and demeaning interpretation favouring the suppression of women.

Sarojini Naidu, dubbed the nightingale of India, published her first set of poems at the age of sixteen and went to England where she was educated at King's College in London, and later at Cambridge. Her writings as an activist and as the governor of Uttar Pradesh reflect her honest and heartfelt concerns about the situation of her country.

Towards the mid-nineteenth century more and more women began to write in English. Some of them, such as Rokeya Sakhawat Hossain, created a world of feminist ideologies. In Sultana's Dream she talks about a world dominated by women; a world which has imprisoned men in a male equivalent of zenanas (women's quarters). She creates a world that is much better than the one men managed. In her woman's world, there are no wars and there is constant scientific progress and love for the environment.

Women's writing in the 20th century moved towards a medium of modernism in which womanist and feminist statements were combined with political messages. The writings of women such as Hamsa Wadkar conveyed an honest impression of a world of professional women whose careers in television and stage segregated them as a class apart, yet subjected them to the same brutality and force of patriarchy. In her autobiography, Hamsa Wadkar talks about her life as an actor from the age of eleven, her marriage to a suspicious and abusive husband, the birth of a daughter, her life after eloping with another man, the imprisonment she faced at his home along with two of his other wives, and her rape by a justice of peace.

Women writers such as Mahashwetadevi combined women's causes with political movements. In Draupadi Mahashwetadevi creates a world of tribal rebels whose fight against a political system of enforced capitalism has driven them to become Naxalites (supporters of a Chinese-style Communism). Others such as Sashi Deshpande build a platform of universal female experiences. In Binding Vines she examines the experiences of women coming from different echelons of society.

Over the years and throughout the political instability which affected Indian society at large, along with a myriad of other influences which have affected culture, language and social patterns, women's literature in India has evolved to show common experiences, a sense of sisterhood and a range of female experiences that question the recurring face of patriarchy.

THE ARYAN INVASION: THEORIES, COUNTER-THEORIES AND HISTORICAL SIGNIFICANCE

The Aryan Invasion theory was first propounded when linguistic similarities between Sanskrit and the major European languages were discovered by European scholars during the colonial era. In an atmosphere of raging eurocentricism, it was inevitable that any explanation of this seemingly inexplicable discovery would taken on racial and ideological overtones.

Colonial Expositions of the Aryan Invasion Theory

British intellectuals were particularly nonplussed by this apparent link between the languages of the conquerors and the conquered. In the earliest phases of British rule in India, the East India Company proceeded largely unconsciously - without moral dilemmas and without overt recourse to ideological or racial superiority. But as the rule of the East India Company expanded, and battles became more hard fought and the resistance to British occupation in India grew, the ideology of European racial superiority became almost essential in justifying British presence in India - not only to assuage British conscience, but also to convince the Indian people that the British were not mere colonial conquerors but a superior race on a noble civilizational mission.

After 1857, the British education system in India had been deliberately designed to assist in the development of a narrow but influential class of deeply indoctrinated and predominantly loyal agents of British colonial rule in India. British elaborations of the Aryan invasion theory became powerful and convenient ideological tools in generating legitimacy for British rule. In it's most classical and colonially tinged incarnation, it portrayed the Aryans as a highly advanced and culturally superior race in the ancient world, locating their original home in Northern Europe. It then went on to suggest that some time in antiquity, the Aryans migrated from their original home in Europe and brought with them their language and their superior culture and transcendental philosophy to civilize the primitive and materially backward Dravidian people of the subcontinent. All the greatness of Indian civilization was ascribed to the Aryans, thus implying that if India were to ever achieve greatness again, a return to Aryan rule was imperative.

And by claiming a cultural continuity between this noble race of ancient times and themselves, the British could become inheritors of the grand Aryan tradition and assert their "legitimate" civilizational right to rule over the people of the subcontinent - not to exploit them, but so as to "reinvigorate" Indian civilization by reintroducing Aryan rule that had been disfigured and corrupted by the violent and barbaric incursions of the Muslims. Preposterous and distorted as it was, this absurdly racist proposition was made palatable to a self-doubting and repressed class of upper-caste Hindus who were told that they were descendants of the Aryans, and could identify with the manifold and globally encompassing achievements of the Aryan people by accepting British authority so as to participate in this great Aryan renaissance in India.

The theory gained rapid currency amongst upper-caste Hindus who had legitimate gripes against the Muslim nobility for having been denied equal access to power in the Muslim courts, but were too enfeebled to put up a fight on their own, and were too alienated from the mass of artisans and peasants to join in popular rebellions against the feudal dispensation. The British rulers offered the opportunity of gaining petty privileges in exchange for acquiescence to colonial rule, and the Aryan invasion theory provided the ideological justification for betraying the rest of ones nation. By placing the ancestral home of the Aryans far off in Northern Europe, the British were putting the idea in the heads of such upper-caste Hindus that they were far removed from the Indian masses and had no good reason to identify with them.

Wittingly or unwittingly, the Aryan invasion theory thus became the emotional bait for a section of the Indian population who were to aid and abet the colonial project in India. Although some of these Indians ultimately did develop national feelings, and forged a national identity that eventually came into conflict with the continuation of colonial rule, the theory continued to play an important role in confusing the psyche of the post-independence Indian intelligentsia.

Since the Aryan invasion belongs to a period of considerable antiquity, and there is little physical evidence to support any authoritative conclusion, theories affirming (or opposing) the invasion hypothesis can vary from being wildly speculative at worst, to being reasonably plausible at best. Even the most diligent and objective of historians can at best come up with informed conjectures, leaving open the possibility for uncertainty, and ideologically-driven diversionary postulations. The absence of concrete data and the ambiguity involved in interpreting surviving texts from the Aryan period makes the task of combating history-writing that has been colored by colonially influenced analysis doubly difficult.

Nevertheless, it is possible to construct the contours of what may be more plausible, and at least eliminate what is obviously fiction or fantasy.

Arguments for and against the Invasion Theory

Opponents of the invasion theory make a somewhat plausible case that the sacrificial rites and rituals described in some of the Vedic texts bear a resemblance to practices that may have been common during the Harappan period. The similiarity of Harappan and Vedic altars is indeed intriguing. This would bolster the argument that Brahmins of the Vedic age emerged from the Harappan priesthood, and not from any Aryan invasion. But a link between the Harappan priesthood and Vedic Brahminism does not preclude the possibility of an invasion or foreign migration. It is not inconceivable that the Vedic Brahmin developed as a composite of the Harappan priest and the priest of an invading (or migrating) tribe or clan. Animal sacrifices were common amongst many tribes in that age - and it is not entirely implausible that some kind of synthesis may have taken place.

Philological Analysis

Proponents of an invasion (or migration) theory feel quite strongly that the Indo-European linguistic commonality cannot be explained in any other way, and cite philological studies that appear to bolster their case.

However, opponents of the invasion theory argue that the structural commonality of the Indo-European group of languages could have been achieved without an Aryan invasion. They observe that the Harappan civilization had extensive trade and commercial ties with Babylon as well as with civilizations to the further West. There is a remarkable similarity in seals and cultural artifacts found in Harappan India, Babylon and even the early civilizations of the Mediterranean such as Crete. Hence, they argue that a linguistic commonality may have developed quite early through trade and cultural contacts and that this common linguistic structure may have subsequently moved from South to North. Since Mediterranean Europe and the Middle

Eastern civilizations developed well before the civilizations of Northern Europe, such a possibility is not altogether inconceivable.

But such a hypothesis does not preclude the possibility that invading or migrating clans may have also introduced non-Indian words into the existing Indian languages - leading to a composite language stream that incorporated both Indo-European and indigenous features. (Urdu is an example of a language that was introduced as a result of a series of invasions, adding a large body of foreign words while maintaining the syntactical structure and vocabulary base of the previous language.)

Since much of the Indo-European linguistic commonality appears to correspond to the basic vocabulary of a pastoral nomadic population, intrusions by patriarchal warrior clans from Central Asia cannot be ruled out. Authors such as Gimbutas (The Civilization of the Goddess, the World of Old Europe) present a reasonably convincing model of how the older matriarchal order in Europe was gradually broken down by migrants/conquerors who spoke a language that might account for certain common elements of the Indo-European group of languages. Although it would be inappropriate to mechanically apply the same conclusions to India, the linguistic and philological arguments are hard to ignore.

It must nevertheless be noted that there are both similarities and differences amongst the various Indo-European languages, and often, historians (and philologists) tend to downplay (or ignore) the contributions of the Adivasi and Tamil language streams in the development of the Indic languages. Philological analysis of the Indian languages points to both Indo-European links, as well as to a considerable degree of independent development. Moreover, just as South Indian languages have absorbed Sanskrit words, North Indian languages have also absorbed words from Tamil and languages related to it.

Another criticism of the inasion theory lies in the interpretation of the word "Arya" to mean race, nationality or even linguistic group. Critics suggest that the word Arya as used in the Rig Veda and other texts is better translated as one who was noble in character (or noble in deed) or perhaps hailing from a noble background. Hence, to use the term "Aryan" to describe the racial or national characteristics of an invading clan or clans would naturally be erroneous. Thus, if an invasion did take place, and if the invaders identified themselves as "Aryans", it would merely reflect their claim to noble status, and would not reflect upon their national or racial origin.

On the other hand, historians favoring the invasion theory have based many of their arguments on postulates connecting the introduction of the horse and chariot in India to invading (or migrating) "Aryans".

They also point to the balladic character of some of the verses in the Rig Veda with references to armed cattle raids and warriors on horse-driven chariots who appear to portray a race or a group of clans of pastoral nomadic warriors. The imagery fits particularly well with artifacts found in Babylon and Ancient Persia (and other regions near the Caspian Sea) that depict warriors riding on horse-driven chariots. Other literary evidence from the Rig Veda also appears to connect the authors of these Rig Veda verses to the "Aryan" identified civilization of ancient Persia.

On the other hand, there is no tangible evidence of warrior clans in the numerous urban settlements that comprise the Harappan civilization. There are also few references to pastoral nomadism or cattle raids. The Harappans appear to have been a relatively urbanized people and based their existence on what seems to be primarily settled agriculture. The character of such verses in the Rig Veda texts does not fit well with a people who designed vast granaries, roads, urban bungalows, and for their time a highly sophisticated drainage system. And while there is evidence to suggest that the Harappans had a priestly class, there is almost no evidence of standing armies.

There is evidence of a local police force but there is little to suggest that the police forces were as well armed or proficient in the use of archery as were the warrior tribes that find mention in the Rig Veda. Unlike the contemporaneous civilizations of Babylon and old Persia, where the institution of monarchy may have been already established, requiring the existence of standing armies and warrior clans to support the monarchy, the Harappan civilization seems to have been largely republican in character, with a much weaker and smaller police force to ensure stability. Based on a survey of surviving physical artifacts, it is possible to surmise that priests may have played a greater role in ensuring the legitimacy of the Harappan state, whereas the warriors may have begun to play a more powerful role in the civilizations of the Middle East and Central Asia.

It is therefore, not unlikely that the introduction of monarchy and standing armies (and the introduction of the Kshatriya caste and the subsequent institutionalization of the caste system) may have come about, at least indirectly, as a consequence of an invasion or conquest. Another argument favoring some kind of an invasion is the evidence for Aryan-like invasions of other settled civilizations such as in Greece, and other parts of the Near East and Europe, and references in the Manusmriti to ruling clans who were clearly of non-Indian origin. Considering how frequently the subcontinent has faced invasions from the North West, an "Aryan" identifying invasion would not be entirely out of character with the experience of the subcontinent. As to the physical origins of these possible invaders, it is very hard to be definitive - but in all likelihood, their origins could not have been too far from the Caspian region.

Some verses in the Rig Veda paint a picture of a people who were familiar with settled agriculture, but whose economic life was dominated by animal husbandry, and who had been exposed to a large body of water such as the Caspian Sea. Geographically, parts of Persia fit quite well with such a description as might other regions bordering on the Caspian or located in the geographical vicinity of the Caspian. These regions offered rather limited possibilities for settled agriculture and shepherding played an important role in the semi-urban civilizations that emerged around the Caspian basin.

The Aryan identifying warrior clans could have been a branch of the ruling warrior clans of early Persia, or else they may have originated in Central Asia or Southern Russia with a civilization that closely resembled the civilization of the old Persians. While some of the verses in the Rig Veda point to a Persian connection, other verses suggest that while these warrior tribes who came to India followed practices that closely resembled those of the Persians, they may not have originated in Persia. The close similarities between names for various kinship ties and familial relationships in India and Russia appears to place these Aryan identifying clans or tribes on the northern side of the Caspian. An explanation that reconciles this apparently conflicting evidence is that there was not a single invasion but a series of intrusions (or migrations) by different Aryan identifying clans - some of whom collaborated with each other while others saw each other as rivals or enemies.

Examples from more recent history might also offer us some clues of what may have occurred. Just as India was confronted by a series of invasions by Islamic rulers from different parts of the Middle East and Central Asia, it is not implausible that several Aryan identifying tribes or clans developed certain common cultural features that spanned Persia, Central Asia and the South Caucasus region and then spread South East towards India, (and also North and West into greater Russia, Europe and the Mediterranean). Of course, it is possible and likely that upon their entry into

India, they also borrowed from the settled agriculture civilizations of India who may have been culturally more advanced in many ways.

Alternatively, the invaders of the Rig-Vedic period may have been like the Rajputs or Gujjars, entering India as warrior clans, conquering territories in India, but adopting the culture of India albeit with certain modifications, and enjoining their balladeers to introduce into the Rig Veda, verses that glorified their conquests, and expressed their particular world view. This would not be too dissimiliar from how the Rajputs and other ruling dynasties had local court chroniclers invent fictional noble lineages to create an impression of continuity.

LINKS BETWEEN HARAPPAN AND VEDIC CIVILIZATION

However, it should be noted that regardless of the geographical origin of such invaders, it is almost certain that the ruling clans of the Gangetic plain included both locals and invaders (or migrants). Later texts (such as the Manusmriti) describe a large number of ruling clans (of varied national origin, including Dravidian origin) as being "Aryan" i.e. of noble descent. Hence, it would be incorrect to argue that the ruling clans of the Vedic period were exclusively made up of "invading Aryans".

There is also compelling circumstantial evidence linking the settlers of the Gangetic plain to earlier Harappan settlements. For instance, emerging geological evidence pointing to ancient river systems drying up and changing course, and the excavation of numerous settlements along the banks of these ancient river systems (such as the Saraswati basin that ran in parallel to the Indus) lends credence to the argument that the settlers of the Gangetic plain must have been predominantly domestic migrants.

Finds of Shatranj (chess) pieces, dice and terracotta animal and goddess figurines also point to connections between Harappan and later civilizations. It is also quite remarkable how the ornamentation of some temples in Rajasthan and Western Madhya Pradesh appears to derive from some of the excavated jewelry from Harappan sites in Northern India.

Some scholars also see a continuity between the Sulva Sutras and the Harappan civilization which owing to it's material advance must have very likely developed a level of arithmetic and ritual and abstract philosophy concomitant with it's achievements in urban planning and agricultural management. The evidence for decimal weights and measures in the Harappan civilization, and the later perfection of a decimal numeral system in India lends further substance to such claims.

RELEVANCE OF THE ARYANS

All this suggests that there is a much greater degree of continuity in Indian civilization than previously realized, and further examination of the Indian historical record will demonstrate that the numerous developments in philosophy and culture that have taken place in India cannot be attributed to "Aryan" invaders. In fact, the main significance of the invasion theory lies not in the determination of whether such an invasion took place or not, but rather in how much of a debt Indian civilization might owe to such an invasion.

For instance, prior to the series of Islamic invasions, and long after the Aryan period of Indian history, there have been numerous other invasions that had an impact on the subcontinent. Yet it is only the "Aryan" invasion that attracts popular and scholarly attention. This is primarily because of the importance ascribed to the "Aryan" invasion by British colonial historians. Before the invention of the "exalted" Aryan by British ideologues, references to the Aryans in the Rig Veda were not treated with any particular importance, and few Indians had any conscious memory of an "Aryan" warrior past. This is not surprising, because the legacy of such invading warrior tribes or clans to Indian civilization is not especially significant.

Prior to any "Aryan" invasion, India already had a relatively advanced settled-agriculture based urban civilization. And within a few centuries after their possible introduction in India, the Aryan-identified gods described in the Rig Veda ceased to be worshipped and gradually faded from Indian consciousness. Brahmin gotra (clan) names mentioned in the Rig Veda also lost their import and the vast majority of Brahmin gotra (clan) names that came into common use could not have had any "Aryan"-invasion connection. As Kosambi convincingly points out in his Introduction to Indian History, many of India's Brahmins rose from 'Hinduised' tribes that earlier practised animism or totem worship, or prayed to various fertility gods (and/ or goddesses), or revered fertility symbols such as the linga (phallus) or the yoni (vagina). A majority of these Hinduised tribes retained many elements of their older forms of worship, and several Brahmin gotra (clan) names are derived from pre-Aryan clan totems and other tribal associations.

For instance, one of the most popular gods in the Indian pantheon - Shiva - appears to have no connection with any Aryan invasion, and may in fact have it's prototype in the fertility god of the Harappans. Similiarly, Hanuman, Ganesh, Kali, or Maharashtra's Vithoba - none could have any Aryan connection, since they don't even find any mention in the Rig Veda. Whether in matters of popular religion or in matters of high philosophy, there is little contribution of note that can be traced directly to an "Aryan invasion".

UNIQUELY INDIAN ASPECTS OF VEDIC LITERATURE

It is important to note that much of the Vedic literature - both in the style and substance of it's verses, appears to be uniquely Indian, and it is not impossible that at least some of the verses may have Harappan origin. Many of the philosophical themes that are explored and developed in the

Vedic literature have insightful naturalist references that are consistent with Indian geography. In addition, there are certain philosophical aspects of the Vedic literature that don't appear to be replicated in quite the same way in any other civilization that was contemporaneous to the Vedic civilization.

The best of the Vedic Shlokas refer to a common life-spirit that links all living creatures, to human social-interconnectedness, to the notion of unity in diversity and how different sections of society might have different prayers and different wishes. Whereas some verses point to god as being a source for wish-fulfillment, in other verses, there are doubts and queries about the nature of god, whether a god really exists, and whether such questions can every be really answered. These aspects of Vedic thought were elaborated upon by later schools of Indian philosophy, and recur frequently in Indian literature and philosophy.

While some of India's rational schools developed in parallel with the Vedas, and are included as appendices to the Vedic texts, others developed practically independently of the Vedas, or even in opposition - as polemics to the Vedas (such as those of the Jains and the Buddhists). The Upanishads, the Sankhya, and the Nyaya-Vaisheshika schools, the numerous treatises on medicine, ethics, scientific method, logic and mathematics clearly developed on Indian soil as a result of Indian experiences and intellectual efforts.

India's great surviving temples and Stupas with their rich carvings and sculpture were all created with aesthetic principles and formulations that developed centuries after any invading or migrating "Aryans" would have completely melted into Indian society. And though it is possible that these foreign "Aryans" may have introduced certain technological innovations and inventions (possibly in the realm of metallurgy, metal tools or carpentry, and may have thus facilitated the spread of settled agricultural civilizations along the Gangetic plain), knowledge of textile production, tool-making, and metallurgy was already available to the Harappans.

The grammar of Sanskrit and its highly systematized alphabet also had little to do with any "Aryan" invasion. Sanskrit is a highly structured and methodical language, optimized for engaging in rational debates and expressing mathematical formulas. And its skillfully organized alphabet bears little resemblance to the rather random and arbitrary alphabet of its European "cousins". Much of its vocabulary and syntax developed long after any supposed invasion, and although the structure of the South Indian languages may differ from those of the North in some respects, the majority of India's languages (both Northern and Southern) share a large base of a common Sanskrit-derived vocabulary. In addition, what is especially significant is how the North Indian scripts share so much in common with the scripts of Southern India.

The phonetic organization of consonants and vowels, phonetic spelling, and the many other commonalities that bind all of India's syllabic scripts weakens the entire linguistic premise of the Aryan invasion theory. In fact, when it comes to scripts, consonant and vowel sounds, all Indian languages are closely related, and their closest relatives are to be found in South East Asia, Ethiopia (and even Korea and Mongolia to some degree) but not in Europe.

It is thus curious, to say the least, when Indian civilization is described as synonymous with an imported "Aryan" civilization - and the self-esteem of so many Indians is tied up with trying to disprove the Aryan invasion theory. Other than perhaps accelerate the demise of republicanism in India, and possibly hasten the spread of settled agriculture along the Northern plains, there appears to be few other tangible and long-lasting effects that could be ascribed to an "Aryan" invasion.

Not only is it unclear as to how much any invading or migrant "Aryan" clan may have introduced into the Vedic literature; Vedic civilization itself is only a subset of Hindu civilization.

While the Aryans of the Vedas may be credited with laying the foundations of "Hindu" civilization in the Gangetic plain, the essence of Hindu civilization emerged gradually, taking several centuries to crystallize. Undergoing both internal reform and fusion with pre-existing tribal and matriarchal cultures, the Hinduism of both the rulers and the masses kept evolving. Even as it retained certain philosophical elements from Vedic literature, it also broadened and in some ways diverged completely from the Vedas.

Beyond the Northern (Yamuna/Gangetic) plains, the influence of Aryan-identified Vedic civilization was generally more limited. Vedic influences on the civilizations in Bengal, Assam and Orissa were initially almost minimal, and these Eastern civilizations largely followed their own (and somewhat unique trajectories), as did the civilizations of South India - absorbing Vedic philosophical concepts gradually and only partially.

Throughout India, Buddhism and Jainism also found converts, and in Kashmir, the North West, and in the East - Buddhism had a particularly profound influence, while in Western India (such as in Rajasthan, Gujarat, Western Madhya Pradesh and Karnataka) Jainism was very influential. In Jharkhand, Chhatisgarh, West Bengal and Orissa, Tantric influences were important.

In essence, Indian civilization whether Hindu, Buddhist or Jain, or any other, developed primarily from the unique (and varied) conditions of Indian geography and the human exertion that went into modifying those conditions to advance agriculture and settled civilization. Taken in the general context of say three or four thousand years of Indian history, it is hard to ascribe to an "Aryan" invasion/s the sort of paramountcy assigned by the British. While British motives in magnifying the "Aryan" character of Indian civilization are only too apparent, this contemporary obsession with the "Aryan" question that appears to have gripped large sections of the Indian intelligentsia suggests that the ideological confusion created by the British has not yet been fully sorted out.

One consequence of this is that the debate on the Aryan question has been highly contentious, with historians adopting strident and extreme positions, not seeing that there can be both continuities and discontinuities in the development of Indian civilization. It has also diverted many of India's historians from equally (or more) important tasks - such as describing and integrating those periods of Indian history where considerable new archeological material is now available and needs to be incorporated into the presently known and documented view of Indian history.

Key aspects of Indian history remain poorly researched and documented. Many Sanskrit and vernacular texts have not been studied and assimilated by English speaking historians. Regional variations in Indian history have not been studied enough. A deeper understanding of some of the lesser known kingdoms all across India is required to correct false generalizations about Indian history. Much more effort is required in understanding social movements, gender and caste equations.

Simplifications and generalizations based on antiquated documents like the Manusmriti (which was mainly resurrected by British historians) provide a very incomplete and distorted picture of actual social relations and practice in India. The Manusmriti also offers little in terms of understanding local and regional peculiarities in matters of social relations.

Considerable work is also required in unifying haphazard and scattered studies in the area of India's economic history and the history of philosophy, science, technology and manufacturing. It is also important that the vast body of work that has been published since independence in English be translated into the nation's many languages and regional dialects. It is tragic that so much of the best research done in Indian history is available only to English speakers. These are just some of the tasks that need greater attention from the community of Indian historians.

Intriguing as the Aryan-origin debate may be, it is in the end only one facet of Indian history, and merits further attention only if historians and archeologists can offer fresh and new insights on this subject and relate them to the broad dynamics of Indian civilization.

2

ENGLISH LITERATURE

The term English literature refers to literature written in the English language, including literature composed in English by writers not necessarily from England; Joseph Conrad was Polish, Robert Burns was Scottish, James Joyce was Irish, Edgar Allan Poe was American, Salman Rushdie is Indian. In other words English literature is as diverse as the varieties of English spoken around the world. In academia, the term often labels departments and programmes practicing English studies.

MIDDLE AGES

Because the Celtic and Roman heritage was almost entirely erased by the invasion of low German and then Scandinavian populations it is only in the early middle ages that appear the first works of English, written in the Anglo-Saxon dialect now called Old English (the oldest surviving text is Cædmon's Hymn). The oral tradition was very strong in early British culture and most literary works were written to be performed. Epic poems were thus very popular and many, including Beowulf, have survived to the present day in the rich corpus of Anglo-Saxon literature.

These are languages that closely resemble today's Norwegian or, better yet, Icelandic, though much Anglo-Saxon verse in the extant manuscripts is probably a "milder" adaptation of the earlier Viking and German war poems from the continent. When such poetry was brought to England it was still being handed down orally from one generation to another, and the constant presence of alliterative verse, or consonant rhyme (today's newspaper headlines and marketing abundantly uses this technique such as in Big is Better) helped the Anglo-Saxon peoples remember it.

Such rhyme is a feature of Germanic languages and is opposed to vocalic or end-rhyme of Romance languages. But the first written literature dates to the early Christian monasteries founded by St. Augustine of Canterbury and his disciples and it is reasonable to believe that it was somehow adapted to suit to needs of Christian readers. Even without their crudest lines, Viking war poems still smell of blood feuds and their consonant rhymes sound like the smashing of swords under the gloomy northern sky: there is always a sense of imminent danger in the narratives. Sooner or later, all things must come to an end, as Beowulf eventually dies at the hands of the huge monster he spends his life fighting. The feelings of Beowulf that nothing lasts, that youth and joy will turn to death and sorrow entered Christianism and were to dominate the future landscape of English fiction. The "ubi sunt" theme is, for example, recurrent in Hamlet ("Alas, poor Yorick"), not to mention much Jacobean poetry.

With the exception of the relatively light-hearted and optimistic Restoration and the Augustan Age, melancholia and angst remain a favorite theme with English-speaking writers, through the Gothic novel and Pre-romanticism to the birth of modern romantic sensibility. When William the Conqueror makes England a part of the Anglo-Norman realm in 1066 bringing Norman, Old English poetry continues to be read and its language widely spoken. It was not until the early 13th century when Albion becomes independent and severs its relations to France that the language really changes.

As the Normans are assimilated into mainstream culture, their French penetrates the lower orders of society changing much of the grammar and lexicon of Old English. Though it does not become a Romance language, Chaucer's English is much closer to present-day English than the language that people spoke a century before. The average English-speaker cannot read Chaucer (Middle English) without difficulty but can nonetheless grasp the gist of the story, while he needs to read Beowulf in modern English -- in translation.

In the late medieval period (1200-1500), the ideals of courtly love entered England and authors began to write romances, either in verse or prose. Especially popular were tales of King Arthur and his court. The poem Sir Gawain and the Green Knight shows many of the key features of literature at this time: a setting in the legendary time of King Arthur, an emphasis on chivalry and knightly behavior, and religious overtones.

English drama at this time was overtly religious. Mystery plays were enacted in cities and towns to celebrate major holidays, and the less formal mummers plays also conveyed Christian themes.

England's first great author, Geoffrey Chaucer (1340 - 1400), wrote in Middle English. His most famous work is The Canterbury Tales, a collection of stories in a variety of genres, ostensibly told by a group of pilgrims on their way to Canterbury. Remarkably, they are from all walks of life, which is reflected as much in the language they use as in the content of their stories. But, though Chaucer is most certainly an English author, he was inspired by literary developments taking place elsewhere in Europe, especially in Italy. Chaucer's The Canterbury Tales are quite indebted to Giovanni Boccaccio's Decameron. The Renaissance was making its way to Britain.

EARLY MODERN (RENAISSANCE)

Following the introduction of a printing press into England by William Caxton in 1476, vernacular literature flourished. The Reformation inspired the production of vernacular liturgy which led to the Book of Common Prayer, a lasting influence on literary English language. The poetry, drama, and prose produced under both Queen Elizabeth I and King James I constitute what is today labelled as Early modern (or Renaissance). This literature is noted for its interest in the human being as a worthy subject (due in large part to the importation of humanism from Italy). Unlike the literature of Medieval England, which was almost entirely religious in nature, Early modern literature offered readers a more secular literature; though it should be noted, Early modern literature does appear overtly religious in many ways when compared with modern secularism.

ELIZABETHAN LITERATURE

The Elizabethan era saw a great flourishing of literature, especially in the field of drama. The Italian Renaissance had rediscovered the ancient Greek and Roman theatre, which was then beginning to evolve apart from the old mystery and miracle plays of the middle ages. The Italians were particularly inspired by Seneca (a major tragic playwright and philosopher, the tutor of Nero) and Plautus (its comic clichés, especially that of the boasting soldier had a powerful influence on the Renaissance and after). However, the Italian tragedies embraced a principle contrary to Seneca's ethics: showing blood and violence on the stage. In Seneca's plays such scenes were only acted by the characters. But the English playwrights were intrigued by Italian model: a conspicuous community of Italian actors had settled in London and Giovanni Florio had brought much of the Italian language and culture to England.

It is also true that the Elizabethan Era was a very violent age and that the high incidence of political assassinations in Renaissance Italy (embodied by Niccolò Machiavelli's The Prince) did little to calm fears of popish plots. As a result, representing that kind of violence on the stage was probably more cathartic for the Elizabethan spectator. Following earlier Elizabethan plays such as

Gorboduc by Sackville & Norton and The Spanish Tragedy by Kyd that was to provide much material for Hamlet, William Shakespeare stands out in this period as a poet and playwright as yet unsurpassed. Shakespeare was not a man of letters by profession, and probably had only some grammar school education. He was neither a lawyer, nor an aristocrat as the "university wits" that had monopolised the English stage when he started writing.

But he was very gifted and incredibly versatile, and he surpassed "professionals" as Greene who mocked this "shake-scene" of low origins. Though most dramas met with great success, it is in his later years (marked by the early reign of James I) that he wrote what have been considered his greatest plays: Hamlet, King Lear, Macbeth, All's Well That Ends Well, Antony and Cleopatra. To this list of works belonging to the later period, we must add The Tempest, a tragicomedy that inscribes within the main drama a brilliant pageant to the new king.

This 'play within a play' takes the form of a masque, an interlude with music and dance colored by the novel special effects of the new indoor theaters. Critics have shown that this masterpiece, which can be considered a dramatic work in its own right, was written for James's court, if not for the monarch himself. The magic arts of Prospero, on which depend the outcome of the plot, hint at the fine relationship between art and nature in poetry. Significantly for those times (the arrival of the first colonists in America), The Tempest is (though not apparently) set on a Bermudan island, as research on the Bemuda Pamphlets (1609) has shown, linking Shakespeare to the Virginia Company itself. The "News from the New World", as Frank Kermode points out, were already out and Shakespeare's interest in this respect is remarkable. Shakespeare also popularized the English sonnet which made significant changes to Petrarch's model.

The sonnet was introduced into English by Thomas Wyatt in the early 16th century. Poems intended for to be set to music as songs, such as by Thomas Campion, became popular as printed literature was disseminated more widely in households. See English Madrigal School. Other important figures in Elizabethan theatre include Christopher Marlowe, Thomas Dekker, John Fletcher and Francis Beaumont. Had Marlowe (1564-1593) not been stabbed at twenty-nine in a tavern brawl, says Anthony Burgess, he might have rivalled, if not equalled Shakespeare himself for his poetic gifts.

Remarkably, he was born only a few weeks before Shakespeare and must have known him well. Marlowe's subject matter, though, is different: it focuses more on the moral drama of the renaissance man than any other thing. Marlowe was fascinated and terrified by the new frontiers opened by modern science. Drawing on German lore, he introduced Dr. Faustus to England, a scientist and magician who is obsessed by the thirst of knowledge and the desire to push man's technological power to its limits. He acquires supernatural gifts that even allow him to go back in time and wed Helen of Troy, but at the end of his twenty-four years' covenant with the devil he has to surrender his soul to him. His dark heroes may have something of Marlowe himself, whose untimely death remains a mystery.

He was known for being an atheist, leading a lawless life, keeping many mistresses, consorting with ruffians: living the 'high life' of London's underworld. But many suspect that this might have been a cover-up for his activities as a secret agent for Elizabeth I, hinting that the 'accidental stabbing' might have been a premeditated assassination by the enemies of The Crown. Beaumont and Fletcher are less-known, but it is almost sure that they helped Shakespeare write some of his best dramas, and were quite popular at the time. It is also at this time that the city comedy genre develops. In the later 16th century English poetry was characterised by elaboration of language and extensive allusion to classical myths. The most important poets of this era include Edmund Spenser and Sir Philip Sidney.

JACOBEAN LITERATURE

After Shakespeare's death, the poet and dramatist Ben Jonson was the leading literary figure of the Jacobean era. However, Jonson's aesthetics harks back to the middle ages rather than to the Tudor Era: his characters embody the theory of humors. According to this contemporary medical theory, and behavioral differences result from a prevalence of one of the body's four "humors" (blood, phlegm, black bile, and yellow bile) over the other three; these humors correspond with the four elements of the universe, air, water, fire, and earth. This leads Jonson to exemplify such differences to the point of creating types, or clichés, while Shakespeare had already abandoned such theory in favor of modern psychology. But Jonson is a master of style, and a brilliant satirist. His Volpone shows how a group of scammers are fooled by a top con-artist, vice being punished by vice, virtue meeting its reward.

Others who followed Jonson's style include Beaumont and Fletcher, who, though not as talented as Shakespeare, wrote nonetheless a brilliant comedy, The Knight of the Burning Pestle, a mockery of the rising middle class and especially of those nouveau riches who pretend to dictate literary taste without knowing much literature at all. In the story, a couple of grocers wrangle with professional actors to have their illiterate son play a leading role in a drama. He becomes a knight-errant wearing, appropriately, a burning pestle on his shield. Seeking to win a princess's heart, the young man is ridiculed much in the way Don Quixote was, although Don Quixote had not yet been written. One of Beaumont and Fletcher's chief merits was that of realising how feudalism and chivalry had turned into snobbery and make-believe and that new social classes were on the rise.

Another popular style of theatre during Jacobean times was the revenge play, popularized by John Webster and Thomas Kyd. George Chapman wrote a couple of subtle revenge tragedies, but must be remembered chiefly on account of his famous translation of Homer, one that had a profound influence on all future English literature, even inspiring John Keats to write some of his great poetry.

The King James Bible, one of the most massive translation projects in the history of English up to this time, was started in 1604 and completed in 1611. It represents the culmination of a tradition of Bible translation into English that began with the work of William Tyndale. It became the standard Bible of the Church of England, and some consider it one of the greatest literary works of all time. This project was headed by James I himself, who supervised the work of forty-seven scholars. Although many other translations into English have been made, some of which are widely considered more accurate, many aesthetically prefer the King James Bible, whose meter is made to mimic the original Hebrew verse.

Besides Shakespeare, whose figure towers the early 1600s, the major poets of the early 17th century included John Donne and the other Metaphysical poets. Influenced by continental Baroque, and taking as his subject matter both Christian mysticism and eroticism, metaphysical poetry uses unconventional or "unpoetic" figures, such as a compass or a mosquito, to reach surprise effects. For example, in one of Donne's Songs and Sonnets, the points of a compass represent two lovers, the woman who is home, waiting, being the center, the farther point being her lover sailing away from her. But the larger the distance, the more the hands of the compass lean to each other: separation makes love grow fonder. The paradox or the oxymoron is a constant in this poetry whose fears and anxieties also speak of a world of spiritual certainties shaken by the modern discoveries of geography and science, one that is no longer the center of the universe. Apart from the metaphysical poetry of Donne, the 17th century is also celebrated for its Baroque poetry. Baroque poetry served the same ends as the art of the period; the Baroque style is lofty, sweeping, epic, and religious.

Many of these poets have an overtly Catholic sensibility (namely Richard Crashaw) and wrote poetry for the Catholic counter-Reformation in-order to establish a feeling of supremacy and mysticism that would ideally persuade newly emerging Protestant groups back toward Catholicism.

CAROLINE AND CROMWELLIAN LITERATURE

The turbulent years of the mid-17th century, during the reign of Charles I and the subsequent Commonwealth and Protectorate, saw a flourishing of political literature in English. Pamphlets written by sympathisers of every faction in the English civil war ran from vicious personal attacks and polemics, through many forms of propaganda, to high-minded schemes aiming to reform the nation. Of the latter type Leviathan by Thomas Hobbes would prove to be one of the most important works of British political philosophy. Hobbes' writings are some of the only political works from the era which are still regularly published whilst John Bramhall, who was Hobbes' chief critic, is mostly forgotten.

The period also saw a flourishing of news books, the precursors to the British newspaper, with journalists such as Henry Muddiman, Marchamont Needham, John Birkenhead representing the views and activities of the contending parties. The frequent arrests of authors and the suppression of their works, with the consequence of foreign or underground printing, led to the idea of licensing being proposed. The Areopagitica, a political pamphlet by John Milton, was written in opposition to licensing and is regarded as one of the most eloquent defences of press freedom ever written.

Other forms of literature written during this period are usually ascribed political subtexts or their authors' are grouped along political lines. The cavalier poets, active mainly before the civil war, owed much to the earlier school of metaphysical poets. The forced retirement of royalist officials after the execution of Charles I was a good thing in the case of Izaak Walton as it gave him time to work on his book The Compleat Angler. Published in 1653 the book, ostensibly a guide to fishing, is much more; being a meditation on life, leisure and contentment. The two most important poets of Oliver Cromwell's England were Andrew Marvell and John Milton with both producing works praising the new government; such as Marvell's An Horatian Ode upon Cromwell's Return from Ireland. Despite their republican beliefs they escaped punishment upon the Restoration of Charles II after which Milton wrote some of his greatest poetical works with any possible political message hidden under allegory. Thomas Browne was another writer of the period; a learned man with an extensive library, he wrote prolifically on science, religion, medicine and the esoteric.

RESTORATION LITERATURE

Restoration literature includes both Paradise Lost and the Earl of Rochester's Sodom, the high spirited sexual comedy of The Country Wife and the moral wisdom of Pilgrim's Progress. It saw Locke's Treatises on Government, the founding of the Royal Society, the experiments of Robert Boyle and the holy meditations of Boyle, the hysterical attacks on theaters from Jeremy Collier, the pioneering of literary criticism from Dryden, and the first newspapers. The official break in literary culture caused by censorship and radically moralist standards under Cromwell's Puritan regime created a gap in literary tradition, allowing a seemingly fresh start for all forms of literature after the Restoration. During the Interregnum, the royalist forces attached to the court of Charles I went into exile with the twenty-year old Charles II. The nobility who travelled with Charles II were therefore lodged for over a decade in the midst of the continent's literary scene. Charles spent his time attending plays in France, and he developed a taste for Spanish plays. Those nobles living in Holland began to learn about mercantile exchange as well as the tolerant, rationalist prose debates that circulated in that officially tolerant nation.

The largest and most important poetic form of the era was satire. In general, publication of satire was done anonymously. There were great dangers in being associated with a satire. On the one hand, defamation law was a wide net, and it was difficult for a satirist to avoid prosecution if he were proven to have written a piece that seemed to criticize a noble. On the other hand, wealthy individuals would respond to satire as often as not by having the suspected poet physically attacked by ruffians. John Dryden was set upon for being merely suspected of having written the Satire on Mankind. A consequence of this anonymity is that a great many poems, some of them of merit, are unpublished and largely unknown.

Prose in the Restoration period is dominated by Christian religious writing, but the Restoration also saw the beginnings of two genres that would dominate later periods: fiction and journalism. Religious writing often strayed into political and economic writing, just as political and economic writing implied or directly addressed religion. Thomas Sprat wrote his History of the Royal Society in 1667 and set forth, in a single document, the goals of empirical science ever after. The Restoration was also the time when John Locke wrote many of his philosophical works. Locke's empiricism was an attempt at understanding the basis of human understanding itself and thereby devising a proper manner for making sound decisions. These same scientific methods led Locke to his three Treatises on Government, which later inspired the thinkers in the American Revolution.

As with his work on understanding, Locke moves from the most basic units of society toward the more elaborate, and, like Thomas Hobbes, he emphasizes the plastic nature of the social contract. For an age that had seen absolute monarchy overthrown, democracy attempted, democracy corrupted, and limited monarchy restored, only a flexible basis for government could be satisfying. The Restoration moderated most of the more strident sectarian writing, but radicalism persisted after the Restoration. Puritan authors such as John Milton were forced to retire from public life or adapt, and those Digger, Fifth Monarchist, Leveller, Quaker, and Anabaptist authors who had preached against monarchy and who had participated directly in the regicide of Charles I were partially suppressed. Consequently, violent writings were forced underground, and many of those who had served in the Interregnum attenuated their positions in the Restoration. John Bunyan stands out beyond other religious authors of the period.

Bunyan's The Pilgrim's Progress is an allegory of personal salvation and a guide to the Christian life. Instead of any focus on eschatology or divine retribution, Bunyan instead writes about how the individual saint can prevail against the temptations of mind and body that threaten damnation. The book is written in a straightforward narrative and shows influence from both drama and biography, and yet it also shows an awareness of the grand allegorical tradition found in Edmund Spenser. During the Restoration period, the most common manner of getting news would have been a broadsheet publication. A single, large sheet of paper might have a written, usually partisan, account of an event. However, the period saw the beginnings of the first professional and periodical (meaning that the publication was regular) journalism in England. Journalism develops late, generally around the time of William of Orange's claiming the throne in 1689. Coincidentally or by design, England began to have newspapers just when William came to court from Amsterdam, where there were already newspapers being published.

It is impossible to satisfactorily date the beginning of the novel in English. However, long fiction and fictional biographies began to distinguish themselves from other forms in England during the Restoration period. An existing tradition of Romance fiction in France and Spain was popular in England. The "Romance" was considered a feminine form, and women were taxed with reading "novels" as a vice. One of the most significant figures in the rise of the novel in the Restoration period is Aphra Behn. She was not only the first professional female novelist, but she may be among the first professional novelists of either sex in England. Behn's most famous novel was Oroonoko in 1688. This was a biography of an entirely fictional African king who had been enslaved in Suriname. Behn's novels show the influence of tragedy and her experiences as a dramatist.

As soon as the previous Puritan regime's ban on public stage representations was lifted, the drama recreated itself quickly and abundantly. The most famous plays of the early Restoration period are the unsentimental or "hard" comedies of John Dryden, William Wycherley, and George Etherege, which reflect the atmosphere at Court, and celebrate an aristocratic macho lifestyle of unremitting sexual intrigue and conquest. After a sharp drop in both quality and quantity in the 1680s, the mid-90s saw a brief second flowering of the drama, especially comedy. Comedies like William Congreve's Love For Love (1695) and The Way of the World (1700), and John Vanbrugh's The Relapse (1696) and The Provoked Wife (1697) were "softer" and more middle-class in ethos, very different from the aristocratic extravaganza twenty years earlier, and aimed at a wider audience. The playwrights of the 1690s set out to appeal to more socially mixed audiences with a strong middle-class element, and to female spectators, for instance by moving the war between the sexes from the arena of intrigue into that of marriage. The focus in comedy is less on young lovers outwitting the older generation, more on marital relations after the wedding bells.

Diarists John Evelyn and Samuel Pepys depicted everyday London life and the cultural scene of the times.

AUGUSTAN LITERATURE

The term Augustan literature derives from authors of the 1720's and 1730's themselves, who responded to a term that George I of England preferred for himself. While George I meant the title to reflect his might, they instead saw in it a reflection of Ancient Rome's transition from rough and ready literature to highly political and highly polished literature. Because of the aptness of the metaphor, the period from 1689 - 1750 was called "the Augustan Age" by critics throughout the 18th century (including Voltaire and Oliver Goldsmith). The literature of the period is overtly political and thoroughly aware of critical dictates for literature. It is an age of exuberance and scandal, of enormous energy and inventiveness and outrage, that reflected an era when English, Scottish, and Irish people found themselves in the midst of an expanding economy, lowering barriers to education, and the stirrings of the Industrial Revolution.

The most outstanding poet of the age is Alexander Pope, but Pope's excellence is partially in his constant battle with other poets, and his serene, seemingly neo-Classical approach to poetry is in competition with highly idiosyncratic verse and strong competition from such poets as Ambrose Philips. It was during this time`that James Thomson produced his melancholy The Seasons and Edward Young wrote Night Thoughts. It is also the era that saw a serious competition over the proper model for the pastoral. In criticism, poets struggled with a doctrine of decorum, of matching proper words with proper sense and of achieving a diction that matched the gravity of a subject. At the same time, the mock-heroic was at its zenith. Pope's Rape of the Lock and The Dunciad are still the greatest mock-heroic poems ever written.

In prose, the earlier part of the period was overshadowed by the development of the English essay. Joseph Addison and Richard Steele's The Spectator established the form of the British periodical essay, inventing the pose of the detached observer of human life who can meditate upon the world without advocating any specific changes in it. However, this was also the time when the English novel, first emerging in the Restoration, developed into a major artform. Daniel Defoe turned from journalism and writing criminal lives for the press to writing fictional criminal lives with Roxana and Moll Flanders. He also wrote a fictional treatment of the travels of Alexander Selkirk called Robinson Crusoe (1719). The novel would benefit indirectly from a tragedy of the stage, and in mid-century many more authors would begin to write novels.

If Addison and Steele overawed one type of prose, then Jonathan Swift did another. Swift's prose style is unmannered and direct, with a clarity that few contemporaries matched. He was a profound skeptic about the modern world, but he was similarly profoundly distrustful of nostalgia. He saw in history a record of lies and vanity, and he saw in the present a madness of vanity and lies. Core Christian values were essential, but these values had to be muscular and assertive and developed by constant rejection of the games of confidence men and their gullies. Swift's A Tale of a Tub announced his skeptical analysis of the claims of the modern world, and his later prose works, such as his war with Patridge the astrologer, and most of all his derision of pride in Gulliver's Travels left only the individual in constant fear and humility safe. After his "exile" to Ireland, Swift reluctantly began defending the Irish people from the predations of colonialism. His A Modest Proposal and the Drapier Letters provoked riots and arrests, but Swift, who had no love of Irish Roman Catholics, was outraged by the abuses and barbarity he saw around him.

Drama in the early part of the period featured the last plays of John Vanbrugh and William Congreve, both of whom carried on the Restoration comedy with some alterations. However, the majority of stagings were of lower farces and much more serious and domestic tragedies. George Lillo and Richard Steele both produced highly moral forms of tragedy, where the characters and the concerns of the characters were wholly middle class or working class. This reflected a marked change in the audience for plays, as royal patronage was no longer the important part of theatrical success.

Additionally, Colley Cibber and John Rich began to battle each other for greater and greater spectacles to present on stage. The figure of Harlequin was introduced, and pantomime theater began to be staged. This "low" comedy was quite popular, and the plays became tertiary to the staging. Opera also began to be popular in England, and there was significant literary resistance to this Italian incursion. This trend was broken only by a few attempts at a new type of comedy. Pope and John Arbuthnot and John Gay attempted a play entitled Three Hours After Marriage that failed. In 1728, however, John Gay returned to the playhouse with The Beggar's Opera. Gay's opera was in English and retold the story of Jack Sheppard and Jonathan Wild. However, it seemed to be an allegory for Robert Walpole and the directors of the South Sea Company, and so Gay's follow up opera was banned without performance. In 1737, 18th century drama almost ends, for that was the year of the Licensing Act. At that point, there was official state censorship of all plays.

An effect of the Licensing Act was to cause more than one aspiring playwright to switch over to writing novels. Henry Fielding began to write prose satire and novels after his plays could not pass the censors. Henry Brooke also turned to novels. In the interim, Samuel Richardson had produced a novel intended to counter the deleterious effects of novels in Pamela, or Virtue Rewarded (1749).

Henry Fielding attacked the absurdity of this novel with Shamela, and then countered Richardson's Clarissa with Tom Jones. Brooke wrote The Man of Feeling and indirectly began the sentimental novel. Laurence Sterne attempted a Swiftian novel with an unique perspective on the impossibility of biography (the model for most novels up to that point) and understanding with Tristram Shandy, even as his detractor Tobias Smollett elevated the picaresque novel with his works.

Each of these novels represents a formal and thematic divergence from the others. Each novelist was in dialog and competition with the others, and, in a sense, the novel established itself as a diverse and open-formed genre in this explosion of creativity. The most lasting effects of the experimentation would be the psychological realism of Richardson, the bemused narrative voice of Fielding, and the sentimentality of Brooke.

18th Century During the Age of Sensibility, literature reflected the worldview of the Age of Enlightenment (or Age of Reason) - a rational and scientific approach to religious, social, political, and economic issues that promoted a secular view of the world and a general sense of progress and perfectibility. Led by the philosophers who were inspired by the discoveries of the previous century (Newton) and the writings of Descartes, Locke and Bacon. They sought to discover and to act upon universally valid principles governing humanity, nature, and society. They variously attacked spiritual and scientific authority, dogmatism, intolerance, censorship, and economic and social restraints. They considered the state the proper and rational instrument of progress. The extreme rationalism and skepticism of the age led naturally to deism; the same qualities played a part in bringing the later reaction of romanticism.

The Encyclopédie of Denis Diderot epitomized the spirit of the age.

Increased emphasis on instinct and feeling, rather than judgment and restraint. A growing sympathy for the Middle Ages during the Age of Sensibility sparked an interest in medieval ballads and folk literature.

ROMANTICISM

The changing landscape of the England brought about by the steam engine has two major outcomes: the boom of industrialism with the expansion of the city, and the consequent depopulation of the countryside as a result of the enclosures, or privatisation of pastures. Most peasants poured into the city to work in the new factories.

This abrupt change is revealed by the change of meaning in five key words: industry (once meaning "creativity"), democracy (once disparagingly used as "mob-rule"), class (from now also used with a social connotation), art (once just meaning "craft"), culture (once only belonging to farming).

But the poor condition of workers, the new class-conflicts and the pollution of the environment causes a reaction to urbanism and industrialisation prompting poets to rediscover the beauty and value of nature. Mother earth is seen as the only source of wisdom, the only solution to the ugliness caused by machines.

The superiority of nature and instinct over civilisation had been preached by Jean Jacques Rousseau and his message was picked by almost all European poets. The first in England were the Lake Poets, a small group of friends including William Wordsworth and Samuel Taylor Coleridge. These early Romantic Poets brought a new emotionalism and introspection, and their emergence is marked by the first romantic Manifesto in English literature, the "Preface to the Lyrical Ballads". This collection was mostly contributed by Wordsworth, although Coleridge must be credited for his long and impressive Rime of the Ancient Mariner, a tragic ballad about the survival of one sailor through a series of supernatural events on his voyage through the south seas which involves the slaying of an albatross, the death of the rest of the crew, a visit from Death and his mate, Life-in-Death, and the eventual redemption of the Mariner at the price of a geas which periodically forces him to tell his tale.

Coleridge and Wordsworth, however, understood romanticism in two entirely different ways: while Coleridge sought to make the supernatural "real" (much like sci-fi movies use special effects to make unlikely plots believable), Wordsworth sought to stir the imagination of readers through his down-to-earth characters taken from real life (for eg. in

"The Idiot Boy"), or the beauty of the Lake District that largely inspired his production (as in "Lines Composed a Few Miles Above Tintern Abbey").

The "Second generation" of Romantic Poets includes Lord Byron, Percy Bysshe Shelley, Mary Shelley and John Keats. Byron, however, was still influenced by 18th-century satirists and was, perhaps the least 'romantic' of the three. His amours with a number of prominent but married ladies was also a way to voice his dissent on the hypocrisy of a high society that was only apparently religious but in fact largely libertine, the same that had derided him for being physically impaired. His first trip to Europe resulted in the first two cantos of Childe Harold's Pilgrimage, a mock-heroic epic of a young man's adventures in Europe but also a sharp satire against English society. Despite Childe Harold's success on his return to England, accompanied by the publication of The Giaour and The Corsair his alleged incestuous affair with his half-sister Augusta Leigh in 1816 actually forced him to leave England for good and seek asylum on the continent. Here he joined Percy Bysshe Shelley, his wife Mary, with his secretary John Polidori on the shores of Lake Geneva in 1816.

Although his is just a short story, Polidori must be credited for introducing The Vampyre to English literature. Percy, like Mary, had much in common with Byron: he was an aristocrat from a famous and ancient family, had embraced atheism and free-thinking and, like him, was fleeing from scandal in England.

Shelley had been expelled from college for openly declaring his atheism, and from England for supporting Irish independence. He had married a 16-year-old girl, Harriet Westbrook whom he had abandoned soon after for Mary (Harriet took her own life after that). Harriet did not embrace his ideals of free love and anarchism, and was not as educated as to contribute to literary debate. Mary was different: the daughter of philosopher and revolutionary William Godwin, she shared his ideals, was a poetess, and a feminist like her late mother, Mary Wollstonecraft.

Shelley's best work was the Ode to the West Wind. Despite his apparent refusal to believe in God, this poem is considered a homage to pantheism, the recognition of a spiritual presence in nature.

Mary Shelley did not go down in history for her poetry, but for giving birth to science fiction: the plot for the novel is said to have come from a nightmare during a stormy night on the lake Geneva. Her idea of making a body with human parts stolen from different corpses and then animating it with electricity was perhaps influenced by Alessandro Volta's invention and Luigi Galvani's experiments with dead frogs. Frankenstein's chilling tale also suggests modern organ transplants, tissue regeneration, reminding us of the moral issues raised by today's medicine. But the creature of Frankenstein is incredibly romantic as well. Although "the monster" is intelligent, good and loving, he is shunned by everyone because of his ugliness and deformity and the desperation that results from social exclusion turns him into a killing machine that eventually murders his own maker.

Probably John Keats does not share Byron's and Shelley's extremely revolutionary ideals, but his cult of pantheism is as important as Shelley's. Keats was in love with the ancient stones of the Parthenon that Lord Elgin had brought to England from Greece, also known as the Elgin Marbles). He celebrates ancient Greece: the beauty of free, youthful love couples here with that of classical art. Keats's great attention to art, especially in his Ode on a Grecian Urn is quite new in romanticism, and it will inspire Walter Pater's and then Oscar Wilde's belief in the absolute value of art as independent from aesthetics.

Jane Austen wrote novels about the life of the landed gentry, seen from a woman's point of view, and wryly focused on practical social issues, especially marriage and money.

VICTORIAN LITERATURE

It was in the Victorian era (1837-1901) that the novel became the leading form of literature in English. Most writers were now more concerned to meet the tastes of a large middle class reading public than to please aristocratic patrons. The best known works of the era include the emotionally powerful works of the Brontë sisters; the satire Vanity Fair by William Makepeace Thackeray; the realist novels of George Eliot; and Anthony Trollope's insightful portrayals of the lives of the landowning and professional classes.

Charles Dickens emerged on the literary scene in the 1830s, confirming the trend for serial publication. Dickens wrote vividly about London life and the struggles of the poor, but in a good-humoured fashion which was acceptable to readers of all classes. His early works such as the Pickwick Papers are masterpieces of comedy. Later his works became darker, without losing his genius for caricature.

An interest in rural matters and the changing social and economic situation of the countryside may be seen in the novels of Thomas Hardy and others.

Leading poetic figures of the Victorian era included Alfred Tennyson, Robert Browning and his wife, Elizabeth Barrett Browning.

Literature for children was published during the Victorian period, some of which has become globally well-known, such as the work of Lewis Carroll who was a proponent of nonsense verse, as was Edward Lear.

EDWARDIAN LITERATURE

The most widely popular writer of the early years of the 20th century was arguably Rudyard Kipling, a highly versatile writer of novels, short stories and poems, often based on his experiences of British ruled India. Kipling was closely associated with imperialism and this has damaged his reputation in more recent times.

GEORGIAN LITERATURE

The Georgian poets maintained a conservative approach to poetry.

The experiences of the First World War were reflected in the work of war poets such as Rupert Brooke, Isaac Rosenberg, Edmund Blunden, Wilfred Owen and Siegfried Sassoon. Many writers turned away from patriotic and imperialist themes as a result of the war, notably Kipling.

John Buchan pioneered a new type of fiction, the spy novel and achieved great popularity during and after the First World War.

MODERNISM

The movement known as English literary modernism grew out of a general sense of disillusionment with Victorian era attitudes of certainty, conservatism, and objective truth. The movement was greatly influenced by the ideas of Romanticism, Karl Marx's political writings, and the psychoanalytic theories of Sigmund Freud. The continental art movements of Impressionism, and later Cubism, were also important inspirations for modernist writers.

Although literary modernism reached its peak between the First and Second World Wars, the earliest examples of the movement's attitudes appeared in the mid to late nineteenth century. Gerard Manley Hopkins, A. E. Housman, and the poet and novelist Thomas Hardy represented a few of the major early modernists writing in England during the Victorian period.

The first decades of the twentieth century saw several major works of modernism works published, including the seminal short story collection Dubliners by James Joyce, Joseph Conrad's Heart of Darkness, Henry James' The Portrait of a Lady, and the poetry and drama of William Butler Yeats.

Important novelists between the World Wars included Virginia Woolf, E. M. Forster, Evelyn Waugh, D. H. Lawrence and T. S. Eliot, the preeminent English poet of the period. Across the Atlantic writers like William Faulkner, Ernest Hemingway, and the poets Wallace Stevens and Robert Frost developed a more American take on the modernist aesthetic in their work.

Perhaps the single most important figure in the development of the modernist movement was the American poet Ezra Pound. Credited with "discovering" both T. S. Eliot and James Joyce, whose stream of consciousness novel Ulysses is considered to be one of the century's greatest literary achievements, Pound also advanced the cause of imagism and free verse, forms which would dominate English poetry into the twenty-first century.

Other notable writers of the period included W. H. Auden, Vladimir Nabokov, William Carlos Williams, Ralph Ellison, Dylan Thomas, and H. D.. However, some of these writers are more closely associated with what has become known as post-modernism, a term often used to encompass the diverse range of writers who succeeded the modernists.

3

POST MODERN LITERATURE

Postmodern literature arose after World War II as a series of reactions against the perceived norms of modernist literature.

MODERNISM AND COMPARISONS WITH POSTMODERNISM

Both modern and postmodern literature represent a break from 19th century realism, in which a story was told from an objective or omniscient point of view. In character development, both modern and postmodern literature explore subjectivism, turning from external reality to examine inner states of consciousness, in many cases drawing on modernist examples in the stream of consciousness styles of Virginia Woolf and James Joyce. In addition, both modern and postmodern literature explore fragmentariness in narrative- and character-construction, reflective of the works of Swedish dramatist August Strindberg and the Italian author Luigi Pirandello.

Unlike postmodern literature, however, modernist literature saw fragmentation and extreme subjectivity as an existential crisis or a Freudian internal conflict. In postmodern literature this crisis is avoided. The tortured, isolated anti-heroes of, say, Knut Hamsun or Samuel Beckett, and the nightmare world of T. S. Eliot's The Waste Land, make way in postmodern writing for the self-consciously deconstructed and self-reflexive narrators of novels by

Vladimir Nabokov, Vladimir Sorokin, John Fowles, John Barth, or Julian Barnes.

SHIFT TO POSTMODERNISM

As with all stylistic eras, no definite dates exist for the rise and fall of postmodernism's popularity. 1941, the year Irish novelist James Joyce and British novelist Virginia Woolf both died, is sometimes used as a rough boundary for postmodernism's start.

Another common divide is the end of the second world war, which saw a critical assessment of human rights in the wake of the Atomic bombings of Hiroshima and Nagasaki, The Holocaust, and Japanese American internment. It also coincides with the beginning of the Cold War, the American Civil Rights Movement (1955-1968) and the beginning of movements which worked towards: (a) the end of Colonialism, (b) the Partition of India, (c) the 1947 UN Partition Plan, and (d) the development of Postcolonial literature. Finally, it reflects the influence of the computer which garnered new importance during thc war. During this time, computers became integrated within postmodern fiction often referred to as Cyberpunk. Indeed, the book Postmodern American Fiction: A Norton Anthology, in section VI, "Technoculture" discusses cyberpunk as a form of postmodern literature:

"Neal Stephenson's Snow Crash (1992) is an exemplar of 'cyberpunk' science fiction...while cyberpunk represents a fast-forward vision of the present, contemporary science fiction is also the site for a peculiarly postmodern technological retrospection. William Gibson's...1984 cyberpunk novel Neuromancer is widely regarded as one of the most influential futuristic visions in American literary history" (page 510).

CRITICISM

Literature of this era does not set itself against modern literature as much as it develops and extends the style, making it self-conscious and ironic. In such literature, one finds a shift in the role of the "inner narrative of the self," from the self at war with itself to the self as arbiter, pointing to the phenomenological roots of postmodern thought. Authors such as David Foster Wallace, Don DeLillo, and Thomas Pynchon in Gravity's Rainbow satirise the paranoid system-building of the kind associated, by postmodernists, with Enlightenment modernity.

Dubbed maximalism by some critics, the sprawling canvas and fragmented narrative of such writers as Dave Eggers has generated controversy on the "purpose" of a novel as narrative and the standards by which it should be judged. The postmodern position is that the style of a novel must be appropriate to that which it depicts and represents, and points back to such examples in previous ages as Gargantua by François Rabelais and the Odyssey of Homer, which Nancy Felson-Rubin hails as the exemplar of the polytropic audience and its engagement with a work.

Many modernist critics attack the maximalist novel as being disorganized, sterile and filled with language play for its own sake, empty of emotional comittment-and therefore empty of value as a novel. Yet there are counter-examples, such as Pynchon's Mason & Dixon, or James Chapman's Stet, where postmodern narrative coexists with emotional commitment.

Indian English Literature (IEL) refers to the body of work by writers in India who write in the English language and whose native or co-native language could be one of the numerous languages of India. It is also associated with the works of members of the Indian diaspora, especially people like Salman Rushdie who was born in India. As a category, this production comes under the broader realm of postcolonial literature- the production from previously colonised countries such as India.

IEL has a relatively recent history, it is only one and a half centuries old. The first book written by an Indian in English was by Sake Dean Mahomet, titled Travels of Dean

Mahomet; Mahomet's travel narrative was published in 1793 in England. In its early stages it was influenced by the Western art form of the novel. Early Indian writers used English unadulterated by Indian words to convey an experience which was essentially Indian. Raja Rao's Kanthapura is Indian in terms of its storytelling qualities. Rabindranath Tagore wrote in Bengali and English and was responsible for the translations of his own work into English. Nirad C. Chaudhuri, a writer of non-fiction, is best known for his The Autobiography of an Unknown Indian where he relates his life experiences and influences. He was a self-confessed Anglophile. P. Lal, a poet, translator, publisher and essayist, is the epitome of the literateur, and besides translating the entire Mahabharata into English, has written many essays in defense of Indian literature in English.

R.K. Narayan is a writer who contributed over many decades and who continued to write till his death recently. He was discovered by Graham Greene in the sense that the latter helped him find a publisher in England. Graham Greene and Narayan remained close friends till the end. Similar to Thomas Hardy's Wessex, Narayan created the fictitious town of Malgudi where he set his novels. Some criticise Narayan for the parochial, detached and closed world that he created in the face of the changing conditions in India at the times in which the stories are set. Others, such as Graham Greene, however, feel that through Malgudi they could vividly understand the Indian experience. Narayan's evocation of small town life and its experiences through the eyes of the endearing child protagonist Swaminathan in Swami and Friends is a good sample of his writing style.

LATER HISTORY

Among the later writers, the most notable is Salman Rushdie, born in India, now living in the United States. Rushdie with his famous work Midnight's Children (Booker

Prize 1981, Booker of Bookers 1992) ushered in a new trend of writing. He used a hybrid language - English generously peppered with Indian terms - to convey a theme that could be seen as representing the vast canvas of India. He is usually categorised under the magic realism mode of writing most famously associated with Gabriel García Márquez.

Bharati Mukherjee, author of Jasmine 1989, has spent much of her career exploring issues involving immigration and identity with a particular focus upon the United States and Canada.

Vikram Seth, author of A Suitable Boy (1994) is a writer who uses a purer English and more realistic themes. Being a self-confessed fan of Jane Austen, his attention is on the story, its details and its twists and turns.

Shashi Tharoor, in his The Great Indian Novel (1989), follows a story-telling (though in a satirical) mode as in the Mahabharata drawing his ideas by going back and forth in time. His work as UN official living outside India has given him a vantage point that helps construct an objective Indianness.

Other authors include Anita Desai, Bapsi Sidhwa, Chitra Banerjee Divakaruni, Raj Kamal Jha, Prakash Kona, and Rohinton Mistry.

DEBATES

It would be useful at this point to bring in the recent debates on IWE.

One of the key issues raised in this context is the superiority/inferiority of IWE as opposed to the literary production in the various languages of India. Key polar concepts bandied in this context are superficial/authentic, imitative/creative, shallow/deep, critical/uncritical, elitist/parochial and so on.

The views of Rushdie and Amit Chaudhuri expressed through their books The Vintage Book of Indian Writing and

The Picador Book of Modern Indian Literature respectively essentialise this battle.

Rushdie's statement in his book - "the ironic proposition that India's best writing since independence may have been done in the language of the departed imperialists is simply too much for some folks to bear" - created a lot of resentment among many writers, including writers in English. In his book, Amit Chaudhuri questions - "Can it be true that Indian writing, that endlessly rich, complex and problematic entity, is to be represented by a handful of writers who write in English, who live in England or America and whom one might have met at a party?"

Chaudhuri feels that after Rushdie, IWE started employing magical realism, bagginess, non-linear narrative and hybrid language to sustain themes seen as microcosms of India and supposedly reflecting Indian conditions. He contrasts this with the works of earlier writers such as Narayan where the use of English is pure, but the deciphering of meaning needs cultural familiarity. He also feels that Indianness is a theme constructed only in IWE and does not articulate itself in the vernacular literatures. (it is probable that the level of Indianness constructed is directly proportional to the distance between the writer and India.) He further adds "the post-colonial novel, becomes a trope for an ideal hybridity by which the West celebrates not so much Indianness, whatever that infinitely complex thing is, but its own historical quest, its reinterpretation of itself".

Some of these arguments form an integral part of what is called postcolonial theory. The very categorisation of IWE - as IWE or under post-colonial literature - is seen by some as limiting. Amitav Ghosh made his views on this very clear by refusing to accept the Eurasian Commonwealth Writers Prize for his book The Glass Palace in 2001 and withdrawing it from the subsequent stage.

The renowned writer V.S. Naipaul, a third generation Indian from Trinidad and Tobago and a Nobel prize laureate, is a person who belongs to the world and usually not classifie under IWE. Naipaul evokes ideas of homeland, rootlessnes and his own personal feelings towards India in many of hi books.

Jhumpa Lahiri, a Pulitzer prize winner from the U.S is a writer uncomfortable under the label of IWE.

Recent writers in India such as Arundhati Roy and Davi Davidar show a direction towards contextuality an rootedness in their works.

Arundhati Roy, a trained architect and the 1997 Booke prize winner for her The God of Small Things, calls herse a "home grown" writer. Her award winning book is set i the immensely physical landscape of Kerala. Davidar se his The House of Blue Mangoes in Southern Tamil Nad In both the books, geography and politics are integral to th narrative.

As the number of Indian writers in English keep increasing, with everyone with a story to tell trying to te a story, and as publishing houses in India vie amon themselves to discover the next new whiz-kid who will lan up with world fame, it could become increasingly difficult separate the wheat from the chaff. Research, debates an seminars on IWE continue with increasing frequenc However,it might be too early a stage in the history of India writing in English to pass any final judgement.

POETRY

A much over-looked category of Indian writing in Englis is poetry. As stated above, Rabindranath Tagore wrote i Bengali and English and was responsible for the translatio of his own work into English. Other early notable poets i English include Derozio, Michael Madhusudan Dutt, Josep Furtado, Armando Menezes, Toru Dutt, Romesh Chand Dutt, Sarojini Naidu and her brother Harendranat Chattopadhyaya.

In modern times, Indian poetry in English was typified by two very different poets. Dom Moraes, winner of the Hawthornden Prize at the precocious age of 19 for his first book of poems "A Beginning" went on to occupy a pre-eminent position among Indian poets writing in English. Nissim Ezekiel, who came from India's tiny Jewish community, created a voice and place for Indian poets writing in English and championed their work.

Their contemporaries in English poetry in India were Arvind Mehrotra, Jayanta Mahapatra, Gieve Patel, AK Ramanujan, Parthasarathy, Keki Daruwala, Adil Jussawala, Arun Kolatkar, Dilip Chitre, Eunice De Souza, Kersi Katrak and Kamala Das among several others.

A generation of exiles also sprang from the Indian diaspora. Among these are names like Agha Shahid Ali, Sujata Bhatt, Melanie Silgardo and Vikram Seth.

The current generation of Indian poets writing in English includes Ranjit Hoskote, Jeet Thayil, Tabish Khair, Vijay Nambisan, H. Masud Taj, Rukmini Bhaya Nair, C.P. Surendran, Moniza Alvi, Imtiaz Dharker, Gayatri Mazumdar, Vivek Narayanan, Gavin Barrett, Anjum Hasan, Jerry Pinto, Smita Agarwal, Arundhathi Subramaniam, Anand Thakore, Meena Alexander, Gayatri Majumdar, Mary Anne Mohanraj, Kumar Vikram and Reetika Vazirani.

4

Indian English Literature

Indian English literature is an endeavour of showcasing the rare gems of Indian writing in English. From being a curious native explosion, Indian English has become a new form of Indian culture, and voice in which India speaks. While Indian authors - poets, novelists, essayists, dramatists - have been making significant contributions to world literature since the pre-Independence era, the past few years have seen a massive flourishing of Indian English writing in the international market. Not only are the works of Indian authors writing in English soaring on the best-seller list, they are also receiving a great deal of critical acclaim. Starting from Mulk Raj Anand, R. K. Narayan, Anita Desai, Toru Dutt to Salman Rushdie, Vikram Seth, Allan Sealy, Amitav Ghosh, Jhumpa Lahiri, Chitra Banerjee Divakaruni, Arundhati Roy,Vikram Chandra ... the parade of fine Indian writers is long and lengthening. Here, you can explore the interesting history of Indian writing in English, and also experience its various facets, as expressed in Indian English literature, plays and movies, and other media.

HISTORICAL PERSPECTIVE

Indian English Literature has grown from a sapling to a strong rooted tree in full bloom. Indians, however, did not start writing in English in a day - it took several historical events and distinguished personalities to bring Indian writing in English to its present eminence. Historical Perspective is an effort to contextualise the growth and rise of Indian English Literature, from its inception to its present glory.

The Beginnings

The East IndiaCompany was formed in 1599 at a meeting attended by leading London merchants and after more than 150years the company had the key to the domination of Bengaland Indiagenerally. The battle of Plassey was fought in 1757 but Clive declined theresponsibility of Diwani or revenue administration and it was in 1722 that theEast India Company took it over and still later in 1790, the responsibility foradministering criminal justice.

The Company was, however, interested in politicaldomination only to the extent such domination increased its own dividends. Itwas directly interested neither in Empire nor in the Kingdom of Christ- and certainly not in the suppression or advancement of indigenous culture. Butthere were exceptions as well. Warren Hastings established the CalcuttaMadrasah in 1781, Sir William Jones established the Royal Asiatic Society ofBengal in 1784 and Sir Thomas Munro too was much impressed by the Indianculture. These men came to be called 'Brahmanised Britons' because they admiredIndian culture and deprecated the idea of introducing Western civilization orChristianity into India.

By the beginning of the 19thcentury, Britain- or East India Company - was more or less the master of the situation in India. In 1813the commercial monopoly of the Company was ended, and the British in India assumed,beside police functions, educating and civilizing mission as well. A tokengrant of Rupees one lakh per year was made for education and the idea was topromote only Oriental education. Printing presses in different parts of thecountry and books in the vernacular as well as in English were coming out sincethe beginning of the 18th century. Along with grammars, dictionariesand translations, the printing presses also gave rise to the first evernewspaper - Hicky's Bengal Gazette (1780), and others followed in due course.Last came the private schools that imparted English education - such schoolshave been started as early as 1717 at Cuddalore near Chennai. 1718 at Mumbai(by Richard Cobbe, a chaplain), and 1720 at Kolkata, endowed by theThomlinsons, culminating in the established of Hindu Collegein 1817. Started by Raja Ram Mohan Roy and his friends - David Hare and SirEdward Hyde East, it became the Presidency College in 1855, stillrecognized as one off the premier educational institutes.

Western education wasspreading fast in different parts of India and was doing much betterthan the institutions imparting oriental education. The Orientalists and theAnglicists continued to wrangle but it was quite evident that the former weresteadily losing ground, and Macaulay'scelebrated Minute settled the issue at last. He declared that it was bothnecessary and possible to "make the natives of this country good Englishscholars and that to this end our efforts ought to be directed." On 7thMarch, 1835, Lord William Bentinck resolved that "the great object of theBritish Government ought to be the promotion of European Literature and scienceamong the natives of India, and all funds appropriated for the purpose ofeducation would be best employed on English education alone." From 1835 was theAnglicizing period.

During the 20 years between 1835 to1855 thenumber of those educated in English had been rapidly increasing. It is saidthat even in 1834-5, 32,000 English books sold in India, as against 13,000 in nativeIndian languages. The vogue for English books increased, and the demand camemore from English educated Indians than from the Englishmen in India. Westernways - in manners and customs- became current in bigger towns and cities. In1853 the first railway was established in India, in 1854 the first telegraphline and a modern postal system were inaugurated. Distance was being abridgedand a common medium of communication was being established. Modern Europeanscientific techniques (including medicine and surgery) were slowly beingintroduced in India.It was thus thought that Indiawas eventually progressing from its static and secure medievalism to a dynamicmodernism.

Indians started with reading, speaking and comprehending English, and they soon started writing also. Once this started,Indian writing in English had to range from the most utilitarian prose to themost ambitious verse-epics, for example.

On the other hand, Indian writing inEnglish was but only one of the manifestations of the new creative urge in India - what is often referred to as theliterary Renaissance in India.The study of English literature stimulated literary creation in Bengali,Marathi, Telegu, Gujrati and other Indian languages.

And Indo-Anglianliterature had the same origin as the other modern literature in India,though here the foreign element seemed more pronounced. The filiations betweenthe modern Indian literatures (including Indian English Literature) and Englishliterature have been close.

Ram Mohan Roy

The renaissance in modern Indian literature begins with Raja Ram Mohan Roy. Roy was born in Radhanagar village in west Bengal's Hooghly district on May 22, 1772, to conservative Bengali Brahmin parents. His father Ramakanta Roy's family belonged to the Vaisnava (who worship Lord Vishnu - the Preserver; followers of Sri Caitanya Maha Prabhu) a liberal sect that flourished in Bengal and South India. His mother Tarini Devi's orthodox priestly family (Bhattacharyas of Chatra) on the other hand belonged to the Shakta sect (worshippers of Godess Kali - the Shakti - the Mother Energy of the universe). Roy did his elementary education in the village school in Bengali, his mother tongue. At the age of 12, Roy went to a seat of Muslim studies in

Patna where he mastered Persian and Arabic. His knowledge of Arabic enabled him to read the Koran in the original, as well as the works of Sufi saints. He also devoured Arabic translations of the works of Aristotle and Plato.

When he was 16, Royclashed with his orthodox father on the issue of idol worship and left home. Toacquaint himself with the Buddhist religion, he travelled across northern India and Tibet for the next three years. Hisquestioning mind objected to the deification of the Buddha and this did not godown well with some of the lamas. He then visited Varanasi where he learnt Sanskrit and studiedancient Hindu scriptures.

In 1803, he secured a job with the East India Company and in 1809, he wasposted to Rangpur. In Rangpur, he learnt about Jainism and studied the Jaintexts. Roy wasdrawn to certain aspects of Christianity that led some of the followers of thereligion to suggest that he convert; but he politely declined.

Roy'sunderstanding of the different religions of the world helped him to comparethem with Vedantic philosophy and garner the best from each religion. Sufimysticism had a great influence on Roy.He loved to repeat three of their maxims: "Man is the slave ofbenefits"; "The enjoyment of the worlds rests on these two points -kindness to friends and civility to enemies"; and "The way of servingGod is to do good to man".

To pursue his interests, Roy resigned from theEast India Company a few years later and came to Calcutta in 1814. Dissatisfied with thesystem of education and the rote method of teaching English, he formed anassociation of English and Hindu scholars. He also invested his own money inthe starting of a school where he introduced subjects like science, mathematics, political science and English. Roy felt that an understanding of these"modern" subjects would give Indians a better standing in the worldof the day.

Though initially antagonistic towards British rule in India, Roylater began to feel that the country would benefit in terms of education and byexposure to the good points of Christianity. For this he was called a stooge ofthe British.

Along with a group of like-minded people, Royfounded the Atmiya Sabha in 1814. The group held weekly meetings at his house;texts from the Vedas were recited and theistic hymns were sung. Roy was drawn to the Unitarian form of Christianity thatresulted in him supporting a Unitarian Mission to be set up in Calcutta in 1824.

Ram Mohan started the Samvad Koumudi - a weekly paper - in 1821, andwith it he was able to make a bolder and more sustained onslaught on the forcesof prejudice and reaction. By 1823, he had fully matured and sharpened hisdialectical instrument. Ram Mohan's interest and inquiries ranged from therights of women and the freedom of the press to English education in India, the revenue and judicial systems in India,religious toleration and the plight of Indian peasantry. He wanted India to becomea new and modern country and the Indians to become a virile new people, byachieving a new integration of our traditional strength with the new scientificdisciplines from the West.

Roy's effortsto abolish the practice of Sati were largely driven by his concern for themoral dimensions of religion. It was the sight of the burning of his brother'swidow on her husband's funeral pyre and his inability to save her that spurredRam Mohan into action.

He delved into the scriptures in great detail and proved that the practice ofSati could not gain moksha (salvation) for the husband as each man wasresponsible for his own destiny. He also realized that very often it was greedyrelatives interested in the property of the dead husband who were behindpromoting the practice.

His relentless efforts in the form of petitions, writings and the organizing ofvigilance committees paid off when the

William Bentinck administration passed alaw in 1829 banning the practice of Sati. Royalso succeeded in starting a revolution for women's education and women's rightto property. By delving into Hindu scriptures, he showed that even ancient Indianwomen enjoyed equal freedom with men.

Among Roy'sother firsts was the publishing of a newspaper in an Indian language. TheAtmiya Sabha brought out a weekly called the 'Bengal Gazette'. He alsopublished a newspaper in Persian called 'Miratul-Akhbar'. Roy placed a great deal of importance on thedevelopment of his mother tongue. His 'Gaudiya Vyakaran' in Bengali is ratedhighly among his writings in prose.

The founding of the Brahmo Samaj was among Roy's most important contributions. Beginningin 1828 as a small group, the Samaj played a major role in Renaissance Bengalof the 19th century by attracting luminaries like Keshub Chandra Sen andRabindranath Tagore and other members of the Tagore family. The objectives ofthe Samaj were to follow a theistic form of Hinduism combining the best of whatRoy inculcatedthrough his exposure to other religions.

Even today, in Brahmo prayer halls all over the country, people meet once aweek, most often on Sundays, and worship the one God or Brahma. At thesegatherings, discourses are offered, Vedic texts recited and hymns sung.Present-day followers try to inculcate his words: "Testing, questing,never resting, with open mind and open heart."

Roy feltstrongly for the downtrodden and his belief in the universal brotherhood of manled him to support many causes and reform movements. A 100 years before theestablishment of the League of Nations, Royexpressed the need for a similar institution. He said that just as twoindividuals resorted to a court of law to settle major disputes, there shouldbe an organization that could help to settle differences between two countries.

Roy feltstrongly for the downtrodden and his belief in the universal brotherhood of manled him to support many causes and reform movements.A 100 years before theestablishment of the League of Nations, Royexpressed the need for a similar institution. He said that just as twoindividuals resorted to a court of law to settle major disputes, there shouldbe an organization that could help to settle differences between two countries.

Roy made his first and only trip to England inNovember 1830 where he lived until his life was tragically cut short onSeptember 27, 1833 after a brief illness. In England, he wrote a briefautobiography on request and it was published in Athenaeum and the LiteraryGazette. He thus started the tradition of Indian leaders writingautobiographies. Modern autobiographers like Gandhi, Nehru, Surendra NathBanerjea, Rajendra Prasad may proudly trace their lineage to him.

Some of Ram Mohan's Major Contributions include:

- Vedantasara 1815,
- Translation of an Abridgment of the Vedant 1816,
- Ishopanishad 1816,
- Kathopanishad 1817,
- A Conference between an Advocate for, and an Opponent of the Practice of Burning Widows Alive (Bengali and English) 1818,
- Munduk Upanishad 1819,
- A Defence of Hindu Theism 1820,
- A Second Defence of the Monotheistical System of the Veds 1820,
- A Second Conference, 1820 (the case for women's rights),
- The Precepts of Jesus - Guide to Peace and Happiness 1820,

- Sambad Kaumudi - a Bengali newspaper 1821,
- Mirat-ul-Akbar - Persian journal 1822,
- Padari Sisya Sambad (Bengali satire) 1823,
- Bengali Grammar 1826,
- Brahmapasona 1828,
- Brahmasangeet 1829 and
- The Universal Religion 1829.

Ram Mohan Roy was the man who fought against superstitions, a pioneer in Indian education, and a trend setter in Bengali Prose and Indian Press. By precept and example he advanced the causes he held dear all along the front, and truly therefore, could he be called the first of the great builders of modern India.

TORU DUTT'S POEMS

Toru Dutt (born on 4th March, 1865)compels attention as a poet, however her life - a combination of beauty andtragedy - equally fascinates and depresses us. Her poetry is reality, no doubt,but the poet too induces interest. She had a rich and respectable ancestry. TheDutts were one of the eminent families in Kolkata.

Her father Govin ChunderDutt, was well-to-do, a good linguist, and a cultured man with literaryleanings and generous impulse. In 1862, when she was just six, the Dutt family embracedChristianity. Initially, this strained the relations between her parents but itturned out to be a temporary phase. Her mother soon reconciled, became a devoutChristian, and translated The Blood of Jesus into Bengali, giving ampleproof of her linguistic abilities and ease in handling the two languages. Toruwas the youngest in the family, having a brother Abju and a sister Aru. Of hisson Govi wrote:

Most loving is my eldest, and I love him most; Almost a man in seeming, yet a child...

And thus of Aru:

My next, the beauty of our home, is meek; Not so deep-loving haply, but less wild Than her dear brother;-brow and blushing cheek Her nature shows serene, and pure, and mild As evening's early star.

And thus to Toru:

Punyand elf-like, with disheveled tresses, Self-willedand shy ne'er heeding that I call, Intentto pay her tenderest addresses Tobird or cat, - but most intelligent...

The children had a private tutor but Govin took personalcare in educating them properly. Toru, was conscious of the influence herfather had exercised in shaping her mental calibre. She recalled gratefully,"without Papa I should never have known good poetry from bad, but he usedto take such pains with us ... When we were quite little ones... I wonder what Ishould have been without my father, nothing very enviable or desirable, Iknow". The first calamity came in 1865 when Abju died. The sisters clungto each other and read Paradise Lost repeatedly, and lost themselves in literary studies.

In 1869, the family left for Europewhere the girls could glean rich treasures of knowledge and become versatile.Their first stay was in Nice, in the South-east of France. Here they attended schooland learnt French - a language in which they attained proficiency to use it forcreativity. The stay at Nice was short and was followed by a visit to Italy and then to England.

In London, the lessons in music aroused thegirls' finer sensitivities and opened new vistas of the world of emotions. Atwo-year period at Cambridgehelped in the blossoming of their personalities further. Toru came into contactwith Mary Martin at Cambridge and the two fostered a life-long bond of friendship and affection. Thecorrespondence with Mary Martin is a valuable source to know the mental make-upof the young poetess. The letters reveal the young writer's childlike joy inlife with her intellectual maturity. They speak of flowers and birds and ofartistic vision, scholarly pursuits and morbid illness.

Soon after their arrival in their London came out The Dutt Family Album (1870), containing about 200 pieces, Govin's contribution being mainly of a didactic nature. His brothers and a nephew called Omesh Chunder were the other contributors to the volume. Of no major literary importance, the volume throws light on the literary exertion and creative atmosphere of the Dutt family house. The family moved back to Kolkata in September 1873 and soon after that, in 1874 July, Aru succumbed to consumption.

Toru's first publication A sheaf Gleaned in French Fields (1876) consisting of translations of seventy French poets (including Hugo, Gautier, Baudelaire, Leconte de Lisle, Nerval, Sainte-Beauve), brought her to the attention of Edmund Gosse. Most of the poems were translated by Toru and her translations are also the more striking:

> *Ha! There's the seagull. See it springs, Pearls scattering from its tawny wings, Then plunges in the gulfs once more, 'Tis lost in caverns of the main! No! No! It upward soars again, As souls from trials upward soar. ('Lines:Victor Hugo')*

The most interesting part of the collection was the Notes appended at the end of volume, consisting of critical comments on the French poetry translated in the volume. They were largely written by Toru. Gosse found them 'curious' and 'bewildering' as 'nothing could be more naïve than the writer's ignorance at some points, or more startling than her learning at others. Thompson admired the 'independence and masculinity' of her criticism.

Shortly after her return to Kolkata, Toru published her first essays, including one on Derozio in the Bengal Magazine (December 1874). She worked hard at learning Sanskrit and writings poems on Hindu mythology. Toru was considering translating Clarisse Bader's La Femme dans l'Inde Antique when she died at the age of only twenty one years and six months. It was 30th August 1877.

A selection of English translation of the sonnets of Comte de Grammont, a sketch for an unfinished romance Bianca, or The Young Spanish Maiden, a complete French novel - Le Journal de Mademoiselle d'Arvers, and a collection of poems Ancient Ballads were left behind by Toru. Bianca was published in Bengal Magazine (1878), while the French novel appeared in 1879 to much critical acclaim. The poems collected in Ancient Ballads were better than anything written up till then by an Indian in the English language. 'Baugmaree' which takes its name from the place where the Dutt country house was situated, is a celebration of trees. In its imagery and description - an affinity might be found between Toru and her contemporary Emily Dickinson. The bulk of the poems in Ancient Ballads is based on Indian mythology.

Toru Dutt's poetry transcends the recognisable school of nineteenth century poetry and evolves a separate identity. The difference lies in the manner in which her language addresses her experience, her vision radiating beyond the boundaries within which most of the nineteenth century poetry in English was confined. Her awareness of her own Indianness is not restricted to Indian historical themes and the reworking of Indian legends. The mythological content of her poems does not exist extrinsically, but is integrated with her consciousness, her memory. In her poetry, we meet for the first time a language that is crafted out of the vicissitudes of an individual life and a sensibility that belongs to modern India.

Rabindranath Tagore

Rabindranath Tagore, the Nobel laureate poet, writer, philosopher was the ambassador of Indian culture to the rest of the world. He is probably the most prominent figure in the cultural world of Indian subcontinent and the first Asian person to be awarded with the Nobel prize. Even though he is mainly known as a poet, his multifaceted talent showered upon-different branches of art, such as, novels, short stories, dramas, articles, essays, painting etc. And his songs, popularly known as Rabindrasangeet, have an eternal appeal and is permanently placed in the heart of the Bengalis. He was a social reformer, patriot and above all, a great humanitarian and philosopher. India and Bangladesh - the national anthems of these two countries are taken from his composition.

Tagore was born on Tuesday, 7th May 1861 in a wealthy family in Calcutta at the address of 6, Dwarakanath Thakur Lane, Calcutta. He was the ninth son of Debenadranath and Sarada Devi. His grand father Dwarakanath Tagore was a rich landlord and social reformer. Even though he was from a very wealthy family, in those days Jorasanko house (Tagore house) was a center of culture.

He was first admitted into Oriental Seminary School. But he did not like the conventional education and started home study under several teachers. Later he went to Normal School, Bengal Academy and St Xaviers School, but all lasted for brief periods. At the age of 7 he wrote a rhyme. Went to visit Northern part of India and Himalayas with this father.

In 1874, his first published poem Abhilaash(Desire) was published anonymously in a magazine called Tattobodhini. Poet's mother Sarada Devi expired in 1875 when he was 13 years old. For the first time a poem with credit to his name was published in Amritabazar Patrika (weekly). He translated Macbeth into Bengali verse which was later published in Bharati magazine. Following the style of Vaisnava Padalvali (verses), he wrote Bhanusingher Padavali under the penname of Bhanusingha. In the beginning of his literary works, there was impact of his elder brother Jyotirindranath and his wife Kadambari Devi. Two magazines, Bharati and Balaka - were used to get published from the Tagore house and he regularly contributed to those.

His first book of poems, Kabi Kahini (tale of a poet) was published in 1878. In the same year, he sailed to England with his brother Satyandranath. He got admitted into the University College in England and started studying under Prof Henry Morley. Retuned to India on 1880. Wrote two musical plays - Valmiki Prativa (The Genius of Valmiki) and Kalmrigaya (The Fatal Hunt). Acted in these plays too. Left for England in 1881, but changed his mind and came back from Madras and went to Mussorie to meet his father. In 1882, he wrote Sandhya Sangeet (Evening Songs) which impressed Bankim Chandra Chatterjee so much that he conferred his garland on Tagore in a function. Wrote a famous poem - Nirjharer Swapnabhanga (The Fountain Awakened from its Dream).

Got married to Bhabatarini Devi in 1883 at the age of 22. Later her name was changed to Mrinalini Devi. In 1884 wrote a collection of poem - Kori-o-kamal (Sharp and Flats). Continued writing in different forms. His first child (daughter) Madhurilata was born in 1886. Wrote musical drama - Mayar Khela. Also wrote dramas - Raja-o-rani (King and Queen) and Visarjan (Sacrifice). In 1890 daughter Renuka was born.

In 1890, Tagore went to Shilaidaha (now in Bangladesh) to look after the family estate. Here, he was influenced by the natural beauty and simple but elegant life of rural Bengal. Attended session of Indian National Congress and sang the song Vandemataram on the opening day. Wrote famous dance/ musical drama - Chitrangada. His youngest daughter Mira was born in 1892. In 1894 , wrote famous collection poems - Sonar Tari (The Golden Boat). Son Samindra was born in 1894.

In 1901 he took the editorial charge of the magazine Bangadarshan. Got involved with freedom fighting movement. Established Bolpur Bramhacharyaashram at Shantiniketan, a school in the pattern of old Indian Ashrama. In 1902, his wife Mrinalini died. Composed Smaran (In Memoriam), a collection of poems, dedicated to his wife.

Within six months from this incident his daughter Renuka expired.

The demise of father Debendranath happened in 1905. He strongly protested Lord Curzcn's decision to divide Bengal on the basis of religion. Wrote a number of national songs and attended protest meetings. He introduced the Rakhibandhan ceremony, symbolizing the underlying unity in undivided Bengal. Was shocked by the sudden death of son Samindra in 1907. In 1909 started writing Gitanjali from Silaidaha. Composed Janaganamana in 1911 which later was selected as the national anthem of India.

In 1912, journeyed to Europe for the second time. On the journey to London he translated some of his poems/songs from Gitanjali to English. He met William Rothenstein, a noted British painter, in London. He was first introduced to Rothenstein in Calcutta in a gathering at Abanindranath Tagore's house.

Rothenstien was impressed by the poems, made copies and gave to Yeats and other English poets. Rothenstien arranged a reading in his house where Yeats read Tagore's poems in front of a distinguished audience comprising of Ezra Pound, May Sinclair, Ernest Rhys etc.

Tagore sailed for America (for the first time) from England. Reached New York, came to Urbana, Illinois, gave a lecture and then went to Chicago. In the mean time, India Society of London published Gitanjali (song offerings) containing 103 translated poems of Tagore. Yeats wrote the introduction for this book and Rothenstein did a pencil sketch for the cover page. The book created a sensation in English literary world. Tagore was traveling America then. Delivered lectures in Rochester, Boston, Harvard University.

Ezra Pound's Poetry Magazine published from Chicago had the honor of publishing first English poem of Tagore. His six Gitanjali poems appeared in Poetry in December, 1912 issue. Th epoet returned back to Calcutta. In 13th

November of 1913, Indians came to know that the Nobel prize for literature has been awarded to Tagore for Gitanjali. On 26th Decemeber, University of Calcutta conferred on him the honorary degree of "D.Litt.". Received Knighthood in 1915.

Proceeded to Japan in 1916. On the way gave speech at Rangoon, Singapore, Hongkong. In Sep 1916, got invitation from different institutions in USA and reached Seattle (Washington). Lectured at Portland, San Fransisco, Los Angeles, Santa Barbara, Salt Lake City, Chicago, Iowa, Milwakee, Detroit, Cleveland, Philadelphia, Boston. At Columbia Theatre, New York read translation from his novel Raja. Returned to Calcutta in 1917. In 1918, his eldest daughter Madhurilata passed away. In 1919, the poet started a tour to South India. Delivered lectures on different topics at Bangalore, Mysroe, Ooty, Coimbatore, Palghat, Salem, Trichy, Sirangapatnam, Kumbakonam, Tanjore and Madras. At Madras spoke as Chancellor of National University, founded by Annie Besant and stayed as a guest of Mr. Besant at Adyar.

In 1919, he wrote a historic letter to Lord Chelmsford repudiating his Knighthood in protest of the massacre at Jalianwalabag, Punjab. In 1920 he went to Gandhiji's Sabarmati Ashram and visited Ahmedabad, Surat and Bombay. Call came from Europe again in 1920. Toured different places in England and Paris, Hague , Brussells. Travelled from Europe to America. Delivered lectures at New York, Princeton, Chicago and came back to Europe. His effort to raise fund for Viswabharati was not very fruitful in America, mostly because he was seen as anti-British and pro-German. He continued talks at Geneva, Zurich, Humburg, Copenhaegen, Stockholm, Berlin, Frankfurt, Vienna, Prague and in other cities.

In 1921, established Viswabharati University. He gave all his money from Nobel Prize and royalty money from his books to this University. Went to Bombay and from there to Poona. Visited and lectured at Mysore, Bangalore,Coimbatore, Trivandam, Cochin and Colombo. Got invitation from China and visited Sanghai, Peiking. Visited Japan again in this tour. Went to South America. Met Argentine poet Madam Victoria Ocampo at Buenos Ayres. The poet gave her a name ,Vijaya and wrote Purabi - a collection of poems dedicated to her. On the return journey visited Italy and lectured in Milan, Venice, Florence. Mahatma Gandhi visited Santiniketan in poet's birthday. In 1926 visited Dacca, Moimonsingha, Comilla (all now in Bangladesh). Visited Europe again and this time went to Norway, Sweden, Denmark, Czechslovakia, Huungary, Bulgaria, Rumania, Greece and Egypt. In 1927 went to Malayasia, Java, Thailand. In 1929 Canada. In 1930 Russia. In 1932 Iran, Iraq. And in 1934 to SriLanka.

In 1940 Oxford University arranged a special ceremony in Santiniketan to honor the poet with Doctorate Of Literature. Tagore passed away on 7th August, 1941 in his ancestral home in Calcutta, the house where he was born.

Sri Aurobindo

Sri Aurobindo was a revolutionary, poet, philosopher, writer, and Spiritual Master. Despite his fascinating life he was sceptical of any biographies saying " No one can write about my life because it has not been on the surface for man to see." - Sri Aurobindo from: On Himself Yet his writings and outer life give a profound glimpse into the life of this unique spiritual master. Sri Aurobindo paved a new approach to yoga, which he termed "Integral Yoga". Unlike the Yogi's of old he felt yoga and spirituality need not involve retreating from the world. Sri Aurobindo wished to bring the Divine into all aspects of life. For the last 40 years of his life he worked tirelessly for this goal of bringing down a new spiritual consciousness.

"We are Sons of God and must be even as He." - Sri Aurobindo.

Early Life - Sri Aurobindo

Sri Aurobindo Ghosh was born on 15th August 1872, to an anglicised father Dr Krishnan Ghosh. He wanted his children to be schooled in English, therefore at the age of 7 Aurobindo was sent to study in England. Aurobindo studied first at St Paul's, London and then at Kings College Cambridge.

Life in England was often tough for Aurobindo; resources were meagre and for many years he had to often survive on a frugal diet. However he proved to be a scholar of great intellect and capacity. He mastered the classics and English poetry (later he wrote extensively on the English poets). The famous don Oscar Browning declared Aurobindo one of the greatest scholars he had seen.

It was at Cambridge university that Aurobindo first became aware of the plight of his country, at the time under the rule of the British Empire. Aurobindo became inspired to join a society committed to overthrowing British rule. This period was an important landmark in Aurobindo's life. With his new political perspective he turned down an opportunity to join the British civil service. He had passed all his exams but failed to turn up for the obligatory horse riding test. Therefore at the age of 21 he returned to India increasingly committed to working for Indian independence.

Sri Aurobindo the Revolutionary

On his return to Indian soil Sri Aurobindo was overwhelmed with a feeling of intense inner peace. This experience came unsought and was an indication of his future spiritual capacity. However at the time Sri Aurobindo's main concern and main passion was political independence of his beloved motherland.

Sri Aurobindo threw himself into revolutionary politics, associating with the great figures of Bengal such as Bipin Pal, B.C Chatterji. He was dismayed with the weakness of

Congress and argued for direct action aiming for complete independence. Through his journal Bande Mataram, Sri Aurobindo was the first leader to call for the full independence for India.

For several years Sri Aurobindo was a pivotal figure in the movement for independence. He had the qualities of a natural leader but was always happy to work in the background as much as possible. It was during this period that Sri Aurobindo also became increasingly interested in Yoga and meditation. Whilst engaged in spiritual disciplines Sri Aurobindo came across a teacher of meditation, Lele Maharaj. He taught Sri Aurobindo how to control thoughts and not let them enter into his mind. Sri Aurobindo followed his instructions to the letter and within 3 days he succeeded in completely emptying the mind and entered into a state of nirvana. This same experience had taken Lele Maharaj over 6 years to attain. Lele Maharaj was amazed at the progress of the young Aurobindo.

However it was the political struggle which held the greatest sway on Aurobindo, the freedom of India was his primary concern.

After a fatal incident involving revolutionaries, Aurobindo became a marked man. In 1908 he was arrested for the possession of weapons and was held in jail for a year before his case came to court. His trial became a major event with much attention placed on the incident. The evidence against Aurobindo was quite weighty and he feared he would be convicted. However Aurobindo was fortunate to have C.R.Das as his defence lawyer. C.R.D as threw himself heart and soul in to Aurobindo's defence. His commitment and capacity meant Sri Aurobindo felt completely assured and did not have to even concern himself with his own defence.

The Spiritual Mission of Sri Aurobindo

By a curious stroke of fate it was in a British jail that Sri Aurobindo began to be seriously awakened to the inner life. Confined to his own prison cell Sri Aurobindo was able to practice meditation and read about the ancient principles of yoga, undisturbed by outer commitments. Sri Aurobindo began to have profound meditations. Entering into higher realms of consciousness he became aware of the omnipresence of God.

As Sri Aurobindo himself said:

"I looked at the jail that secluded me from men and it was no longer by its high walls that I was imprisoned; no, it was Vasudeva who surrounded me. I walked under the branches of the tree in front of my cell but it was not the tree, I knew it was Vasudeva, it was Sri Krishna whom I saw standing there and holding over me his shade. I looked at the bars of my cell, the very grating that did duty for a door and again I saw Vasudeva. It was Narayana who was guarding and standing sentry over me. Or I lay on the coarse blankets that were given me for a couch and felt the arms of Sri Krishna around me, the arms of my Friend and Lover. This was the first use of the deeper vision He gave me. I looked at the prisoners in the jail, the thieves, the murderers, the swindlers, and as I looked at them I saw Vasudeva, it was Narayana whom I found in these darkened souls and misused bodies. Amongst these thieves and dacoits there were many who put me to shame by their sympathy, their kindness, the humanity triumphant over such adverse circumstances." - from The Uttarpada Speech 30 May 1909

It was also in prison that Sri Aurobindo was visited by the soul of Swami Vivekananda, who instructed Sri Aurobindo about the workings of the superconsciousness which was above the mind. Sri Aurobindo also became aware of a divine inner guidance, that was never to leave him. From this divine source he was given an Adesh "inner command" that henceforth he should not worry about politics. India would gain her independence in due course but this would be achieved by others. The task for Sri Aurobindo was the renewal of "sanatana dharma, the eternal religion." To pursue this spiritual task it was necessary for Sri Aurobindo to leave the political arena. In his own words Sri Aurobindo said of his mission.

> *"We must return and seek the sources of life and strength within ourselves... It is the spiritual revolution we forsee and the material is only its shadow and reflex."*

After gaining a dramatic acquittal Sri Aurobindo was released, but was still pursued by the British, who considered him "the most dangerous man we have to reckon with..." It was around this time that he again came into contact with Sister Nivedita, a disciple of Swami Vivekananda and fellow revolutionary. She warned Sri Aurobindo of the dangers he was in. After a while Sri Aurobindo followed another "Adesh" to move to the French province of Pondicherry. At Pondicherry Sri Aurobindo was able to dedicate himself fully to his spiritual disciplines. Despite frequent requests to return to politics, Sri Aurobindo spent much of his time in meditation becoming more aware of the supramental consciousness. Through his practise of Yoga Sri Aurobindo also gained the capacity to be a prolific writer producing many articles, writings and poetry.

Gradually spiritual seekers began to be attracted to Pondicherry and so an informal ashram began to be set up. A significant moment in the life of Sri Aurobindo and the fledgling ashram was the arrival of a French women, Mira Richards, who would later be affectionately known as the Mother of the Sri Aurobindo ashram. The Mother instantly recognised Sri Aurobindo as the one who had been guiding her sadhana (spiritual practices). In turn Sri Aurobindo entrusted the organisation of the ashram to the Mother and under her guidance, which continued for nearly fifty years, the Ashram grew into a dynamic spiritual community. The Sri Aurobindo Ashram still flourishes today and has a unique character in the sense that it does not involve retreating from the world. In Sri Aurobindo's words:

"The way of Yoga followed here has a purpose different from others, - for its aim is not only to rise out of the ordinary ignorant world-consciousness into the divine consciousness, but to bring the supramental power of that divine consciousness down into the ignorance of mind, life and body, to transform them, to manifest the Divine here and create a divine life in Matter."

Sri Aurobindo was a rare combination of poet, philosopher, writer and spiritual Master. During his time in Pondicherry he wrote several books explaining his view on Yoga and spirituality. His most notable exposition was perhaps in "The Life Divine" which is a comprehensive explanation of his integral yoga. Sri Aurobindo was also a noted poet. Many of his poems are vivid and soulful portrayals of his supramental experiences. For example.

Only the illimitable Permanent Is here. A Peace stupendous, featureless, still. Replaces all, - what once was I, in It A silent unnamed emptiness content Either to fade in the Unknowable Or thrill with the luminous seas of the Infinite. (last verse of Nirvana by Sri Aurobindo)

In November 1926 Sri Aurobindo would retreat from Ashram life, (he felt this withdrawal was necessary to be able to complete his work) however he spent many hours every day carefully replying to the letters of his disciples. These letters were an opportunity to explain his yoga and how it applied in particular situations. With good humour and great compassion he was able to relieve the fears and anxieties common to many seekers. Sri Aurobindo's letters show great wisdom and he often displayed a good sense of humour as he said himself:

"A God who could not smile could not have created this humorous universe." - Sri Aurobindo.

It is rewarding to read these letters and also stories by disciples such as Dilip Kumar Roy who maintained a long and fruitful written communication with his Guru. In these letters and other writings Sri Aurobindo gives an insightful look into the play of cosmic forces that work unseen behind external circumstances.

Although distanced from any direct involvement in politics Sri Aurobindo still took a keen interest in political events from around the world.

In particular he saw in Hitler and Nazi Germany a great threat to the whole of civilisation. Therefore at the outbreak of the Second World War, Sri Aurobindo, the former revolutionary against the British Empire, came out with his full public support for the Allies and their cause. Some Indians who still saw Britain as the main enemy did not always appreciate this decision.

However although Sri Aurobindo was a prolific writer he felt his main task was to bring down a new consciousness, which would usher in a new era where spirituality and truth were given a higher profile. But Sri Aurobindo went to great pains to say he did not wish to bring about a new religion or creed. As he wrote in his article "Sri Aurobindo On Himself.

"This is Sri Aurobindo's teaching and method of practice. It is not his object to develop any one religion or to amalgamate the older religions or to found any new religion - for any of these things would lead away from his central purpose. The one aim of his Yoga is an inner self-development by which each one who follows it can in time discover the One Self in all and evolve a higher consciousness than the mental, a spiritual and supramental consciousness which will transform and divinise human nature."

August, 1934 From SABCL, Vol. 26, "Sri Aurobindo on Himself "

He offered a new vision of yoga and a spiritual path that could be followed by sincere seekers. However Sri Aurobindo never desired to have a large numbers of disciples or followers. He admitted his path was not always easy and could be quite arduous. But to attain a real transformation of one's nature was not possible without maintaining certain spiritual standards and spiritual discipline.

Sri Aurobindo taught that the different world religions were right in their own way. However Sri Aurobindo also stated that there was no need to repeat what had happened in the past. The world is in continuous evolution and there is a need to bring down a higher truth with each age. Continuing the vision of Swami Vivekananda, Sri Aurobindo sought to combine the best from Eastern spirituality and Western materialism.

> *"I saw them cross the twilight of an age The sun-eyed children of a marvelous dawn... The massive barrier-breakers of the world.. The architects of immortality... Bodies made beautiful by the Spirit's light, Carrying the magic word, the mystic fire, Carrying the Dionysian cup of joy.. "*

From: Savitri - Sri Aurobindo

After a short illness Sri Aurobindo entered his mahasamadhi on 5th December 1950. During his last illness Sri Aurobindo refused any major surgery or even to heal himself. He said by leaving his body he would most effective in continuing his spiritual mission.

Sri Aurobindo's life was of constant service to bringing down a higher ideal and vision.

> *"The vast universal suffering feel as thine: Thou must bear the sorrow that thou claimst to heal; The day-bringer must walk in darkest night. He who would save the world must share its pain. If he knows not grief, how shall he find grief's cure? If far he walks above mortality's head, How shall the mortal reach that too high path? If one of theirs they see scale heaven's peaks, Men then can hope to learn that titan climb. God must be born on earth and be as man That man being human may grow even as God." - From Savitri by Sri Aurobindo*

SAROJINI NAIDU

Sarojini Chattopadhyay was born at Hyderabad on February 13, 1879 the eldest of a large family, all of whom were taught English at an early age. At the age of twelve she passed the Matriculation of the Madras University, and awoke to find herself famous throughout India.

Before she was fifteen the great struggle of her life began. Dr. Govindurajulu Naidu, later to become her husband was, though of an old and honourable family, not a Brahmin. The difference of caste roused an equal opposition, not only on the side of her family, but of his; and in 1895 she was sent to England, against her will, with a special scholarship from the Nizam. She remained in England, with an interval of travel in Italy, till 1898, studying first at King's College, London, then, till her health again broke down, at Girton. She returned to Hyderabad in September 1898, and in the December of that year, to the scandal of all India, broke through the bonds of caste, and married Dr. Naidu.

During her stay in England she met Arthur Symons, a poet and critic. They corresponded after her return to India. He persuaded her to publish some of her poems as The Golden Threshold(55K e-text available through Project Gutenberg). her collection of poems was published in 1905 under the title "Golden Threshold". After that, she published two other collections of poems--"The Bird of Time" and "The Broken Wings". In 1918, " Feast of Youth" was published. Later, "The Magic Tree", "The Wizard Mask" and "A Treasury of Poems" were published. Mahashree Arvind, Rabindranath Tagore and Jawaharlal Nehru were among the thousands of admirers of her work. Her poems had English words, but an Indian soul.

Then in 1916, she met Mahatma Gandhi, and she totally directed her energy to the fight for freedom. She would roam around the country like a general of the army and pour enthusiasm among the hearts of Indians. The independence of India became the heart and soul of her work.

She was responsible for awakening the women of India. She brought them out of the kitchen. She traveled from state to state, city after city and asked for the rights of the women. She re-established self-esteem within the women of India.

In 1925, she chaired the summit of Congress in Kanpur. In 1928, she came to the USA with the message of the non-violence movement from Gandhiji. When in 1930, Gandhiji was arrested for a protest, she took the helms of his movement. In 1931, she participated in the Round Table Summit, along with Gandhiji and Pundit Malaviyaji. In 1942, she was arrested during the "Quit India" protest and stayed in jail for 21 months with Gandhiji.

After independence she became the Governor of Uttar Pradesh. She was the first woman governor. She passed away on March 2, 1949.

This bio was partly condensed from the introduction and dedication of The Golden Threshold.

MAHATMA GANDHI

Mohandas Karamchand Gandhi (October 2, 1869 - January 30, 1948), was a major political and spiritual leader of India and the Indian independence movement. In India, he is recognized as the Father of the Nation. October 2nd, his birthday, is each year commemorated as Gandhi Jayanti, and is a national holiday. He was the pioneer of Satyagraha-the resistance of tyranny through mass civil disobedience, firmly founded upon ahimsa or total non-violence-which led India to independence and inspired movements for civil rights and freedom across the world. Gandhi is commonly known in India and across the world as Mahatma Gandhi from Sanskrit, mahatma: Great Soul) and as Bapu (in Gujarati, Father)

A British-educated lawyer, Gandhi first employed his ideas of peaceful civil disobedience in the Indian community's struggle for civil rights in South Africa. Upon his return to

India, he organized poor farmers and labourers to protest against oppressive taxation and widespread discrimination. Assuming leadership of the Indian National Congress, Gandhi led nationwide campaigns for the alleviation of the poverty, for the liberation of women, for brotherhood amongst differing religions and ethnicities, for an end to untouchability and caste discrimination, and for the economic self-sufficiency of the nation, but above all for Swaraj-the independence of India from foreign domination.

Gandhi famously led Indians in the disobedience of the salt tax on the 400 kilometre (248 miles) Dandi Salt March in 1930, and in an open call for the British to Quit India in 1942. He was imprisoned for many years on numerous occasions in both South Africa and India.

Throughout his life, Gandhi remained committed to non-violence and truth even in the most extreme situations. A student of Hindu philosophy, he lived simply, organizing an ashram that was self-sufficient in its needs.

Making his own clothes-the traditional Indian dhoti and shawl woven with a charkha, he lived on a simple vegetarian diet. He used rigorous fasts, for long periods, for both self-purification and protest. Gandhi's life and teachings inspired Dr. Martin Luther King Jr., Steve Biko and Aung San Suu Kyi and through them the American civil rights movement and the freedom struggles in South Africa and Myanmar respectively.

Gandhi in Film, Literature, Plays, and Popular Culture

Main article: List of artistic depictions of Mahatma Gandhi Mahatma Gandhi has been portrayed in film, literature, and in the theater. Ben Kingsley portrayed Gandhi in the 1982 award-winning film, Gandhi. Gandhi is also a central figure in the 2006 Bollywood film Lage Raho Munna Bhai. The philosophy of Gandhism is an important thematic component of both the 2005 film, Water and the novel by author Bapsi Sidhwa based on the film, also called Water

(Gandhi also appears as a character in both). The Making of the Mahatma documents Gandhi's 21 years in South Africa. The play Mahatma vs. Gandhi explores his troubled relationship with his eldest son Harilal Gandhi. A 2002 play Mohandas Karamchand Gandhi (play) gives the life story of Gandhi from the age of twelve until his death. The opera Satyagraha, composed by Philip Glass (in 1980), with a libretto by himself and Constance De Jong is based on the life of Gandhi. The tamil film 'Hey Ram' deals with the theme of Gandhi's assassination and its precursors.

JAWAHARLAL NEHRU

Jawaharlal Nehru was born on 14 November 1889 at Allahabad and educated in England, at Harrow and Cambridge. In 1912, Nehru returned home to play a central role in India's struggle for freedom from British colonial rule, and then, as prime minister of independent India for seventeen years, went on to shape the nation's future as a modern, secular and democratic state. He died in office, on 27 May 1964. Visionary and idealist, scholar and statesman of international stature, Nehru was also an outstanding writer. His three most renowned books-An Autobiography, Glimpses of World History and The Discovery of India-have acquired the status of classics, and are all published by Penguin.

Book(s) by Jawaharlal Nehru:

- A Bunch of Old Letters
- Glimpses of World History
- Letters from a Father to His Daughter
- An Autobiography
- The Discovery of India

MULK RAJ ANAND

Indian novelist, short-story writer, and art critic writing in English. Mulk Raj Anand was among the first writers to render Punjabi and Hindustani idioms into English. Called the Zola or Balzac of India, Anand drew a realistic and sympathetic portrait of the poor of his country. With Raja Rao and R.K. Narayan he has been regarded as one the "founding fathers" of the Indian English novel.

"And he had soon become possessed with an overwhelming desire to live their life. He had been told they were sahibs, superior people. He had felt that to put on their clothes made one sahib too. So he tried to copy them as well as he could in the exigencies of his peculiarly Indian circumstances." (from Untouchable, 1935)

Mulk Raj Anand was born in Peshawar, as the son of Lal Chand, a coppersmith and soldier, and Ishwar Kaur. Anand rebelled early on against his father's subservience to the British authorities. His first texts were born as a reaction to the trauma of the suicide of an aunt, who had been excommunicated for dining with a Muslim woman. An unhappy love for a Muslim girl, who was married, inspired some of his poetry.

Anand attended Khalsa College, Amritsar, and entered the University of Punjab in 1921, graduating with honors in 1924. Thereafter Anand did his additional studies at Cambridge and at London University, receiving his Ph.D. in 1929. He studied-and later lectured-at League of Nations School of Intellectual Cooperation in Geneva. Between 1932 and 1945 Anand lectured, on and off, at Workers Educational Association in London.

In the 1930s and 1940s, Anand divided his time between literary London and Gandhi's India. He joined the struggle for independence, but also fought with the Republicans in the Spanish Civil War. During World War II, he worked as a broadcaster and scriptwriter in the film division of the BBC in London. Among his friends was George Orwell.

After the war Anand returned permanently to India, making Bombay his hometown and center of activity. In

1946 he founded the fine-arts magazine Marg. He also became a director of Kutub Publishers. From 1948 to 1966 Anand taught at Indian universities. In the 1960s he was Tagore Professor of Literature and Fine Art at the University of Punjab and visiting professor at the Institute of Advanced Studies in Simla (1967-68). Between the years 1965 and 1970 Anand was fine art chairman at Lalit Kala Akademi (National Academy of Arts). In 1970 he was appointed president of Lokayata Trust, for creating a community and cultural center in the village of Hauz Khas, New Delhi.

Anand started to write at an early age. Although Punjabi and Hindustani were Anand's mother tongues, he wrote in English, because English language publisher did not reject his books due to their themes. His career as a writer Anand began in England by publishing short notes on books in T.S. Eliot's magazine Criterion. His acquaintances from this time included such authors as E.M. Forster, Herbert Read, Henry Miller, and George Orwell, who tired to get Anad a full-time post at the BBC. The most important influence upon Anand was Gandhi, who shaped his social conscience.

In the early 1930s Anand focused on books on art history. It was not until the appearance of the novels Untouchable (1935) and Coolie (1936), the story of a fifteen year-old child-labourer who dies of tuberculosis, that Anand gained a wide recognition. Untouchable narrates a day in the life of Bakha, an unclean outcaste, who suffers a number of humiliations in the course of his day. Bakha is eighteen, proud, "strong and able-bodied", a child of modern India, who has started to think himself as superior to his fellow-outcastes. The "touching" occurs in the morning, and subsequently shadows the rest of the day. Due to his low birth, Bakha's fate is to work as a latrine sweeper.

The powerful critique of the Indian caste system suggested that British colonial domination of India has actually increased the suffering of outcastes, such as Bakha. After 19 rejection slips Anand's novel was published in England with a preface by E.M. Forster: "Untouchable could only have been written by an Indian. and by an Indian who observed from the outside. No European, however sympathetic, could have created the character of Bakha, because he would not have known enough about his troubles. And no Untouchable could have written the book, because he would have been involved in indignation and self-pity."

In Two Leaves and a Bud (1937) Anand continued his exploration of the Indian society. The story told about a poor Punjabi peasant. He is brutally exploited in a tea plantation and killed by a British official, who tries to rape his daughter. The socially conscious work shared much with the proletarian novels published in Britain and the United States during the 1930s.

Anand's famous trilogy, The Village (1939), Across the Black Waters (1940), and The Sword and the Sickle (1942), was a strong protest against social injustices. The story follows the life of Lai Sing from adolescent rebellion through his experiences in World War I, to his return home and revolutionary activities. In Anand's early novels his social and political analysis of oppression grows clearly from his involvement with the Left in England. Among Anand's later and most impressive works is The Private Life of an Indian Prince (1953). This time Anand focused more on human psyche and personal struggles than on class conflicts. The story had its origins in the betrayal of a hill-woman with whom the author was romantically involved while married to his first wife, the actress Kathleen van Gelder. Anand had met Gelder in London; they married in 1939.

After divorce in 1948, Anand married Shirin Vajibdar, a distinguished dancer. Anand's daughter from his first marriage became a writer, too. Since the 1950s, Anand intermittently worked on a projected seven-volume autobiography, entitled Seven Ages of Man. From the project appeared Seven Summers (1951), Morning Face (1968), Confessions of a Lover (1976), and The Bubble (1984). Anand also published books on subjects as diverse as Marx and Engels in India, Tagore, Nehru, Aesop's fables, the Kama Sutra, erotic sculpture, and Indian ivories. Mulk Raj Anand died in Pune on September 28, 2004. Along with the novelista and short story writer Munshi Premchand (1880-1936), Anand was involved in forming dalit literature, used to refer to the "untouchable", casteless sects of India.

For further reading: Mulk Raj Anand: A Revaluation by P. Rajan (1994); Studies in Indian and Anglo-Indian Fiction by Saros Cowasjee (1993); The Novels of Mulk Raj Anand, ed. by R.K. Dhawan (1992); The Wisdom of the Heart by M. Fisher (1985); Mulk Raj Anand by by G. Packham (1979); The Yoke of Pity by A. Niven (1978); So Many Freedoms by S. Cowasjee (1977); Coolie: An Assessment by S. Cowasjee (1976); Mulk Raj Anand by M. Berry (1971); Mulk Raj Anand by M.KL. Naik (1968); The Elephant and the Lotus by J. Lindsay (1965) - See also: World Hello Day Letters; Indian Literature.

Selected works:

- Persian Painting, 1930
- Curries and Other Indian Dishes, 1932
- The Hindu View of Art, 1933
- The Golden Breath, 1933
- The Lost Child and Other Stories, 1934
- Untouchable, 1935
- Coolie, 1936
- Two Leaves and a Bud, 1937
- Lament on the Death of a Master of the Arts, 1938
- Marx and Engels on India, 1939
- The Village, 1939
- Across the Black Waters, 1940
- Letters on India, 1942

- The Sword and the Sickle, 1942
- India Speaks, 1943 (play)
- The Barber's Trade Union, and Other Stories, 1944
- The Big Heart, 1945
- Apology for Heroism, 1946
- Homageto Tagore, 1946
- Indian Fairy Tales, 1946 (retold by M.R.A.)
- The Tractor and the Corn Goddess, and Other Stories, 1947
- The Bride's Book of Beauty, 1947 (with K. Hutheesing)
- On Education, 1947
- Indian Short Stories, 1947 (ed., with I. Singh)
- The King-Emperor's English, 1948
- The Story of India, 1948
- Letters Written to Indian Air, 1949
- The Indian Theatre, 1950
- Seven Sumers, 1951
- The Story of Man, 1952
- The Private Life of an Indian Prince, 1953 (rev.ed. 1970)
- Reflections on the Golden Bud and Other Stories, 1954
- Selected Stories, 1954
- The Story of Man, 1954
- The Dancing Foot, 1957
- The Hindu View of Art, 1957
- India in Colour, 1958
- Kama Kala, 1958
- The Power of Darkness, and Other Stories, 1959

- Aesop's Fables, 1960 (retold by M.R.A.)
- The Old Woman and the Cow, 1960 (as Gauri, 1976)
- Homage to Khajuraho, 1960
- The Road, 1961
- More Indian Fairy Tales, 1961 (retold by M.R.A.)
- Homage to Khajuraho, 1962
- Is There a Contemporary Indian Civilization?, 1963
- Death of a Hero, 1963
- The Third Eye, 1963
- The Story of Chacha Nehru, 1965
- Bombay, 1965
- Lajwanti and Other Stories, 1966
- The Volcano, 1967
- The Humanism of M.K. Gandhi, 1967
- Morning Face, 1968
- Annals of Childhood, 1968 (ed.)
- Contemporary World Sculpture, 1968 (ed.)
- Experiments, 1968 (ed.)
- Grassroots, 1968 (ed.)
- Delhi, Agra, Sikri, 1968
- Konorak, 1968 (with others)
- Indian Ivories, 1970
- Ajanta, 1970
- Roots and Flowers, 1972
- Author to Critic: The Letters of Mulk Raj Anand to Saros Cowasjee, 1973
- Between Tears and Laughter, 1973
- Album of Indian Paintings, 1973

- Folk Tales of Punjab, 1974 (ed.)
- Apology for Heroism: a Brief Autobiography of Ideas, 1975
- Roots and Flowers, 1975
- Confessions of a Lover, 1976
- Homage to Amritsar, 1977 (ed.)
- Homage to Jaipur, 1977 (ed.)
- Selected Short Stories, 1977
- Alampur, 1978 (ed.)
- Seven Little Known Birds of the Inner Eye, 1978
- Tales from Tolstoy, 1978 (ed.)
- Tantra Magic, 1978 (with A. Mookerjee)
- The Humanism of Jawaharlal Nehru, 1978
- Only Connect: Letters to Indian Friends - E.M. Forster, a Profile, 1979
- Homage to Kalamkari, 1979 (ed.)
- The Humanism of Rabindranath Tagore, 1979
- Golden Goa, 1980 (ed.)
- Splendours of Tamil Nadu, 1980 (ed.)
- Splendours of the Vijayanagara, 1980 (ed.)
- Maya of Mohenjo-Daro, 1980
- Conversations in Bloomsbury, 1981
- Maharaga Ranit Singh as Patron of the Arts, 1981 (ed.)
- Treasures of Everyday Art, 1981 (ed.)
- Kama Sutra of Vatsyayana, 1982 (ed. with L. Dane)
- Ellora, 1984
- Madhubani Painting, 1984
- The Bibble, 1984

- Pilpali Sahib: the Story of a Childhood under the Raj, 1985
- Poet-Painter: Paintings by Rabindranath Tagore, 1985
- Panorama, 1986 (ed. with S.B. Rao)
- Ajanta, 1988
- Three Eminent Personalities on the Ram Janambhoomi, 1989
- Amrita Sher-Gil, 1989
- Pilpali Sahib: The Story of a Big Ego in a Small Boy, 1990
- Old Myth and New Myth: Letters from Mulk Raj Anand to K.V.S. Murti
- Anand, 1991
- Little Plays of Mahatma Gandhi, 1991
- Caliban and Gandhi: Letters to 'Bapu* from Bombay, 1991

R. K. NARAYAN

R. K. Narayan was born in Madras in 1906 and educated there and at Maharajah's College in Mysore. He has lived in India ever since, apart from his travels. Most of his work, starting from his first novel Swami and friends (1935) is set in the fictional town of Malgudi which at the same time captures everything Indian while having a unique identity of its own. After having read only a few of his books it is difficult to shake off the feeling that you have vicariously lived in this town. Malgudi is perhaps the single most endearing "character" R. K. Narayan has ever created.

He has published numerous novels, five collections of short stories (A Horse and Two Goats, An Astrologer's Day, Lawley Road, Malgudi Days, and The Grandmother's Tale), two travel books (My Dateless Diary and The Emerald Route), four collections of essays (Next Sunday, Reluctant Guru, A

Writer's Nightmare, and A Story-Teller's World), a memoir (My Days), and some translations of Indian epics and myths (The Ramayana, The Mahabharata, and Gods, Demons and Others).

In 1980, R. K. Narayan was awarded the A.C. Benson award by the Royal Society of Literature and was made an Honorary Member of the American Academy and Institute of Arts and Letters. In 1989 he was made a member of the Rajya Sabha (the non-elective House of Parliament in India). He received the Sahitya Akademi Award for The Guide (1958).

R. K. Narayan's full name is Rasipuram Krishnaswami Ayyar Naranayanaswami. In his early years he signed his name as R. K. Narayanaswami, but apparently at the time of the publication of Swami and Friends, he shortened it to R. K. Narayan on Graham Greene's suggestion.

Book(s) by R. K. Narayan:

- 1935: Swami and friends
- 1937: Bachelor of Arts
- 1938: The Dark Room
- 1939: Mysore
- 1945: The English Teacher
- 1947: An Astrologer's Day, and other stories
- 1949: Mr. Sampath - The Printer of Malgudi
- 1952: The Financial Expert
- 1953: Grateful to Life and Death
- 1955: Waiting for the Mahatma
- 1956: Lawley Road, and other stories
- 1958: The Guide
- 1960: Next Sunday : sketches and essays
- 1961: The Man-Eater of Malgudi

- 1964: My Dateless Diary: An American Journey
- 1965: Gods, Demons, and others
- 1967: The Vendor of Sweets
- 1970: A Horse and two Goats, stories
- 1972: The Ramayana; a shortened modern prose version
- 1974: My Days
- 1974: Reluctant Guru
- 1976: The Painter of Signs
- 1978: The Mahabharata: a shortened modern prose version
- 1980: The Emerald Route
- 1982: Malgudi Days
- 1983: A Tiger for Malgudi
- 1985: Under the Banyan Tree and other stories
- 1986: Talkative Man
- 1988: A Writer's Nightmare : selected essays
- 1989: A Story-Teller's World: Stories, Essays, Sketches
- 1990: The World of Nagaraj
- 1992: Malgudi Landscapes: the best of R.K. Narayan
- 1993: The Grandmother's Tale: three novellas
- 1993: Salt & sawdust : stories and table talk

RAJA RAO

Indian writer of novels and short stories, whose works are deeply rooted in Brahmanism and Hinduism. Raja Rao's semi-autobiographical novel, The Serpent and the Rope (1960), is a story of a search for spiritual truth in Europe and India. It established him as one of the finest Indian stylists. "Writing is my dharma," he once said.

I hear you saying that liberation is possible and that Socratic wisdom is identical with your guru's. No, Raja, I must start from what I am. I am those monsters which visit my dreams and reveal to me my hidden essence. (Czeslaw Milosz in 'To Raja Rao')

Raja Rao was born on November 8, 1908 in Hassan, in the state of Mysore in south India, into a well-known Brahman family. His native language was Kanarese, but his post-graduate education was in France, and all his publications in book form were in English. Like the Nigerian novelist Chinua Achebe, writing in English, Rao was concerned with language and consciousness. In the foreword to Kanthapura (1938) he admitted the difficulties in using "a language that is not one's own the spirit that is one's own," and conveying "the various shades and omissions of certain thought-movement that looks maltreated in an alien language."

Rao was educated at Muslim schools. After taking a degree from Madras University, he left India for Europe, where he remained for a decade. He studied at the universities of Montpellier and the Sorbonne, doing research in Christian theology and history. In 1931 he married a French academic, Camille Mouly. Later he depicted the breakdown of their marriage in The Serpent and the Rope. His first stories Rao published in French and English. During 1931-32 he contributed four articles written in Kannada for Jaya Karnataka, an influential journal.

When his marriage disintegrated in 1939, Rao returned to India and began his first period of residence in an ashram. During WW II, he travelled widely in India in search of his spiritual heritage. In 1942 he was active in an underground movement against colonial rule. During these years he edited the literary magazine Tomorrow.

Rao's involvement in the nationalist movement is reflected in his first two books. The novel Kanthapura (1938) was an account of the impact of Gandhi's teaching on non-violent resistance against the British. The story is seen from the perspective of a small Mysore village in South India. Rao borrows the style and structure from Indian vernacular tales and folk-epic. The narrator is an old woman. She tells how the community obtains from daily life, with its millennia-old worship of the local deity, the strength to stand against the British Raj.

In the character of the young Moorthy, who comes back from the city, Rao portrays an idealist and supporter of ahimsa and satyagraha, who wants to cross the traditional barriers of caste. The younger generation has city ways, they read city books, and they even call themselves Gandhi-men. Doré, as the old woman calls the "university graduate," has given up his "boots and hat and suit and had taken to dhoti and khadi, and it was said he had even given up his city habit of smoking." The work was highly praised by the English writer E.M. Forster, whose masterwork A Passage to India (1924) criticized British imperialism. However, Rao's India is not a certain geographical or historical entity, but more of a philosophical concept and a symbol of spiritual calling.

Rao returned to the theme of Gandhism in the short story collection The Cow of the Barricades (1947). In 1998 he published Gandhi's biography Great Indian Way: A Life of Mahatma Gandhi. After the war, Rao spent much of his time in France and travelling throughout the world. He visited America in 1950 and later spent some more time living in an ashram. In 1965 he married an actress, Katherine Jones. From 1965 to 1983 Rao lectured on Indian philosophy at the University of Texas, Austin. In 1988 he received the prestigious Neustadt International Prize for Literature. Several Neustadt Laureates have also received the Nobel Prize for literature, among them Gabriel García Márquez, Czeslaw Milosz, and Octavio Paz.

The Serpent and the Rope was written after a long silence during which Rao lived India, where he renewed a connection with his roots in the modern rendering of the

Mahabharata legend of Satayavan and Savithri. The work also dramatized the relationships between Indian and Western culture. Ramaswamy, a young Brahmin studying in France, is married to a French college teacher, Madeleine, who sees her husband above all as a guru. As Ramaswamy struggles with commitments imposed on him by his Hindu family, his wife becomes a Buddhist in her spiritual quest and renounces worldly desires. She leaves her husband to find his own true self. The serpent in the title refers to the illusion and the rope to the reality.

Cat and Shakespeare (1965) was a metaphysical comedy that answered philosophical questions posed in the earlier novels. In the book the Hindu notion of karma is symbolized by a cat. The hero discovers in his attempts to receive divine grace, that there is no dichotomy between himself and God. Comrade Kirillov (1976) was written early in Rao's career and was first published in French. It satirized communism as an ideological misunderstanding of man's ultimate aims, and argued that all foreign creeds gradually become Indianized.

The Chessmaster and His Moves (1988) is peopled by characters from various cultures seeking their identities. Like Nabokov, Rao used the metaphor of the chess game to animate philosophical and psychological ideas. In the story Sivaram Sastri, an Indian mathematician in Paris, meets Proust, and recounts his love affairs and friendships. Rao has confessed: "I am no scholar. I am a creative writer. I love to play with ideas. It is like a chess game with horses, elephants, chamberlains and kings which might fight with one another. The game is not for winning. It is for rasa-delight." Raja Rao died of heart failure on July 8, 2006, at his home in Austin, Texas. He was 97.

Selected works:

- Kanthapura, 1938
- Changing India, 1939 (ed., with I. Singh)

- The Cow of the Barricades, and Other Stories, 1947
- Whither India, 1948 (with I. Singh)
- The Serpent and the Rope, 1960
- The Cat and Shakespeare, 1965
- Comrade Kirilov, 1976
- The Policeman and the Rose, 1978
- The Chessmaster and His Moves, 1988
- On the Ganga Ghat, 1993
- The Meaning of India, 1996
- Great Indian Way: A Life of Mahatma Gandhi, 1998
- The Best of Raja Rao, 1998

EMINENT AUTHORS

Indian authors writing in English have conquered the world. These eminent writers have won coveted national and international Literary Awards, attracted vast media attention and made the publishing industry breath afresh. With a rising readership, they are the centre of critical attention, scholarly works and research activities of International academia. Showcased here are the brief biographical details of these eminent authors, along with their noteworthy works and critical response.

A. K. Ramanujan

Attipat Krishnaswami Ramanujan or A. K. Ramanujan, as he is known, was born in Mysore, India in 1929. He was a transitional figure in the history of Indian English Literature, and also a trans-disciplinary scholar, working as a poet, translator, linguist, and folklorist. Although he wrote primarily in English, he was fluent in both Kannada and Tamil, the language of his family. Ramanujan received his BA and MA in English language and literature from the University of Mysore. He then spent some time teaching at several universities in South India before getting a graduate diploma in theoretical linguistics from Deccan University in Poona in 1958. He went to the U.S. in 1959.

In 1962, he became an assistant professor at the University of Chicago, where he was affiliated throughout the rest of his career. The following year, he went to Indiana University where he got a Ph.D. in linguistics in 1963. He taught at several U.S. universities, including Harvard, University of Wisconsin, University of Michigan, University of California at Berkeley, and Carlton College. At the University of Chicago, Ramanujan was instrumental in shaping the South Asian Studies program. He worked in the departments of South Asian Languages and Civilizations, Linguistics, and with the Committee on Social Thought. In 1976, the government of India awarded him the honorific title "Padma Sri," and in 1983, he was given the MacArthur Prize Fellowship. Ramanujan breathed his last in Chicago on July 13, 1993.

Selected bibliography of Ramanujan's works:

Books:

The Striders. London: Oxford U. Press, 1966.

Interior Landscapes: Love Poems from a Classical Tamil Anthology. Bloomington: Indiana U. Press. 1967.

Hokkulalli Huvilla, No Lotus in the Navel. Dharwar, 1969.

Relations. London, New York: Oxford U. Press, 1971.

Speaking of Siva. Harmondsworth, Great Britain: Penguin Books, 1973.

(with Edwin Gerow, eds.) The Literatures of India. Chicago: University of Chicago Press, 1974.

Selected Poems. Delhi, New York: Oxford U. Press, 1976.

Samskara. Delhi: Oxford U. Press, 1976.

Mattu Itara Padyagalu And Other Poems. Dharwar, 1977.

Hymns for the Drowning. Princeton: Princeton U. Press, 1981.

The Epic of Palnadu: A Study of Translation of Palnati Vinula Katha, a Telugu Oral Tradition from Andhra Pradesh, India. New York: Oxford University Press, 1982.

Poems of Love and War. New York: Colombia U. Press, 1985.

Second Sight. New York: Oxford U. Press, 1986.

(with S. Blackburn, eds.) Another Harmony New Essays on the Folklore of India. Berkeley: University of California Press, 1986. 294-344.

(with Vinay Dharwadker, eds.) The Oxford Anthology of Modern Indian Poetry. 1990

Folktales from India, Oral Tales from Twenty Indian Languages. New York: Pantheon Books, 1991.

The Collected Poems of A. K. Ramanujan. Delhi: Oxford University Press, 1995.

A Flowering Tree and Other Oral Tales from India.

Essays :

(with W. Bright.) "Sociolinguistic Variation and Language Change." In Sociolinguistics: Selected Readings. J.B. Pride and J. Holmes, eds. London: Penguin, 1964.

"The Indian Oedipus." In Oedipus: A Folklore Casebook. Alan Dundes and Lowell Edmunds, eds. New York: Garland Press, 1983. 234-261.

"On Folk Puranas." Conference on Puranas, University of Wisconsin, Madison, August, mss. 1985.

"Two Realms of Kannada Folklore." In Another Harmony New Essays on the Folklore of India. Blackburn and Ramanujan, eds. Berkeley: U of California Press, 1986. 41-75.

"Introduction." In Indian Folktales, Beck et al., 1987. xxv-xxxi.

"The Relevance of South Asian Folklore." In Indian Folklore II, Peter Claus, J. Handoo, and D.P. Pattanayak, eds. Mysore: Central Institute of Indian Languages, 1987. 79-156.

"Classics Lost and Found." In Contemporary India: Essays on the Uses of Tradition. Carla M. Borden, ed. Delhi: Oxford University Press, 1989.

"Where Mirrors are Windows: Toward an anthology of reflections." In History of Religions 28.3 (1989): 187-216.

1990 "Is There an Inidan Way of Thinking?" In India Through Hindu Categories. McKim Marriott, ed. New Delhi/ London: Sage publications, 1990.

"Three hundred Ramayanas." In Many Ramayanas: The Diversity of a Narrative Tradition. Paula Richman, ed. Berkeley: U Cal Press, 1991.

"Toward a Counter-System: Women's Tales." In A. Appadurai, F. Korom, and M. Mills, eds. Philadelphia: U Penn Press, 1991.

"A story in search of an audience." In Parabola 17.3 (1992): 79-82.

"On Folk Mythologies and Folk Puranas." In Purana Perennis: Reciprocity and Transformation in Hindu and Jaina Texts. Wendy Doniger, ed. Albany: State University of New York Press, 1993.

1994 "Some Thoughts on 'Non-Western' Classics, with Indian Examples." World Literature Today, 1994. 68.

Achievements :

- Contributions to South Asian Studies
- Sociolinguistic Theory
- Folklore Studies
- Translation Works
- Ramanujan's Poetry

CONTRIBUTIONS TO SOUTH ASIAN STUDIES

Ramanujan was a major figure in shaping South Asian studies. According to him, the Indian way of thinking is "context-sensitive" as opposed to "context-free." Context-sensitive is, he suggests, the more appropriate term for what others have taken for an Indian tendency toward inconsistency and hypocrisy, as well as, perhaps tolerance and mimicry. Ramanujan cites Said's Orientalism here, suggesting a European source for these stereotypes created out of a necessity to essentialize and exoticize the Eastern world. These terms, he takes from linguistics, in which they refer to different kinds of grammatical rules. In applying them to cultures or ways of thinking, Ramanujan relies primarily on a text-based analysis.

He cautions that they are "overall tendencies." "Actual behavior may be more complex, though the rules they think with are a crucial factor guiding the behavior". Context-free thinking, which he attributes to Euro-American culture, gives rise to universal testaments of law, such as in the Judeo-Christian tradition and in the European philosophical tradition, e.g. Hegel. Context-sensitive thinking, on the other hand, gives rise to more complicated sets of standards such as the Laws of Manu, by which appropriateness depends on various factors, especially factors of identity and personhood, such as birth, occupation, life stage, karma, dharma, etc. Ramanujan stresses that this difference in philosophical outcome is not a symptom of irrationality, but a different kind of rationale.

SOCIOLINGUISTIC THEORY

Ramanujan's work in sociolinguistics also speaks to the critique of Sanskritic Indology. As shown in his 1964 essay with W. Bright, Sociolinguistic Variation and Language Change, Ramanujan opposes those who would conceive a monolithic standard grammar for Indian languages. Rather, he seeks to legitimize the vast variety of linguistic dialects.

Specifically, here, Ramanujan and Bright compare a Brahmin Tamil dialect with a non-Brahmin Tamil dialect. The Brahmin dialect, they found, was much more inflected with Sanskrit loan words and styles, whereas the non-Brahmin dialect tended to shift by innovation on existing phonologic and morphologic features rather than by foriegn adoption. Ramanujan and Bright do not address the political and economic implication of this differential grammatical shift. However, their point, in 1964, was only to acknowledge and legitimize linguistic innovation as it occurs in various social groups in India.

FOLKLORE STUDIES

In Ramanujan's writing about Indian folklore and classic poetry, the theme of context-sensitivity reappears. In Where Mirrors are Windows (1989) and in Three Hundred Ramayanas (1991), he discusses the "intertextual" nature of written and oral Indian literature. By this, he means that Indian stories refer to one another and sometimes to other versions of the very story being told. He says, "What is merely suggested in one poem may become central in a 'repetition' or an 'imitation' of it. Mimesis is never only mimesis, for it evokes the earlier image in order to play with it and make it mean other things". It is important for Ramanujan to note that these intertextual influences do not occur in a unidirectional pattern. He emphasizes that the oral and written traditions, the Sanskritic and local traditions are in dialogue with and mutually influence one another.

TRANSLATION WORKS

Ramanujan worked to make non-Sanskritic Indian literature acknowledged in the realm of South Asian studies through the translation of works in the South Indian languages Kannada and Tamil. His translation works include Interior Landscapes: Love Poems from a Classical Tamil Anthology (1967), Speaking of Siva (1973), Hymns for the Drowning (1981), and A Flowering Tree and Other Oral

Tales from India. In The Interior Landscape (1967), Ramanujan covers another sense of intertextuality which lies in the symbolic evocation common in Tamil poetry. Here, he discusses the highly stylized symbol system of Tamil poetry in which different landscape features evoke emotional tones, meanings and relational qualities. Necessary to understanding any Tamil poem is knowledge of the symbolic context and tradition in which it was written.

RAMANUJAN'S POETRY

Ramanujan wrote poetry almost entirely in English. The poet is known for his rather atavistic poetic arguments - arguments which disrupt common expectations. Ramanujan is not a poet of easy moral expectations. Where conventional morality collapses, poetry takes off. In Ramanujan's quirky universe, excellence in human affairs is more a product of one's compulsions or handicaps rather than one's innate genius. Reviewer Bruce King called Ramanujan one of the "Indo-Anglian harbingers of literary modernism". This description highlights several characteristics of Ramanujan's poetry, perhaps less common in other transcultural poetry. Characteristics of his modernist style include an almost jarring realism and hints at a kind of confessional style. Themes of hybridity and transculturation are also highlighted in his poetry.

Selected reviews and commentaries on Ramanujan

Book reviews :

Chandran, K. Narayana. "The Collected Poems of A. K. Ramanujan." In World Literature Today 70 (1996): 762.

Venkateswaran, P. "The Collected Poems of A. K. Ramanujan." In Choice 34 (1996): 121.

Essays :

Dharwadker, Vinay. "A. K. Ramanujan: Author, Translator, Scholar." In World Literature Today 68.2 (1994): 279.

Jha, Rama. "A Conversation with A. K. Ramanujan." Humanities Review 3.1 (1981).

Naik, M. K. "A. K. Ramanujan and the Search for Roots." In Living Indian English Poets: An Anthology of Critical Essays. M. Prasad, ed. New Delhi: Sterling Publishers Private Ltd, 1989.

Parthasarathy, R. "How it Strikes a Contemporary: The Poetry of A. K. Ramanujan." Literary Criterion 12.2-3 (1976).

Patel, Geeta. "King, Three Indian Poets: Nissim Ezeliel, A. K. Ramanujan, Don Moraes." In The Journal of Asian Studies 51.4 (1992): 960.

Ramazani, Jahan. "Metaphor and Postcoloniality: The Poetry of A. K. Ramanujan." In Contemporary Literature 39.1 (1988): 27.

Shulman, David. 1994. "Attipat Krishnaswami Ramanujan (1929-1993)." In The Journal of Asian Studies 53.3 (1994): 1048.

Singh, Rajendra and Jyant K. Lele. "The Autonomy of Social Variables: The Indian Evidence Revisited." In Explorations in Indian Sociolinguistics. Rajendra Singh, Probal Dasgupta, and Jayant K. Lele, eds. New Delhi: Sage Publications, 1995.

Venkatachalapathy, A. R. "Obituary: A. K. Ramanujan." In Economic and Political Weekly 28.31 (1993): 1571.

ABHA DAWESWAR

"Fun Fearless Female" - is how Abha Dawesar has been crowned by Cosmopolitan, a monthly magazine of India. Femina magazine in India named her one of India's 12 remarkable women and one of India's leading national English language newspapers, The Hindustan Times, included Dawesar with a list of eleven other authors in its Next Big Things for 2005. New York's weekly magazine Time Out listed Dawesar as one of 25 People to make their mark in

2005. This young and promising author was born in New Delhi in 1974. She graduated with a degree in political philosophy from Harvard University after writing an honors thesis examining the conception of human greatness in Nietzsche's On the Genealogy of Morals. She currently works in Business Development for a software company in New York. She is the receipient of the New York Foundation of the Arts Fellowship in Fiction for 2000.

Dawesar's debut novel Miniplanner was chosen as a "Season's best pick" by the NY publication LGNY. It was also published in India by Penguin Books under the title The Three of Us and hailed as "a coming-of-age of Indian diaspora writers."

Babyji, her second novel, is the winner of the American Library Association's Stonewall Award for 2006. The novel was also named one of the ten best books of fiction for 2005 by the Boston Phoenix. It was reviewed nationally and internationally in the US media, India, Italy, Germany, and Spain.

That Summer in Paris is Abha Dawesar's third novel and it is to be released on 20th June, 2006.

Bibliogarphy

This is a story about Andre Bernard, a white male financial analyst. Andre, a freshly minted 24-year-old college grad, soon finds himself on both a corporate fast track and a sexual roller coaster. On moving to Manhattan for a corporate job he finds himself having sex with Nathan, his boss' boss. Things become even more intriguing when he later meets Nathan's wife. He is seduced by the elegant Sybil, Nathan's young wife. Before long he's half heartedly sleeping with the office secretary, Martha (eventually getting her pregnant). Along the way he reconnects with level headed Madhu, the Indian woman he dated and nearly married in college. The story progresses through ever more complicated sexual triangles, all kept in order through his mini-planner.

The comic surface of the story with juicy intricacies of sex, belies an under-plot about growing up, assuming responsibility, and learning to-trust oneself.

Babyji

Babyjiis the story of Anamika Sharma, a sexy, surprising, and subversively wise student growing up in Delhi. At school she is number one at quantum physics. At home she sneaks off to her parents' scooter garage to read the Kamasutra. Before long she has seduced an elegant older divorcée and the family servant, and has caught the eye of a classmate coveted by all the boys. After studying chaos theory in her high school physics textbook, Anamika feels justified in pursuing three simultaneous same-sex affairs, with her doting servant, her impressionable schoolmate and a beautiful older woman who inspires such complicated feelings that Anamika nicknames her India, after their vast and varied homeland. Anamika uses sex as a means to investigate life's chemistry and her autonomy outside of rigid Brahmin mores. As issues of caste, meritocracy and self-sacrifice arise; Anamika purifies her intentions by channelling them into helping a troubled male student, Chakra Dev, who's almost as oversexed as she is. If the unusual secondary characters occasionally seem as gratuitous as pornographic movie extras, Anamika's ponderings and emotional reversals are lavished with as much attention as a 16-year-old girl would demand. With adulthood setting in, Anamika confronts questions that would test someone twice her age.

That Summer in Paris

Written with sureness of style and tempo, That Summer in Paris reflects on how art informs love-and love, literature. Prem Rustum, a celebrated aging Indian novelist, unexpectedly meets Maya, a vibrant aspiring writer, and surprises himself by following her to Paris. In the slow, sensuous summer that follows, Prem looks back on his muses, his art, and his lost loves. Maya's presence brings Prem into direct confrontation with his mortality and desires. As he struggles anew with the eternal question of love, Prem's longstanding friendship with Pascal, a fellow writer, illuminates them both in the final chapter of their lives.

Abha Dawesar's Miniplanner does not Skirt the Issue

When writer Abha Dawesar began to work on her first novel Miniplanner, she had an image in her mind - a strip club in New York City. In the opening chapter of Miniplanner (Cleis Press, 2000), Dawesar's 24-year old protagonist, André Bernard visits Skirts -- a strip club, with his boss, Nathan Williams, where women in G-strings perform lap dances for male customers.

Although they are visiting a heterosexual establishment, André and Nathan will soon start a torrid gay relationship. And by the time you are into the first 50 pages, getting through the steamy sexual sequences between the two, André has also started an affair with Nathan's wife Sybil. His after-work social life will get so complicated that he will need a miniplanner to keep track of his evening/night schedules.

"I had the initial scene in my mind -- the strip club scene -- and once I started writing, I really got into it," Dawesar says, sipping a cappuccino at a coffee shop in Manhattan's Lower East Side. The strip club image is familiar to Dawesar, since her day-job is in the financial services industry.

"I thought it was interesting that all these people from Wall Street, accountants and consultants go to strip clubs and behave this way," Dawesar says, adding that she has visited a strip club with office mates. "Many people I work with do this kind of thing. Often, the whole group will go out to entertain a business client visiting from outside. This is corporate entertainment."

How does a 26-year-old raised in New Delhi (she attended Army Public School and her parents, both doctors, still live in India), with an undergraduate degree in philosophy from

Harvard University, get into the mind and under the skin of a white, male, bisexual investment banker - André Bernard?

"Living in New York you have exposure to a lot of different communities and different types of people," Dawesar says. "I hadn't really intended to write a book about André. It was really my imagination taking over. The imagination is limitless. You can be anything you want, whenever you want."

"The way the world is, there are so many different types of identities you have and so many different compartments, but there is also so much crossover. In some ways, André is nothing of what I am, but on the other hand I can write in his voice. Because in some ways, I can be him in my mind."

She wrote the book two years ago, over a five-week stretch. It was an easy write, she says. Once she finished it, she showed the manuscript to friends, who were more familiar with André's lifestyle.

"No even one commented on things I expected to be problematic, whether André's representation was accurate. And that was fantastic," she says.

She pitched the book to a couple of agents, and when things were not working out, she decided to send manuscript to Cleis Press -- a small publishing house in San Francisco.

"One thing I like about Cleis is that they do a lot of gender bending stuff and so hopefully the book won't get slotted as a gay book," she says. "It was heartening that they thought the primary readership will be heterosexual women in big cities."

Since November 2000, when the book was published, Dawesar has been on a limited promotion tour to Los Angeles, San Francisco, Boston and New York, reading at independent and specialized bookstores. Her audience, she says, has been young city dwellers, though varied in race (including South Asian men and women) and gender.

She has read at Manhattan's Joseph Papp Public Theater and at an Asian studies conference at Columbia University. She has also been interviewed at the Asia Pacific Forum on the WBAI radio station in New York City.

Slowly, the book it finding its way in gay and lesbian publications and web sites.

Writing on planetout.com, Richard Labonte said: Dawesar has crafted an intricate, often hilarious story...(with) steamy sex scenes, tender family moments and passages of reflective introspection."

And a reviewer on LesbianNation.com said: "Dawesar exhibits talent when it comes to hot sex scenes, and she's a keen and witty observer of corporate life."

Although she dedicated Miniplanner to her parents, Dawesar was quite clear that she did not want them to read the book.

"I love my parents. This my first book. I dedicated the book to them, but that doesn't mean I wanted them to read it."

Miniplanner has not been released in India, but her parents managed to acquire a copy through friends in Vermont.

"I was aghast," she says. "And so I called them up and said please don't read it, but my mother said she was definitely going to read it. So I said fine, but please don't let anyone else at home read it."

The next time she called home her father was 50 pages into the book. "He said it was quite remarkable," she says with a nervous giggle. "So I was kind of shell-shocked."

She thinks her father liked the book more than her mother. In fact, her mother has pointed out that Miniplanner could have accomplished the things it did, without being so explicit.

"But if you are living in 1999 in New York as a gay man, I don't think you are going to be coy," she says. "You are going to speak the way gay men do and not talk about sex as a young Indian woman, who is 26 or for that matter a middle aged Indian woman in New Delhi. This book has to be authentic to that. I certainly think I made the right choice."

A Life Less Ordinary

Abha Dawesar's: The Three of Us is a rather hatke se debut. The 28-year-old writer from Delhi's Army Public School who went on to do a thesis on Nietzsche's On the Genealogy of Morals from Harvard chose to make her debut with a novel about a white male protagonist.

In town visiting relatives, Abha is a petite personification of calling a spade a spade. "I am not obsessed with South Asian identity. I just want to write fiction and the whole idea of fiction is creating something, isn't it? I am not writing a memoir."

The Three of Us tells the story of Andre Bernard who comes to New York on his first job in a Japanese investment bank. Before we are through with the first chapter, Andre has been taken out to a strip club by his boss's boss, Nathan, and seduced by him.

The book follows a sexual merry-go-round where Andre sleeps with Nathan, Nathan's wife, the office secretary, a French tourist and his ex-girlfriend. While there is so much sex in the book, the treatment is amazingly matter-of-fact.

"I did not put in the sex to titillate - I was just being authentic to Andre's voice." At book readings in Bangalore and Delhi, "there were quite a few raised eyebrows but in the final count most people were pretty open-minded."

The novel started off as a short story according to Abha. "There are a lot of corporates taking freshers to strip clubs and I thought it would make an interesting story. But even

35 pages on, the story showed no signs of getting over which is how the book was born."

About the difference between writing a short story and novel, Abha comments, "Short stories offer immediate gratification as there is a specific plot and a quick resolution, while with a novel it becomes difficult to sustain atmosphere and quite often the novel develops into something totally different from what you set out to do in the first place."

Abha insists that Andre "is a regular guy in New York. Homosexuality is not such a big deal there. I am not speaking for the whole of America. But in New York the assimilation of gay people is very high. I did not plan to make Andre gay. The character just developed like that."

The description of women is striking in the book mainly because they are not objectified. "That is in character - Andre has discovered he is gay and so his vision is slightly askew. He notices men rather than women."

Working in an investment bank on Wall Street (she quit 13 months ago to concentrate on writing) provided Abha with the backdrop for the novel. Having a lot of gay friends also helped. There were other areas that Abha had to do research on like "Monk fish. I spoke to a lot of people about how it is made."

A vegetarian, Abha finds "long descriptions of meat unappetising" which is one of the reasons the book has so many vegetarians in it. "It was not conscious decision. And vegetarianism is a popular trend now."

The Three of Us was originally published as The Miniplanner in 2000 in San Francisco. "When it was being published in India, Penguin India suggested a change of name as people would not relate to the Miniplanner. I picked out The Three of Us among the titles they suggested."

Abha chose a male voice as "it is fun and partly because I wanted to see if I could get away with it." Abha has set her second novel, Babyji, (it has been bought by Random House), in India and the novel has a female voice. Abha describes the book, which is scheduled for publication next year, as having "a wider canvas."

Fond of classical music ("I cannot play music in my head like Andre"), Abha is not a fan of Hollywood or Bollywood. "Unless I am brain dead or on a plane, I would not like to spend two or three hours of my time watching these utterly predictable movies. I know they are entertainment but I would like some sort of artistic satisfaction." Abha is a fan of contemporary French cinema.

Abha chose to go West to study the arts in an atmosphere "where the arts are appreciated. I did not want to study literature as I did not want to be told how to appreciate a work of art." Abha chose to study philosophy as "life is about choices and philosophy educates us about the choices we can make."

An only child, Abha says her parents have been very supportive. Her New York state of mind is mainly echoed in her choice of clothes - "I do not like to dress up. I prefer trousers and kurtas or tops - that is the American side of me," she says with a smile.

"I am saving up all my personal memories for my 4,000-page autobiography that I will write when I am 80 years old," she says with a laugh. And then will we get all the salacious details of a life less ordinary? "Salacious or boring? There might be a reason I chose to write fiction you know!"

There does not seem any danger of that as boring is hardly a word you would associate with Abha Dawesar.

MANHATTAN MASALA

Abha Dawesar's: The Three Of Us has descriptions of sex every few paragraphs and has none of the lyrical eroticism of Lolita. But the novel, the New York-based author insists, holds a mirror to the post-modern world where science has stripped us of all mystery and dignity. After the reading at Sankar's, Abha Dawesar didn't have too many questions to answer. Someone asked if her novel had a moral, and she said it didn't. What her narrative offered, she said, was an observation on the Manhattan life. And she wound up soon. For a book with descriptions of sex every few paragraphs, this was a tame Q&A session.

Many have asked Abha why The Three of Us can't be called a pornographic book. And things on the home front haven't been as easy as at the bookstore. Her doctor-mother, who lives in Delhi, thought she could have told the story without getting into all those details. Her cousins, some of whom had come to visit their relatives in N.R. Colony, were curious how she could have written "all that".

That is a curiosity that Abha has now learnt to live with. "In the U.S., the South Asian community is more interested in me than in the book," she says. When the 28-year-old New Yorker came to Bangalore for a weeklong visit, she was interviewed by several newspapers, and by E-TV, for which she attempted to speak in her "rusty" Kannada. Her mother hails from these parts, but Abha spent all her schooling years in Delhi.

She later went to Harvard, where she studied political philosophy, particularly Nietzsche. Then she wanted to live in New York, and scanned the newspapers to see if she could get a job. A firm headquartered in London was setting up shop in New York, and offered her one. "I learnt on the job," she says. She worked for seven years, first in a financial services firm and later in an investment bank. In the last few months, she has been a fulltime writer, and hopes to make a living that way.

Some of what she observed at the investment bank job has come into her debut novel. The Three of Us, called Miniplanner in the U.S., is the story of Andre, an investment banker, who is seduced by Nathan, his boss's boss. As the book opens; we see Nathan taking Andre to a strip club in New York, and sex happens between them and a "regular girl". "It is a common practice among investment bankers to take their out-of-town clients to strip clubs," explains Abha.

Soon Andre is in bed with Nathan's elegant wife Sybil. He is sleeping with husband and wife every alternate day and has landed in the "inconvenient" situation of having to juggle them around. After an office party, Andre gets involved with Martha, who works as a secretary, and ends up impregnating her.

And then there is Madhu, his ex-girlfriend caught in a bad marriage, who comes by and finds consolation in his bed. When he has a spare day in his miniplanner, he contacts the Gay and Lesbian Center, hoping to find a lover. His typical week is choc-a-bloc with day and night appointments with his lovers.

In all her works published so far (the novel and two short stories on her website), Abha writes in a male voice. "I am writing my second novel from a woman's perspective," she says. But many have asked her the question how, given her Indian origins, she could write from a white male perspective. "It was interesting when the gay white press loved the book and didn't seem to notice or care that I was an Indian or a woman," she says. Abha is described as a South Asian writer - a label the Americans give writers from India to avoid confusing them with their native Indians.

Nathan comes across as a just man, less given to jealousy and unreasonableness than Andre's other lovers, which could explain the favourable reaction of the gay press. But Abha is aware the book could also be read as an adolescent fantasy. "In some ways, Andre has suddenly entered this stage in life where he finds himself in a sexual utopia," she says. "In some ways it is his adolescence. Andre is not the most mature of people... adolescence comes at different ages to different people."

Abha's essay on Nietzsche (1844-1900), posted on her website (www.abhadawesar.com) , says both the Left and the Right have misappropriated him. "The politicisation of university education, 20th Century pogroms for cleansing humanity, the displacement of philosophy by the behavioural sciences, and pseudo-Gothic industrial music all have one thing in common - Friedrich Wilhelm Nietzsche," she writes.

Where does Andre fit in this spectrum? "Nietzsche was a very good diagnostician of what's wrong with the modern world," she says. "In very broad philosophical terms, he tells us where we have failed, what our modern problems are, where democracy has failed..." She says she places Andre in the "modern or post-modern world where modern science has stripped us of our mystery, stripped us of the dignity of what was and not given us a new dignity".

Andre, for Abha, is a post-Nietzschean character who chooses "hedonism over something else, and a lot of it comes from a lack of understanding of where he fits in". His problems, she says, stem essentially from the denigration of the status of the human being "from being a soul to being a psyche". Nietzsche, she points out, saw democracy as a "bulldozer of greatness".

The sexual permutations and combinations in The Three of Us push it in the direction of situational comedy, or what Abha calls "sexual farce". Abha's characters make Woody Allen, that well-known Manhattan chronicler, look old-fashioned and conservative. Abha hasn't read him, but has watched his films. "In the past 10 or 15 years things have changed. Gay couples don't even get a second glance. New York is one of the most open cities in the world if you consider the amount of diversity, the amount of variations it allows. People walk on the streets with blue hair and nobody even notices them. This is definitely set in that New York."

Abha has read Nabokov's Lolita, but his erotic lyricism, she says confidently, is not her style. The narrative in The

Three of Us is snappy in a journalistic sort of way. "That really is a matter of taste," she says. "The style is enhanced in this direction because of the pace of the city, and the pace of its life."

Alan Bloom is Abha's favourite writer. His book, The Closing of the American Mind, is close to her heart. "He was a professor of political philosophy who lived in Chicago and died some years ago. I never met him, but when I read him, I feel that he is my guru." Abha is floored by many of his ideas, including the suggestion that the beat of rock is the beat of sex, and represents the desire for continual climax.

AKHIL SHARMA

Akhil Sharma was born in Delhi, India, in 1971. He grew up in Edison, New Jersey.

His stories have appeared in the Best American Short Stories anthology, the O. Henry Award Winners anthology, The Atlantic Monthly, and The New Yorker. He is a winner of The Voice Literary Supplement's Year 2000 "Writers on the Verge" Award. A portion of An Obedient Father was excerpted in the debut fiction issue of The New Yorker in June 2000. Sharma lives in New York City, where he is an investment banker at a major Wall Street firm.

Recent reviews...

> *"Sharma's sharply realistic fiction effortlessly interweaves one man's life, one family's history, and one country's fate into a compelling debut novel ... Sharma allows his fiction to unfold through wonderfully rich details. From Karan's cajoling of bribes from a school principal to his memories of his childhood in Beri to the minutiae of his sad domestic life with his daughter, the facts of this novel fascinate the reader. Combine this with Karan's greedy, comic, petty, and ultimately horrifying voice, and the result is a tale that haunts us long after we've finished it. A remarkable first novel."*

"A supernova in the galaxy of young, talented Indian writers, Sharma debuts with a bold and shocking novel that casts a mesmerizing spell. Ram Karan is a widower whose widowed daughter, Anita, and eight-year-old granddaughter, Asha, live with him in a tiny apartment in one of Delhi's poorer sections. Nominally a functionary in the physical education department of the city's schools, Ram is in fact 'Mr. Gupta's moneyman'; that is, he coerces bribes for his boss, who funnels the money to the Congress Party.

At first, Ram's candid admissions of 'general incompetence and laziness' are perversely endearing, but when the real cause of his self-hatred comes to light, the reader's perceptions begin to change. In a moment of temptation, Ram commits a furtive sexual act with his unwitting granddaughter - and his downfall begins. Twenty years ago, he had repeatedly raped Anita, who now becomes unhinged at the thought that her daughter may be in peril. Anita's bizarre revenge will result in Ram's complete degradation; ironically, the repercussions of her obsessive need for disclosure cause even more emotional damage to everyone involved. Concurrent with these personal tragedies and the breakdown of one family, Sharma draws an acid-etched picture of modern Indian society, in which the corrupt political system victimizes all citizens ... Sharma's depiction of a society riddled with graft, violent religious prejudice, male chauvinism and bigoted cultural attitudes is a cautionary tale about what happens to the individual spirit when poverty, superstition, racial tension and general hopelessness are exacerbated by the absence of judicial morality. This caustic yet darkly comic story resonates powerfully, as the reader comes to sympathize with fallible human beings trapped in circumstances that corrupt the soul."

AMIT CHAUDHURI

Born in Calcutta, India, in 1962, Amit Chaudhuri was brought up in Bombay. He graduated from University College,

London, and was a research student at Balliol College, Oxford. He was later Creative Arts Fellow at Wolfson College, Oxford, and received the Harper Wood Studentship for English Literature and Poetry from St John's College, Cambridge. He has contributed fiction, poetry and reviews to numerous publications including The Guardian, the London Review of Books, the Times Literary Supplement, the New Yorker and Granta magazine.

His first book, A Strange and Sublime Address (1991), a novella and a number of short stories, won the Betty Trask Prize, the Commonwealth Writers Prize (Eurasia Region, Best First Book) and was shortlisted for the Guardian Fiction Prize. His second novel, Afternoon Raag (1993), won both the Southern Arts Literature Prize and the Encore Award (for best second novel of the year). The novel adopts the metaphor of Indian classical music, the raag, to evoke the complex emotions displayed by the narrator, a young Indian student at Oxford. It was followed by Freedom Song (1998), set in Calcutta during the winter of 1992-3 against a backdrop of growing political tension between Hindus and Muslims. The US edition of Freedom Song won the Los Angeles Times Book Prize (Fiction) in 2000. A New World (2000) is the story of Jayojit Chatterjee, a divorced writer living in America, and the visit he makes with his son Vikram to his elderly parents' home in Calcutta. His latest book, Real Time (2002), includes a number of short stories set in Bombay and Calcutta, some of which have been published in the London Review of Books, the Times Literary Supplement and the New Yorker, as well as 'E-minor', a memoir written in verse. D. H. Lawrence and 'Difference': Postcoloniality and the Poetry of the Present, exploring Lawrence's position as a 'foreigner' in the English canon, was published in 2003.

Amit Chaudhuri lives in Calcutta with his wife and daughter. He is editor of The Picador Book of Modern Indian Literature, published in 2001. His most recent book is St. Cyril Road and Other Poems (2005).

Bibliography of Amit Chaudhuri

A Strange and Sublime Address Heinemann, 1991

Afternoon Raag Heinemann, 1993

Freedom Song Picador, 1998

A New World Picador, 2000

The Picador Book of Modern Indian Literature (editor) Picador, 2001

Real Time Picador, 2002

D. H. Lawrence and 'Difference': Postcoloniality and the Poetry of the Present (with foreword by Tom Paulin) Oxford University Press, 2003

St. Cyril Road and Other Poems Penguin, 2005

Prizes and Awards

1991 Betty Trask Prize A Strange and Sublime Address

1991 Guardian Fiction Prize (shortlist) A Strange and Sublime Address

1992 Commonwealth Writers Prize (Eurasia Region, Best First Book) A Strange and Sublime Address

1993 K. Blundell Trust Award

1993 Southern Arts Literature Prize Afternoon Raag

1994 Encore Award Afternoon Raag

2000 Los Angeles Times Book Prize (Fiction) Freedom Song: Three Novels (US edition)

2003 Sahitya Akademi Award A New World

AMITAV GHOSH

Amitav Ghosh is one of the most widely known Indians writing in English today. His books include The Circle of Reason, The Shadow Lines, In An Antique Land, Dancing in Cambodia, The Calcutta Chromosome, and most recently,

The Glass Palace. Amitav Ghosh was born in Calcutta in 1956. He studied at St. Stephens College, Delhi; St. Edmund Hall, Oxford; and the Faculty of Arts, University of Alexandria. He worked for the Indian Express newspaper in New Delhi and he earned his doctorate in Oxford before he wrote his first novel.

The Circle of Reason won the Prix Medici Etranger, one of France's top literary awards, and The Shadow Lines won the Sahitya Akademi Award , India's most prestigious literary prize.

The Calcutta Chromosome won the Arthur C. Clarke Award for 1997 and The Glass Palace won the Grand Prize for Fiction at the Frankfurt International e-Book Awards in 2001.

Amitav Ghosh was the winner of the 1999 Pushcart Prize, a leading literary award, for an essay that was published in the Kenyon Review.

He lives with his wife, Deborah Baker and their children, in Brooklyn, USA.

Bibliography of Amitav Ghosh

Read more on Amitav Ghosh

The Hungry Tide

The Imam and the Indian

The Glass Palace

Dancing in Cambodia and at large in Burma

The Calcutta Chromosome

In An Antique Land

The Shadow Lines

The Circle of Reason

The Hungry Tide

The Hungry Tide

Book Type: Novel

ISBN No : 0007141777

Publisher's Name: HarperCollins

Published On : 2004-00-00

Synopsis

In between the sea and the plains of Bengal, on the easternmost coast of India, lies an immense archipelago of islands. Some of these islands are vast and some no larger than sandbars; some have lasted through recorded history while others have just washed into being. These are the Sundarbans - the beautiful lands. Here there are no borders to divide fresh water from salt, river from sea, even land from water. The tides reach more than two hundred miles inland, and every day thousands of acres of mangrove forest disappear only to re-emerge hours later. For hundreds of years, only the truly dispossessed and the hopeless dreamers of the world have braved the man eaters and the crocodiles who rule there, to eke a precarious existence from the unyielding mud.

The settlers of the Sundarbans believe that anyone who dares venture into the vast watery labyrinth without a pure heart, will never return. It is the arrival of Piyali Roy, of Indian parentage but stubbornly American, and Kanai Dutt, a sophisticated Delhi businessman, that disturbs the delicate balance of settlement life and sets in motion a fateful cataclysm. Kanai has come to visit his widowed aunt and to review some writings left behind by her husband, a political radical who died mysteriously in the aftermath of a local uprising. He meets Piya on the train from Calcutta and learns she has come to the Sundarbans in search of a rare species of river dolphin. When she hires Fokir, an illiterate, yet proud local fisherman to guide her through the mazelike backwaters, Kanai becomes her translator. From this moment, the tide begins to turn.

Amitav Ghosh has discovered yet another new territory, summoning a singular place from its history, language and myth and bringing it to life. Yet the achievement of The Hungry Tide is in its exploration of a far darker and more unknowable jungle, the human heart. It is a novel that asks at every turn: what danger resides there, and what delusion? What man can take the true measure of another?

The Hungry Tide is a whirlwind work of the imagination, every bit as epic in scope and ambition as his beloved and bestselling work, The Glass Palace.

IMAM AND THE INDIAN

There are about seven-eight essays that hinge around Amitav Ghosh's experiences in Egypt as researcher in early 80s. The title essay "The Imam and the Indian" brings out the pathos of two "superceded civilizations" - one of ancient Egypt and other of India - "vying with each other to lay claim to the violence of the West." In "The Relations of Envy in an Egyptian Village," Ghosh, like an astute anthropologist, works out the relation of Evil Eye practices with conditions of production in rural economy of Egypt.

In another essay, "Categories of Labour and the Orientation of the Fellah Economy," the notion of labour as mere performance of a technically necessary technical function is dispensed with. Ghosh investigates into the history and metaphysics of labour as it manifests itself in various forms in rural set-up. These essays are more or less corollaries to the writer's travelogue entitled In An Antique Land (1992) - an account of Egypt, which is reckoned most authentic even by the Egyptians themselves. Its in these essays that Amitav Ghosh approximates Clifford Geertz ideal of 'author as anthropologist.'

Amitav Ghosh is not a professional academic critic, yet at times he is simply impelled to write about writers that overwhelm him. The essay on Agha Shahid Ali's poetry, "The Ghat of the Only World," is lyrical and analytical at the same time; it is obituary and critique at one go. Another highlight of Amitav's critical methodology is the simultaneous presence of various timeframes and cultural contexts that he employs to understand the implications of a work of art in the larger civic context. Ghosh has the flexibility to invoke Cervantes to understand Babar's Babur-nama. He has the range to discuss writers as different as Michael Ondaatje, Agha Shahid Ali, Shyam Sevadorai in the larger context of civil strife and ethnic violence all across the subcontinent.

Spice-encounter at the beginning of the colonial period becomes a cultural correlative of Oil-Encounter in 70s. But despite all his anthropological, academic and activist predilections, it is ultimately Amitav Ghosh, the writer of fine literary sensibili who excels. A rural landscape is described thus: "a maze of low mud huts huddled together like confectionery on a tray." The singing of the bride is likened to the "the bloom of pomegranate." "An Egyptian in Baghdad" is more a tragic short story of Egyptian migrants to Iraq who send money towards the building of their pucka houses back home but never come back to occupy them. "The Slave of MS.H6" has the trappings of an anthropological detective fiction.

The essays which deal with the ethnography of the UN peacekeeping force in Combodia, the non-institutional character of Indian diaspora, the fundamentalist challenge in the Post-Cold War period are equally remarkable for their analytical rigour and poetical vigour. The self-critical, perceptive title essay relates an incident from his time doing fieldwork in Egypt. He argues with an intolerant village imam over the relative merits of cremating the dead, as Indian Hindus do, and the Egyptian Muslim practice of burying them. The imam calls the Hindu custom "primitive" and argues that the "advanced" West doesn't burn dead bodies.

Ghosh, soon incensed, lashes out, saying that even Western countries burn their dead: "They have special electric furnaces meant just for that." Both sides are stung. The imam accuses Ghosh of lying, with the logic that the West cannot be so ignorant, as they "have guns, tanks and bombs". Ghosh retorts that India not only has those heavy armaments but also nuclear weapons: a response that shocks Ghosh himself. "So there we were," Ghosh concludes, "the imam and I, delegates from two superseded civilizations vying to lay claim to the violence of the West." This subtle, all encompassing worldview is vintage Ghosh. His historian's eye takes in the breadth of peoples' experiences, and his anthropologist's mind makes connections between their religions, wars, cultures and ways of life. Above all, he describes these complex connections with simple profundity - with the skill of the novelist that he is. Ghosh can be jocular, too, without being trite. His essay "Four Corners" about a road trip in the US illustrates his keen observational powers and ability to relate the commonplace to history.

America's recreational vehicles (RVs), are, in his words, "if not quite palaces, then certainly midtown condos on wheels". He notices their curious names, Native American words like Winnebago and Itasca. "The names of the dispossessed tribes of the Americas hold a peculiar allure for marketing executives of automobile companies. Pontiac, Cherokee - so many tribes are commemorated in modes of transport," Ghosh observes. And then, as always, the summing up: "It is not a mere matter of fashion that so many of the cars that flash past on the highways carry those names, breathing them into the air like the inscriptions on prayer wheels. This tradition of naming has a long provenance: Did not Kit Carson himself, the scourge of the Navajo, name his favorite horse Apache?"

Why doesn't Ghosh come off as a know-it-all? With disarming frankness, he acknowledges that he doesn't have all the answers, or even explanations, for the fascinating quirks of culture he describes. In a short essay about a New York fundraising party for Tibet, for instance, Ghosh confesses that as an undergraduate, he and his friends would get drunk when they went to eat Tibetan food at a Tibetan refugee camp in Delhi. "You couldn't help doing so - it was hard to be in the presence of so terrible a displacement." As Ghosh muses thus in the trendy Manhattan restaurant, he catches the eye of the sole monk at the gathering and finds that "... his smile seemed a little guilty: the hospitality of a poor nation must have seemed dispensable compared to the charity of a rich one." Or perhaps he was merely bewildered, Ghosh continues. "It cannot be easy to celebrate the commodification of one's own suffering." Despite the mysterious omission of Ghosh's marvelous essays on Cambodia The Imam and the Indian is one collection that should be on the bookshelves of all who call themselves readers. The 18 essays in The Imam and the Indian were written over a 16-year time span - from 1986 to 2002. Which partly explains the eclecticism of this collection. A translation of Tagore's "Kshudhita Pashan", two essays on the social anthropology of an Egyptian village, an elegy to the Kashmiri poet, Agha Shahid Ali, a travel piece on the Four Corners, some incidental pieces like "A Tibetan Dinner" and "The Ghosts of Mrs Gandhi" - the diversity of genres, subjects, dictions would seem much too heterogenous for compilation in a single volume.

But for Amitav Ghosh, "connections are of greater importance than disjunctions" in the imaginative sphere.One of these "connections", very obviously, is the fact that the pieces were written in the gaps between the novels and hence trace the evolution of the author's interest and ideas that later were transmuted into fiction. Those familiar with Ghosh's fictional career will run into many familiar themes, motifs and characters here. But more notable is Ghosh's fixation with "encounters" between cultures and the modes of thought they embody. It could result, at times, in scepticism - the Imam's suspicion of the doctor al-Hindi, who comes from the land where cows are worshipped and the dead are burnt. Or, it could give rise to conflict like the one between the Navajos and the early settlers in North America. In most cases, the humans caught up in the clash of cultures are unaware of its historical import.

Look at Babur's near dislike for the kingdom that he won in the battle of Panipat and which was to earn him a place in history. In the modern world, however, such encounters are almost always violent and throw up a detritus in the form of an uprooted populace. Like the Tibetan monk Ghosh encounters at a New York charity dinner for the Tibetan cause. Some, like Nabeel, are lost to friends and relations forever.

Others, like the Sylheti UN peace-keeper entrusted with clearing the Khmer Rouge's mines in Cambodia, learn to cope as best as they can and soon become inured to the brutality around them. And most touchingly, Agha Shahid Ali, a resident of "the country without a pos-office" - Kashmir - who must die of cancer in Northampton, denied the right to go back to his homeland in his last days. What comes in the way of peaceful coexistence between two peoples? And what happens to the people caught in the midst of war or civil violence? Are their any alternative patterns of relations between different cultures - one that does not lead to strife?

In the present global scenario, the artist cannot but state which side of the political fence he is on. Thus art itself is a political stratagem. As Ghosh writes in The Shadow Lines, "Every word I write...is the product of a struggle with silence." And memories of violence, experienced or heard of, a weapon of defiance that helps to destroy the "thickening crust of awareness that is both a sign and a reminder of our unwitting complicity in the evolution of violence".

Which is why all fundamentalist regimes consider the destruction of literature and art - a way of ordering memory and human values - an article of faith. As every Kashmiri would say with Shahid: "Your history gets in the way of my memory / I am everything you lost. Your perfect enemy."

Reviews

The Imam and the Indian written over a 16-year time span (1986-2002), is a fascinating compilation of Amitav Ghosh's articles, lectures and translations spanning over two decades where the author's deceptively gentle style conceals cavernous depths of imagination and erudition. The book comprises a translation of Tagore's "Kshudhita Pashan", two essays on the social anthropology of an Egyptian village, an elegy to the Kashmiri poet, Agha Shahid Ali, a travel piece on the Four Corners, some incidental pieces like "A Tibetan Dinner" and "The Ghosts of Mrs Gandhi" - the diversity of genres and issues would seem too diverse for compilation in a single volume.

But for Amitav Ghosh, "connections are of greater importance than disjunctions" in the imaginative scheme of things.

The author digs out lost lives from centuries past and he explicitly portrays how the metaphysical is contained within the mundane. With subtlety, Ghosh hints that a critique of the Enlightenment need not lead directly to nativism if such critiques are grounded in meticulous research. He is continually thoughtful, vivacious, responsible rather than rakish.

One of his essays titled, The Slave Of MS.H.6, is indeed a quest for the subaltern. Ghosh's search for an individual who lived in the 12th century, wrote nothing about himself and thus left behind no records of his life. Ghosh depicts the slave as a phantom, who appears only coincidentally in a set of letters exchanged between two 12th century merchants. But this unknown slave may have witnessed the Crusades and his life might provide important clues about the fact that "slavery" was not slavery as we comprehend it today but a quasi-professional relationship between groups unrelated by blood. Ghosh indulges in ghost-hunting and finally finds the spirit of "Bomma the Slave," hiding eerily in a research institute.

In The Ghosts of Mrs Gandhi, Ghosh vividly narrates the endless tragedies (read riots) that gripped the Capital following the murder of Indira Gandhi in 1984. With sensitivity he describes how an elderly Sikh couple in desperation to save their lives clambered over a wall into their neighbours' welcoming South Delhi home. In other words, the author displays with alacrity of how the stories of every act of violence conceal the civil response to them.

Ghosh's brilliance and his nostalgic memories of his stint in Egypt are rekindled in the books' first essay, The Imam and the Indian. Ghosh gives a sparkle to the thematic element in this essay through an argument between an Indian student (himself) and the imam of an Egyptian village. The author opines, "two delegates of superseded civilisations vying with each other to lay claim to the violence of the West".

And in yet another essay, Ghosh answers the call of the desert. Travelogues, the author opines, are an integral part of Bengali literature- Fluent in Arabic, he reflects on the romanticism associated with the adventures of a Bengali traveller.

Meanwhile, in the modern world, encounters are often violent and throw up debris in the guise of an uprooted populace. Like the Tibetan monk, Ghosh encounters at a New York charity dinner for the Tibetan cause. Some, like Nabeel, are lost to friends and relations forever. Others, like the Sylheti UN peace-keeper entrusted with clearing the Khmer Rouge's mines in Cambodia, learn to cope as best as they can and soon become accustomed to the brutality around them. And most touchingly, Agha Shahid Ali, a resident of "the country without a post-office" - Kashmir - who must die of cancer in Northampton, is denied the right to go back to his homeland in his last days.

Above all, Ghosh remains fascinated by the mysticism within whose periphery the written word leaves its mark on earth. The author, also the exponent of the dilemmas between the physical and the metaphysical, the tangential oddities between the erudite and the earthy in the Imam and the Indian, exploresand discusses various issues with remarkable sensitivity and precision.

The Glass Place

The Glass Palace is a masterful novel of love, war and family and presents us with a band of memorable characters, spread across Burma, Malaya and India, and across three generations - before the door to Burma closes behind them, and the glittering light of that civilisation seems extinguished.

Starting in Mandalay at the time of the exile of King Thebaw and Queen Supayalat, THE GLASS PALACE is compelling historical fiction that tells the story of three families during a time of transition for India and its people. Politics, business, love, and war intertwine with unforgettable characters to immerse you in the story of a land and its people.

Rajkumar is a poor orphan boy stranded in Mandalay while the sampan on which he's working gets repaired. While working for a food vendor, he meets Saya John and his son, Matthew, who is a few years younger than he.

The locals loot the palace during the unsettled days of the King and Queen's disposition. While there, Rajkumar sees the most beautiful girl he's ever seen, the youngest of the Queen's maids. Rajkumar only has time to learn her name before the approaching soldiers force the looters to leave. He sees Dolly once more when the Royal Family is being led to the boat that will bring them to their home in exile. Years later, he'll go in search of the gi rl he cannot forget.

After the King and Queen are forced to leave, Mandalay is like a ghost town. The food vendors can no longer afford to stay open, leaving Rajkumar without a job. Rajkumar again goes to Saya John to find employment.

The Royal Family is exiled to Ratnagiri where they become the responsibility of the District Collector, a member of the Indian Civil Service, who ruled Britain's Indian possessions. In 1905, an Indian District Collector is appointed who brings with him his wife Uma. She becomes a lifelong friend of Dolly's and a voice for India's independence.

Ties between the orphan Rajkumar, Dolly, Saya John's family, and Uma's family span generations; their story is woven into the history of Burma, India, and Malaya. One generation works within the British-ruled system to build their dynasty, harvesting teak and rubber using slave labor. The next generation confronts a rising consciousness of Indian independence, which is intensified during World War II. Indians in the British Indian Army confront racism within their army as well as in the Indian National Army fighting for India's freedom.

Editorial Reviews

From Publishers Weekly

Ghosh's epic novel of Burma and Malaya over a span of 115 years is the kind of "sweep of history" that readers can appreciateDeven loveDdespite its demands. There is almost too much here for one book, as over the years the lives and deaths of principal characters go flying by. Yet Ghosh (The Calcutta Chromosome; Shadow Lines) is a beguiling and endlessly resourceful storyteller, and he boasts one of the most arresting openings in recent fiction: in the marketplace of Mandalay, only the 11-year-old Indian boy Rajkumar recognizes the booming sounds beyond the curve of the river as English cannon fire. The year is 1885, and the British have used a trade dispute to justify the invasion and seizure of Burma's capital. As a crowd of looters pours into the fabled Glass Palace, the dazzling throne room of the nine-roofed golden spire that was the great hti of Burma's kings, Rajkumar catches sight of Dolly, then only 10, nursemaid to the Second Princess. Rajkumar carries the memory of their brief meeting through the years to come, while he rises to fame and riches in the teak trade and Dolly travels into exile to India with King Thebaw, Burma's last king; Queen - Supayalat; and their three daughters.

The story of the exiled king and his family in Ratnagiri, a sleepy port town south of Bombay, is worth a novel in itself, and the first two of the story's seven parts, which relate that history and Rajkumar's rise to wealth in Burma's teak forests, are marvelously told. Inspired by tales handed down to him by his father and uncle, Ghosh vividly brings to life the history of Burma and Malaya over a century of momentous change in this teeming, multigenerational saga. (Feb. 6) Forecast: Novels by Indian authors continue to surge in popularity here, and this title not only ranks among the best but differs from the pack for its setting of Burma rather than India

From Library Journal

In an industry not known for risk-taking, the publisher is to be congratulated for offering Ghosh (The Calcutta Chromosome) a contract on his as-yet-unwritten novel. Set primarily in Burma, Malaya, and India, this work spans from 1885, when the British sent the King of Burma into exile, to the present. While it does offer brief glimpses into the history of the region, it is more the tale of a family and how historical events influenced real lives. As a young boy, Rajkumar, an Indian temporarily stranded in Mandalay, finds himself caught up in the British invasion that led to the exile of Burma's last king.

In the chaos, he spies Dolly, a household maid in the royal palace, for whom he develops a consuming passion and whom years later he tracks down in India and marries. As their family grows and their lives intersect with others, the tangled web of local and international politics is brought to bear, changing lives as well as nations. Ghosh ranges from the condescension of the British colonialists to the repression of the current Myanmar (Burmese) regime in a style that suggests E.M. Forster as well as James Michener.

AMITAVA KUMAR

Amitava Kumar was born in Ara, Bihar, and grew up in the nearby town of Patna, famous for its corruption, crushing poverty and delicious mangoes.

Kumar's writings have appeared in The Nation, Harper's, New Statesman, Transition, American Prospect, Toronto Review, Colorlines, Biblio, Outlook, Frontline, India Today, The Hindu, Himal, Herald, The Friday Times, The Times of India, and other publications. He has also been a literary columnist at Tehelka.com.

Kumar is the author of Passport Photos (University of California Press and Penguin-India, 2000) and Bombay-London-New York (Routledge and Penguin-India, forthcoming in 2002). Passport Photos was the winner of an "Outstanding Book of the Year" Award from the Myers Program for the Study of Bigotry and Human Rights in North America. Kumar is also the scriptwriter and narrator of the prize-winning documentary, Pure Chutney (1997).

He has been awarded a Barach Fellowship at the Wesleyan Writers Festival and a SAJA prize in 2001 for op-ed writing. He has won fellowships from the NEH, Yale University, SUNY-Stony Brook, Dartmouth College, and University of California-Riverside. Kumar is a professor in the English department at Penn State University. He and his wife live in State College, only a few blocks away from three equally bad Indian restaurants.

AMULYA MALLADI

Amulya Malladi was born and raised in India. She graduated with a bachelor's degree in engineering from Osmania University, Hyderabad, India and received a master's degree in journalism from The University of

Memphis, Tennessee, USA. After living in the United States for several years, Amulya now lives in Copenhagen, Denmark with her husband and two sons.

Amulya's fourth novel, Song of the Cuckoo Bird was released by Ballantine Books on December 27, 2005. She is currently working on her fifth novel, tentatively titled, The Sound of Language, which is set in Denmark.

ANITA DESAI

Anita Desai was born in Mussoorie, a hill station north of Delhi, as the daughter of a D.N. Mazumdar, a Bengali businessman, and the former Toni Nime, of German origin. She grew up speaking German at home and Bengali, Urdu, Hindi and English at school and in the city streets. She has said that she grew up surrounded by Western literature and music, not realizing until she was older that this was an anomaly in her world where she also learned the Eastern culture and customs. She married a businessman at twenty-one and raised several children before becoming known for her writing. Her first book, Cry,the Peacock was published in England in 1963, and her better known novels include In Custody (1984) and Baumgartner's Bombay (1988). She once wrote: "I see India through my mother's eyes, as an outsider, but my feelings for India are my father's, of someone born here" (Griffiths).

She never considered trying to first publish in India because there was no publisher in India who would be interested in fiction by an Indian writer (Jussawalla) and it was first in England that her work became noticed. U.S. readers were slower to discover her, due, she believes to England's natural interest in India and the U.S.'s lack of comprehension regarding the foreignness of her subject.

But Desai only writes in English. This, she has repeatedly said,was a natural and unconscious choice for her: "I can state definitely that I did not choose English in a deliberate and conscious act and I'd say perhaps it was the language that chose me and I started writing stories in English at the age of seven, and have been doing so for thirty years now without stopping to think why "(Desai).

She is considered the writer who introduced the psychological novel in the tradition of Virginia Woolf to India. Included in this, is her pioneer status of writing of feminist issues. While many people today would not classify her work as feminist, she believes this is due to changing times: "The feminist movement in India is very new and a younger generation of readers in India tends to be rather impatient of my books and to think of them as books about completely helpless women, hopeless women. They find it somewhat unreal that the women don't fight back, but they don't seem to realize how very new this movement is" (Jussawalla).

Also, she says, her writing is realistic: "Women think I am doing a disservice to the feminist movement by writing about women who have no control over their lives. But I was trying, as every writer tries to do, even in fiction, to get at the truth, write the truth. It would have been really fanciful if I had made [for example, in Clear Light of Day] Bim and Tara modern-day feminists "(in Griffiths).

Desai considers Clear Light of Day, her most autobiographical book, because she was writing about her neighborhood in Delhi, although the characters are not based on her brothers and sisters. What she was exploring in this novel, she has said, was the importance of childhood and memories as the source of a life. She had wanted to start the book at the end and move backwards, into the characters' childhood and further, into the childhood of their parents etc., but in the end: "When I had gone as far back as their infancy the book just ground to a halt; it lost its momentum. It told me that this was done, that I couldn't carry it further. But I still have a sense of disappointment about that book, because the intention had been different" (Jussawalla). The character of Raja is identified with her in the sense that he is so immersed in all different types of literature and culture, and is so concerned with protecting the multicultural heritage of India. His worries about the Muslim neighbor family is not just about them particularly, but rather worry about the loss of all that the Muslim culture and literature contributes to India.

While Desai has taught for years at Mount Holyoke and MIT, and spends most of the year outside of India, she does not consider herself part of the Indian Diaspora. Although she does not fit in the Indian box anymore (Griffiths) as she said, she considers herself lucky for having not left India until late in her life, because she feels that she has been drifting away from it ever since: "I can't really write of it with the same intensity and familiarity that I once had." Yet she cannot feel at home in any other place or society (Griffiths).

ANITA RAU BADAMI

Anita Rau Badami was born in 1961, in the town of Rourkela in ,Orissa, India. Her father, a mechanical engineer who designed trains, was transferred every two or three years, so that she had a mobile childhood. She grew up in a household where English was the primary language spoken and attended Catholic schools in India, because, as she explains, until around twenty years ago, these were the good schools in India.

At age 18, Anita Rau Badami borrowed money from her father to buy novels at a book fair in Chennai, India. To pay him back she took her first writing assignment, an article in a local newspaper, and earned 75 rupees. She holds degrees in Communication Media, English Literature, and Journalism from universities in Bombay and Madras. Badami began her career as a freelance writer in India with regular features in The Hindu, The Deccan Herald, and Indian Express.

She worked as a copywriter for advertising agencies in Bombay, Bangalore and Madras, and wrote stories for children's magazines. She married in 1984, had a son in 1987, and moved to Calgary in 1991. In 1995, she graduated from the University of Calgary where she received an M.A. degree in English. She submitted her first work to Penguin Books. Penguin published her work, and soon Badami was touring North America, reading from her best-selling debut novel Tamarind Mem.

Several of her short stories appeared in Canadian literary journals such as The Malahat Review, Event, Toronto Review of Contemporary Fiction among others. The Hero's Walk was the winner of the Marian Engel Award for excellence in fiction for a body of work; a Finalist in the 2000 Kiriyama Pacific Rim Prize for fiction; and on the longlist for the 2002 Orange Prize for Fiction.

The Hero's Walk was nominated for the 2002 International IMPAC Dublin Literary Award. The Hero's Walk also won the Commonwealth Best Book Prize in the Canada/ Caribbean region, as well as the Washington Post Best Book of 2001. Ms. Badami has taught writing at University of British Columbia.

Since moving to Montreal two years ago when her husband, Madhav, got a job teaching at McGill University, she has been working quietly on her third novel. A year ago, she received a call from Concordia offering her the position.

It was in Vancouver that she began working on her third novel, Can You Hear the Night Bird Sing, to be published next fall. She has been contacted by her publishers in India and England to republish her children's stories, and she has had an idea for book number four. The working title is The Guest.

ANJANA APPACHANA

Anjana Appachana was born in India, received her education and also worked there for a few years before moving to USA. She has degrees from Delhi University,

Jawaharlal Nehru University, and in Creative Writing from Pennsylvania State Univeristy.

One of her short stōries Sharmaji was included in the anthology on 50 years of Indian writing (by Salman Rushdie and Elizabeth West). Her focus, as evinced by the theme of her novel Listening Now is the experience of the ordinary Indian woman: her dreams and passions frustrated and realised, through and in spite of the mundane, repetitive and domestic pattern of her life.

Anjana Appachana is the recipient of an O. Henry Festival Prize and a National Endowment for the Arts Creative Writing fellowship. She lives in Tempe, Arizona.

ANURAG MATHUR

Anurag Mathur was born in Delhi and educated at Scindia School, Gwalior, St Stephen's College, Delhi, and the University of Tulsa, Oklahoma, USA. He is a journalist in the print and electronic media and loves reading, music, eating out and tennis. His published books include the best-selling novels The Inscrutable Americans and Making the Minister Smile.

ARUNDHATI ROY

Arundhati Roy is known as an award winning author and also as a social activist and inspiration to all those who seek to support the poor and oppressed. Roy came in the limelight in 1997 when her book The God of Small Things fetched the coveted Booker Prize. This down-to-earth girl-next-door whisked off a whirlwind of controversy through her pen and her association with various social movements and activities. And this year again she is back in the public eye having been awarded the prestigious Sahitya Akademi Award (2005) for her collection of Essays The algebra of infinite justice. Arundhati Roy - the multifaceted talent - is In Focus this week.

Life : Born in 1961 in Bengal, Arundhati Roy grew up in Kerala, the Indian state where The God of Small Things is set.

The tale is based on twin children battling with the caste structures in India. Roy, herself, is the product of an inter-caste marriage. Her father is from a Hindu family of Bengal while her mother is a Christian. From the time she was very young, she knew in her heart that she wanted to be a writer. She studied architecture and taught aerobics but once Roy began writing screenplays, her writing career took off. Roy's debut novel, The God of Small Things, was published in 1997. It became an international bestseller, and in October 1997 won the coveted Booker Prize. Roy has since involved herself in causes such as the anti-nuclear movement and the Narmada Bachao Andolan and has written several essays in support of the causes she so strongly believes in. Arundhati is a towering intellect with a poetic fluency with words delivered in a soft modulated voice. She is also a dog-lover and her past times are writing and running.

ASHOK BANKER

Ashok Kumar Banker (born 1964) is a novelist and short story writer born and living in Mumbai, India. He has written professionally since his early teens, and has worked as a print journalist, columnist, scriptwriter for television series and documentaries, and in advertising.

Banker has published in several genres, ranging from contemporary fiction about urban life in India to multi-volume mythological epics, as well as science fiction, fantasy, and cross-genre works. His first three novels to be published were crime thrillers, claimed to be the first written by an Indian novelist in English. They gained him widespread attention and a reputation for being a crime novelist that has clung to him despite his not having written crime novels since, though he has written short crime fiction, some of which involves characters from the novels. The stories of his

"Devi" series are short works featuring avatars of the Hindu goddess Devi, and have appeared in various science fiction, fantasy, and horror magazines.

Bibliography

The Ramayana series:

- The Prince of Ayodhya (2003)
- Siege of Mithila (2003)
- Demons of Chitrakut (2004)
- Armies of Hanuman (2005)
- Bridge of Rama (2005)
- King of Ayodhya (2006)

The Mahabharata series:

- The Seeds of War (2006)

His other novels include:

- The Iron Bra (1993)
- Murder & Champagne (1993)
- Ten Dead Admen (1993)
- Vertigo (1993)
- Byculla Boy (1994)
- The Missing Parents Mystery (1994)
- Beautiful Ugly

The Reality of Illusions

A study of Aparna Sen's 15, Park Avenue.

Physical disability, mental disorder, sexual orientation, and religious background, in general, are the parameters of excluding people from the mainstream of society, the rules and regulations of which are determined by those who define themselves as "normal". Consequently, a physically disabled person or somebody who's suffering from some mental illness is often marginalized and looked upon with pity. The basic human rights are sometimes denied to them; they are often treated as inanimate objects sans feelings. Aparna Sen makes an attempt to reveal to us the reality of these people who are mercilessly sidelined. Schizophrenia has always interested the director.

We come across schizophrenic characters in almost all her films. Schizophrenic people are driven to the margins simply because the reality, in which they seem to have unwavering faith, appears hallucinatory to others. Sen delves deep into this unreal reality and goes to the extent of identifying reality as multiple...no reality is more real than the other.

15, Park Avenue featuring Mithi (Konkona Sensharma) as its protagonist is another attempt on the director's part to show the reality of the unreal a schizophrenic person believes in. In Paromitar Ekdin Sen had introduced us to a schizophrenic girl Khuku, who knows that she is brainsick. She sings marvelously but can't even tie her hair properly. Her reality was set against Sanaka, her mother and Paromita, her sister-in-law, both of whom go on defining for themselves their identities.

In the process, Sanaka, a half-literate woman doesn't seem much different from the post-graduate copywriter Paromita. Both feel victimized as women in a patriarchal society and in contrast to them, Khuku lost in her own world seems luckier. As she sings "Hriday aammar prakash holo, ananta aakashe" (My heart finds expression in the boundless firmament) with Sanaka and Paromita gazing at her with wet eyes, we feel how fortunate she is on being able to move effortlessly between the world of mundane reality and her own reality which is as boundless as the sky.

15 Park Avenueis a profounder study of schizophrenic disorders. The film is well researched. Before going into a detailed analysis of the film, we may examine what "schizophrenia" connotes.

The term was introduced in 1911 by a Swiss psychiatrist, Eugen Bleuler. The word comes from the Greek schizo meaning "split" and phrenia meaning "mind." Bleuler wanted to convey the split between what is perceived, what is believed, and what is objectively real. He did not mean that the person with schizophrenia is split into two personalities, but that there is a splitting away of the personality from reality. The concept of "split," however, has led to schizophrenia being confused with multiple personality, a less common and very different psychiatric disorder, much publicized through such stories as Dr. Jekyll and Mr. Hyde, The Three Faces of Eve, and Sybil. Today, many health care professionals regret the existence of the term "schizophrenia" because of the confusion and misunderstanding that surround it.

Added to this basic confusion is a history of blame. Families agree that blame is a major stumbling block to seeking and receiving support.

In the late 1800s and the early part of this century, three competing views about the nature of mental illness gained acceptance in the psychiatric profession. Biological psychiatry grew from the research of Dr. Emil Kraepelin in Germany; psychoanalysis from the findings of Dr. Sigmund Freud and his colleagues in their studies on neuroses in Austria; and behaviorism from the work of Dr. John B. Watson in the United States. Kraepelin's views predominated the thinking of psychiatrists in Europe, while both psychoanalysis and behaviorism flourished in North America (Andreasen, The Broken Brain, pp. 11-20).

In the 1950s, many North American psychiatrists began to believe that schizophrenia resulted from a form of psychic trauma inflicted on the individual early in life, typically by parents. Mothers of those with schizophrenia were believed to be over-anxious, obsessive, and domineering. These women were labeled "schizophrenogenic." One mother said she almost understood this. "When you are pushing to get help for your child, it is easy for some to 'put the cart before the horse' and point to this pushiness and tension as the cause of your child's problem, rather than the result of it." Gradually, blame was placed on the family as a unit. Theorists noticed poor family functioning where there was someone with schizophrenia, and confused the effect of the illness with its cause.

Two other theories contributed to the mythology surrounding schizophrenia. The American psychoanalyst Thomas Szasz pronounced that schizophrenia, like all other mental illnesses, is a set of behaviors, not a disease. The late R.D. Laing, a British psychiatrist, suggested that it is really a "healthy" response to an insane world. People burdened with terrible stress act "crazy" in an effort to adapt.

Scientific research and factual data have discredited these theories. Unfortunately, they were all popular enough at one time to have gained public attention. You may still run into health care professionals who will suggest that you "caused" your relative's illness, and that a continuing family relationship may hinder recovery.

Aside from the history of blame, the symptoms of the illness itself can often add to the stigma of schizophrenia. The odd and unpredictable behavior, poor functioning, or lack of good health habits can be disturbing to others. News coverage on acts of violence or suicides committed by people reported as having schizophrenia serves to add to the stigma, even if unintentionally.

Aparna Sen is medically correct in the chalking out of the screenplay, but she goes a step further to show if a schizophrenic person is frantically in search of an identity in which the world has no faith, we all are schizophrenic in our own ways.

Mithi's (Konkona Sensharma) disease is detected quite late, though symptoms were rather apparent from a very young age. She maintained distance from other children, was noticeably quiet and thoughtful. Psychiatrists identify these as strong symptoms of schizophrenia. However, she is left completely devastated after she suffers gang rape on a journalistic trip to cover post-poll agitations in Dhanbad. Interestingly, the director mingles the protagonist's own reality with the reality of the devastating Iraq war. She imagines Saddam Hussein talking to her from the television. It is this illusory Hussein who informs her that her boyfriend Joydeep (Rahul Bose) is presently working in Baghdad and Ballygunge Park Road has been renamed 15, Park Avenue. The film begins with an exasperated Anjali (Shabana Azmi) driving Mithi along Park Road. The latter claims that she has a house at No.15 on that road.

She inhabits a delusional world of her own with her five imaginary children and her husband. She hears voices, voices of her children pleading with her to come back. This world is so real to her that she starts looking upon her half-sister Anjali as her sole enemy who keeps her away from 15, Park Avenue.

The most important question the film raises is that whether "reality" is something what the majority approves of. The crux of the film perhaps lies in the scene where Anjali asks Kunal (Dhritiman Chatterjee) whether Mithi's reality is real enough. In reply, Kunal asks her to turn around and say what she sees on the table behind her. She finds a vase. Kunal jokingly contradicts her saying that he sees a table lamp. Bewildered, Anjali gestures disbelief when Kunal asks her whether she would continue to see a vase if everyone else in the restaurant claims it to be a table lamp.

What comes out of this conversation is that "reality" is a construction. All the "realities" we believe in are mere constructions. Does Anjali realize that her "reality" lies in seeing herself as the captain of the ship with her old mother (Waheeda Rahman) and her schizophrenic sister on board? Does she realize that the "reality" that sustains her is that she has sacrificed everything for her responsibilities? Then, why does she take pride in her decision of turning down

Sanjeev's (Kanwaljeet Singh) offer? In the process, she does not recognize how she moves between her real self and the mask she wears. Anjali looks upon herself as invincibly strong, invulnerable and practical. But we often see her breaking down emotionally, exasperated with Mithi's hallucinations. But Anjali refuses to see herself like that. Hence, if the identity of Mrs. Joydeep Roy is real to Mithi, the role Anjali defines for herself is equally real. Anjali's "role-playing" cannot be named "schizophrenic" but it is "role-playing" after all.

The portrait of Joydeep is no less layered than that of Anjali. Given the standards of the world, it was quite natural for him to opt out of Mithi's life. Yet years later, when he happens to see her wandering by the river, he can't help going back to her. A sense of guilt haunts him deep down. Torn between his wife and his schizophrenic girlfriend, an overwhelming sense of duty propels him to participate in Mithi's delusions.

But Mithi doesn't recognize him as her beloved Jojo. The father of five children she has in her imagination is a different person altogether. In her own imaginative world, Joydeep is so "real" that the "real" Joydeep makes no difference to her. The same person is split into two------- the loving husband and the repenting traitor. We are left to speculate which of the Joydeeps is more real.

Mithi continues to exist in two worlds simultaneously-the world of domestic fulfillment and the world that treats her as "mad" and takes resort to broom-thrashing in order to bring her back to her senses. Significantly, the scene where Mithi is given to the whims of the saffron-clad sham is intercut by the scene of the classroom where Anjali lectures on Quantum Mechanics. On a superficial level the scene may be interpreted as a contrast between mindless superstitions and something as advanced as the laws of Quantum Mechanics. But the implications are profounder than that: Quantum Mechanics, a development of Einstein's theory of

Relativity, goes to the extent of claiming that an atom can exist at two different locations at the same time.

This calls for looking at the film from the perspective of the physicist. It is not without significance that Anjali is a professor of Quantum Mechanics. She knows her subject to the core, yet cannot sympathize with Mithi who exists in two different worlds at the same time. A potential professor of Physics, Anjali, ironically, fails to realize when Mithi comes back to the so-called "real" world and complains to her about the ritual broom-thrashing. Unable to convince Anjali, Mithi slashes her wrist. If Quantum Mechanics approves of the relative existence of two locations, why can't Anjali?

Theories of Quantum Mechanics and psychology mingle in the fictional world of 15, Park Avenue and reality is described in scientific terms. Ironically enough, Sen proves the multiplicity of reality through an intelligent application of scientific laws that generally defines "realism" to be that what the rational mind sees.

The film comes to a full circle with Joydeep and Mithi looking for the house at 15, Park Avenue. Anjali and Kunal follow them. Mithi treats Joydeep as her confidant and believes that he will be able to help her find the house. In fact, Mithi does find her house this time, with Jojo sitting on the doorstep, and the children playing in the garden. We see her moving out from our real world to her own world of reality. At this point a question that nags us is that why does Mithi find the house now but she doesn't when she comes there with Anjali? Is it because Anjali has no faith in her world and Joydeep, at least pretends that he has? Then, shall we say, that the reality of the minority (represented by Mithi) exists only when it is approved by the majority (represented by the "normal" Joydeep)? We are left to speculate when Mithi is not found again. In a twinkling of an eye she vanishes as if she weren't there at all. The camera zooms out with the frenzied trio of Anjali, Kunal, and Joydeep and a group of curiously bewildered passers-by chanting "15, Park Avenue? 15, Park Avenue!" The voices soon overtaken by silence are symbolic of the search of identity everybody has embarked upon. But what becomes of Mithi? The film provides no answer. It almost concludes with a jolt...perhaps deliberately, to leave you thinking how volatile is the "reality" you think you inhabit?

Doshor : Estranged Companions?

How difficult or easy is it to forgive a philandering husband or an unfaithful wife? What solemnizes marriage which is presumably the most pure relationship on earth? Trust or a series of compromises? Rituparno Ghosh's Doshor raises all these questions and leaves them to the audience to answer.

Women and their role in the domestic sphere have been Ghosh's putative concern. Through Unishe April, Dahan, Subho Muharat, and Chokher Bali,Ghosh has gone out of his way to show how women continue to play second fiddle to men, in spite of themselves. Yet, he has shown how women can rise above crises and define for themselves an identity of their own. If Rangapishima of Subho Muharat reinvents herself as a detective, Binodini of Chokher Bali abandons both her lovers and embarks on a journey to discover for herself the meaning of "nation". It was, therefore, really surprising for such a strong-willed woman as Kaberi (Konkona Sensharma) to stay on with Kaushik (Prasenjit Chatterjee), even though he fails to justify his relationship with Mita (Chandrayee Ghosh). The film could have been more radical if Kaberi had walked out of the relationship after Kaushik had recovered. Although it would have been A Doll's House kind of ending, it would have been a Rituparno Ghosh kind of ending as well.

Kaberi is almost shattered on discovering her husband's liaison with his office colleague Mita. This might not have ever been discovered if Mita had not died in an accident in which Kaushik is almost mortally injured. Both of them were returning by car after a sojourn at a resort outside the city, while Kaberi thought that Kaushik was on some business tour. Kaberi is in double crisis: on the one hand, she has to look after an ailing husband; on the other hand, she has to suffer the insult of being betrayed by someone she had unconditionally trusted.

Initially, she decides to walk out of the relationship and asks her brother-in-law to file a divorce case immediately. She feels no sympathy for Kaushik and in a deliberate attempt to hurt him she conveys the news of Mita's death rather insipidly without any introduction. Back home, when Kaushik pleads with her to look after him and listen patiently to what he has to say about his extra-marital affair, Kaberi's rejoinder is just too brilliant: "I can't really take the responsibility of your catharsis." She is remarkably indifferent to him; yet, she cannot help but sponge him as he is too seriously handicapped to do anything on his own. What surprises us is that Kaushik does not really suffer from any sense of dependence and almost shamelessly endeavors to get intimate with her once again. Though Kaberi shows apathy and indifference, she gradually gives in and the relationship is saved.

On the other hand, there is the betrayed husband Mr. Biswas (Shankar Chakraborty). He is unnaturally silent and is unwilling to discuss anything about it with Kaberi who voluntarily goes over to his place after the incident. In fact his very act of returning to Kaberi a packet of rubber found in his wife's bag seems brutally inhuman, a deliberate attempt to hurt somebody else in the absence of his wife. Another instance of his displaced aggression is seen in his brutal act of intercourse with the prostitute (Moumita Gupta) who slaps him really hard: "Aren't you satisfied by murdering your wife that you want to kill me as well?"...

Then there is a third couple---- Bobby (Parambroto Chatterjee) and Brinda (Pallavi Chatterjee). Brinda seems completely frustrated with Subir, her legal husband. She seeks in Bobby a friend, a lover and everything else which apparently she has not got from her husband. Yet, many a times she notices that Bobby sounds very much like her husband. The relationship reveals its emptiness the day Brinda tells Bobby that she is pregnant. Bobby's reaction puts down Brinda completely. He refuses to take responsibility of the child on the grounds that Brinda couldn't just be too sure that the child is his, for, all these days, she has been sleeping with her husband as well.

As expected of a Rituparno Ghosh film, Doshor too is an out-and-out a feminist film. Taslima Nasreen in her review of the film praises the director for his realization of the one and only truth that defines a man-woman relationship: the man is all powerful and the woman is absolutely powerless. In the game of power politics it is the man who always wins. But since any form of art, especially cinema is expected to have a social message, then, Doshor has nothing new to offer if it shows what is just too evident.

Elaine Showalter in A Literature of Their Own (1977) talks about three different stages of the feminist movement: the "feminine" (1840-1880), the "feminist" (1880-1920), and the "female" (1920 onwards). In the first stage, women's literature aimed to equal men while assimilating men's assumptions about women. In the second stage, women rebelled against patriarchal norms and advocated their rights and values. In the third stage, women turned inward and tried to discover for themselves their own identities, independent of men. Doshor may be a representative work of the second stage of the feminist movement, although our expectation was to see it conforming to the parameters of the third stage. However, as third-world feminism markedly differs from the feminism that originated in the west, Rituparno Ghosh may not have conformed to any of these stages deliberately. In any case, a theory remains a theory and generally refuses to apply to practical situations. Consequently, Ghosh may have intentionally circumvented theoretical assumptions in an attempt to bring home to his audience the practical reality.

Therefore, those who know Rituparno too well felt disappointed when Kaberi forgives Kaushik in the end. However, what's really disappointing is her encouraging Brinda and Bobby to carry on with their relationship. She rages and sulks on discovering Kaushik's liaison with Mita, yet she goes on indulging Brinda and Bobby. Almost as a saving grace, as if to vindicate her moral uprightness, the director gives her that one dialogue in support of Brinda's husband Subir: "I guess you must tell Subir da what you two are planning to do. What's the use in keeping him in the dark?"...

Again, if she supports Brinda for walking out of the marriage, then how much have we seen of Kaberi to put the blame on Kaushik for being adulterous? The film begins rather abruptly with Kaberi discovering her husband's infidelity. The director doesn't create a platform strong enough for the audience to sympathize with Kaberi. How pretentiously faithful was Kaushik that Kaberi is awfully shattered when his relationship with Mita is uncovered accidentally? We are given no hint as to what kind of an equation Kaberi shared with Kaushik. Consequently, the audience fails to suffer Kaberi's trauma.

It is, however, easier to empathize with Mita. Kaushik is informed that the company has erased her name from all its records as if she never existed at all. Mita continues to live with the blemish of infidelity even after death while Kaushik emerges unstained, unconditionally forgiven. Women have to bear the brunt of humiliation and insult; men remain officially chaste in spite of themselves.

Yet a pertinent question that arises at this point is that how could have Mita defended herself for being unfaithful to her husband? Taslima Nasreen points out that the imbecile manner in which Mita's husband treats the prostitute in bed, speaks volumes about their relationship. Presumably a victim of "legal" rape, Mita had no choice but to look for "love" outside. But this is a mere assumption. We cannot be too certain of this inference. Even if we believe in this hypothesis, then wasn't it too selfish for Mita to break a home in search of love? Yet, before blaming her, we must consider the fact that Kaushik must have been inviting enough to encourage Mita to make advancements. What emerges from these speculations is that none of the characters is simple enough to be described in black-and-white terms. Hence Rituparno's resorting to black-and-white color tone seems more than ironical.

In the end, Kaberi fails to put her foot down in deciding in favor of divorce. The film comes to a close with Kaushik posing an important question:"Would you have forgiven me, if Mita were alive? " Kaberi does not answer the question. Instead, she starts reciting a poem composed by Mita----- a poem that is repeated like a refrain throughout the film. A sense of dissatisfaction sets in as the curtain falls...we keep on wondering why weren't we made to live through Kaushik's "catharsis". What made Kaberi forgive him so easily?

Whatever it is, the film leaves the impression that the trust factor that is famed to strengthen marital bonds is frightfully missing. Infidelity has spread like a pestilence to estrange "companions" forever. The black-and-white tone attributes to the film a kind of gloominess in which conjugal love seems to suffocate to death. To escape this gloominess, men and women look outside in search of true love only to extend the claustrophobia infinitely.

ABOL TABOL : THE NONSENSE WORLD OF SUKUMAR ROY

If you thought that writing nonsense verse and prose was the exclusive preserve of the likes of Lear and Carrol then its time you start thinking again. More than a century ago one person from Bengal had explored and conquered the strange world of nonsense literature and that world revives in Sampurna Chatterjee's translation: Abol Tabol - the nonsense world of Sukumar Roy. The Bengali language has never been quite so much a living, breathing creature of whimsy as in Sukumar Ray's hands, and his creations-wild and wicked, dreamy and delirious-have thrilled children and adults alike. Roy's creative play with words and images earned him the title of the "Master of nonsense" and his magic is recreated amply in Sampurna Chatterjee's work.

Abol Tabol - the nonsense world of Sukumar Roy offers the best of Roy's pun-riddled, fun-fiddled poetry from Abol Tabol and Khai-Khai, stories of schoolboy pranks (Pagla Dashu) and madcap explorers (Heshoram Hushiyarer Diary), and the unforgettable harum-scarum classic of Haw-Jaw-Baw-Raw-Law. All the stories and poems are accompanied by Sukumar Ray's inimitable illustrations that make the book come alive with life and laughter. If translating verse is a tough assignment, translating nonsense verse is tougher still. Sampurna Chattarji has, indeed, done a commendable job of translating Abol Tabol. In this volume she has successfully transcreated everything in the world that is happy and mischievous. The Nonsense World of Sukumar Ray lives up to its name in such an endearing manner that you enjoy every minute of your stay there. Part prose, part verse, the common thread running through the book is its unbridled sense of fun. Devoid of the staple ingredients of children's literature, this book offers a roller-coaster ride with characters who are as fun as they are weird, as interesting as they are outlandish. With their simple charm and wacky wickedness, they can bring a smile to adults as easily as they can to children.

SUKUMAR ROY

Roy, Sukumar (1887-1923) children's writer, was born in Kolkata on 30 October 1887. His family was originally from Masua in Mymensingh. His father, Upendra Kishore

Roychowdhury, who also wrote for children, was a musician and mechanic and his son was the Oscar-winning filmmaker Satyajit Roy.-

After passing the Entrance examination from the City School, Sukumar Ray took his BSc (1911) in chemistry from Presidency College. He then went to England on the Guruprasanna Ghosh Scholarship to study photography and printing technology. Sukumar studied at the Manchester School of Technology, where he proved the effectiveness of photo printing in halftone invented by his father.

At the East and West Society, Sukumar Roy read an essay called 'Spirit of Rabindranath', which was later published in The Quest magazine. This earned him the opportunity to speak at various meetings in England. He was selected fellow of the Royal Photographic Society; he was the second Indian to earn this distinction. Back home in 1913, he took over his father's enterprise called U Roy and Sons.

Sukumar Roy was a versatile genius. He used to compose rhymes at an early age. Along with photography he learnt painting. While at college, he used to write comedies and act in them. He also acted in a play called Goday Galad with Rabindranath Tagore and Abanindranath Tagore at Santiniketan. He composed some songs during the Swadeshi Movement and also sang the songs himself. After his father's death, he took over the Sandesh, a magazine published by his father. While in England, he sent stories, poems and paintings to be published in the magazine.

While studying at Presidency College, he set up an organisation called 'Nonsense Club' and published the magazine Sade-Batrish-Bhaja as its mouthpiece. On his return from England, he started the 'Monday Club' where he used to arrange discussions along with refreshments, which earned the club another name, Monda (Bangla for sweetmeat) Club.

Sukumar Roy was principally noted for his writings for young children. He mixed comic elements and subtle satire in all his works-poems, plays, stories or paintings. His satire is marked by his social consciousness. His prominent writings include, Ha-Ya-Ba-Ra-La (Topsy-Turvy, 1928), Pagla Dashu (1940), Bahurupi (The Jester, 1944), Khaikhai (I Want More, 1950), Abak Jalpan (Strange Drink), Shabdakalpadrum (The Tree of Words) and Jhalapala (Irritation). He also wrote some serious essays in Bangla and English. He wrote a collection of belles-lettres called Hesoramer Dairi, written in the form of a diary.

Sukumar Ray's finest work Abol-Tabol the nearest English translation of which can be 'nonsense' or 'gibberish,' was written in the last two and a half years of his life. He died in 1923, nine days before his best-loved book 'Abol Tabol' was published. Anyone who has had his early schooling in Bengal, has grown up with the delightfully crazy verses of Abol Tabol that children love to recite. The poems of Abol Tabol had been gathered out of various issues of the children's magazine, Sandesh, which Sukumar Ray had been editing. The comic fantasies of Abol Tabol display a special brand of anarchic madness which bears the distinctive stamp of Sukumar Ray. Among his fantastic characters is an old man who survives on boiled wood and can tell you the taste and smell of different kinds of wood ("Kaath Buro"). There is the old woman whose rickety house has been put together with spit. There is a singer whose voice echoes from Delhi to Burma and makes animals faint. Roy's artistry and genius is best portrayed in this collection of fine verses and if he had not written a single word elsewhere - Abol Tabol would have anyways made him what he is today.

TWENTIETH CENTURY

Representing the Great War : Overview

Today we know it as World War I, but those who lived through it called it the Great War. At first, the war was predicted to last only a few months and to result in a resounding success for the British Empire and its allies. But as the years passed and the casualties mounted into the millions, it became clear that this conflict was quite different from its predecessors. With nearly nine million soldiers killed (one in five of those who fought) and survivors afflicted with prolonged physical and mental suffering, the war marked a sea-change in the course of military and political history. It also represented a challenge to anyone wishing to give meaning to the enormity of the death toll and the futility of trench warfare. Soldiers living in rat-infested and water-saturated trenches fired machine-guns at unseen soldiers in other trenches; when they went "over the top" into no-man's-land, they became completely vulnerable. The use of the term "Great War" suggests the challenge of representing something so new and awful, so vast and traumatic.

Once it became clear that both sides had settled into their trenches, which stretched from Switzerland to the North Sea, people naturally wondered what had gone wrong. Patriotic poems and songs from previous wars, such as Henry Newbolt's "Vitaï Lampada" (1897-98), linked the British soldier's fighting prowess with his moral superiority, fairness, and skill. World War I also elicited representations that blurred the line between war and athletics, such as Jessie Pope's jingoistic poem "The Call" (1915) and the recruiting poster "The Army Isn't All Work." But as soldiers' expectations of a just, valorous, sporting war gave way to hideous, anonymous carnage, characteristic expressions of irony emerged.

For soldier poets such as Siegfried Sassoon and Wilfred Owen, irony proved a useful means of representing the gulf between expectation and reality, the murderous war and the unsuspecting nation, the soldier's comrades in the trenches and the unseen enemy across no-man's-land. Bitterly ironic statements such as Siegfried Sassoon's "A Soldier's Declaration" helped call attention to the rage and bewilderment of the trench soldier; but their chilly reception by an equally bewildered reading public reinforced cultural divisions. Some readers at home condemned the war poets' attacks as unpatriotic, and opinion remained divided between those who had fought and knew, and those who preferred not to know.

Some poets also disliked the soldier poets' graphic and caustically ironic depictions of the war. In the words of W. B. Yeats in his 1936 preface to The Oxford Book of Modern Verse, the bitterness of war poets was an unconstructive "passive suffering." Yeats refused to include in his anthology combatant poets such as Owen and Sassoon. He preferred in poetry a more active heroism, such as that he invented for the speaker of "An Irish Airman Foresees His Death."

As casualties from both the Allied and Central Powers ran into the millions, military tactics became increasingly desperate. These included the deployment of mustard gas, submarine attacks on shipping lines, and howitzer shelling and zeppelin bombings of cities miles behind the front lines. Such tactics signaled a breakdown of the rules of warfare in favor of indiscriminate killing of both the soldiers and the civilians they protected. Civilian artists now found they had an authentic, lived experience of war they could express.

The involvement of millions of women in the war effort, such as those depicted in the poster "We Need you, Redcross," eroded the distinction between civilian women and the men who went off to save the country. Munitions, factory, and textile jobs were vacated by enlistees and quickly filled by women for whom the war represented an economic opportunity. Although recruiting posters such as "Women of Britain say-GO!" associated women with the English countryside that valiant soldiers ought to defend, poems such as Jessie Pope's "War Girls" represent women as empowered by the challenge of their wartime jobs.

Frustrated by the war's length and carnage, some poets, such as Sassoon and Ezra Pound, allude disparagingly to the women and the civilization soldiers were supposedly protecting. Pound's Hugh Selwyn Mauberley, for example, refers to Britain as "an old bitch gone in the teeth."

Because of its massive scale and controversial impetus, monuments to the war often indicate the difficulty of representing it. Commemorative physical structures tend to look like a mixture of massiveness and stripped-down, minimalist gestures, as if trying to speak volumes and remain silent at the same time. The Menin Gate and the Cenotaph of Whitehall both stand in mute remembrance of a massive loss that can barely be imagined, much less represented.

The spareness of the Cenotaph, meanwhile, allowed two contemporaries to draw different conclusions about its significance: Henry Morton's Heart of London records his impression of the monument as a symbol of unity and communal reverence, while Charlotte Mew cannot help but notice, in her poem "Cenotaph," how incongruous this great static symbol of grief appears in the middle of a degraded mercantile hub. Like the divergences between jingoists and satirists, soldiers and civilians, feminists and antifeminists, these differences over war memorials reflect competing views over how to represent a war that ultimately defies representation.

The early part of the twentieth century saw massive changes in the everyday life of people in cities. The recent inventions of the automobile, airplane, and telephone shrank distances around the world and sped up the pace of life.

Freud's theory of the unconscious and infantile sexuality radically altered the popular understanding of the mind and identity, and the late-nineteenth-century thinkers Karl Marx and Friedrich Nietzsche in different ways undermined traditional notions of truth, certainty, and morality. Theoretical science, meanwhile, was rapidly shifting from two-hundred-year-old Newtonian models to Einstein's theory of relativity and finally to quantum mechanics.

At least partly in response to this acceleration of life and thought, a wave of aggressively experimental movements, sometimes collectively termed "modernist" because of their emphasis on radical innovation, swept through Europe. In Paris, the Spanish expatriate painter Pablo Picasso and the Frenchman Georges Braque developed cubism, a style of painting that abandoned realism and traditional perspective to fragment space and explode form. In Italy, the spokesperson for futurism, F. T. Marinetti, led an artistic movement that touched on everything from painting to poetry to cooking and encouraged an escape from the past into the rapid, energetic, mechanical world of the automobile, the airplane, and Marinetti's own "aeropoetics."

Dadaists such as the Frenchman Marcel Duchamp, author of the ready-made Fountain (1917), a urinal, began a guerilla campaign against established notions of sense and the boundaries of what could be called art. In music, meanwhile, composers such as the Frenchman Claude Debussy and Russian-born Igor Stravinsky were beginning experiments with rhythm and harmony that would soon culminate in the outright atonality of composers such as the Austrians Arnold Schoenberg and Alban Berg.

In England, this outbreak of modernist experiment influenced a loosely interrelated network of groups and individuals, many of them based in London. In anglophone literature, "modernism" more nearly describes an era than a unitary movement. But what connects the modernist writers-aside from a rich web of personal and professional connections-is a shared desire to break with established forms and subjects in art and literature. Influenced by European art movements, many modernist writers rejected realistic representation and traditional formal expectations.

In the novel, they explored the Freudian depths of their characters' psyches through stream of consciousness and interior monologue. In poetry, they mixed slang with elevated language, experimented with free verse, and often studded their works with difficult allusions and disconnected images. Ironically, the success of modernism's initially radical techniques eventually transformed them into the established norms that would be resisted by later generations.

Among the earliest groups to shape English-language modernism were the imagists, a circle of poets led initially by the Englishman T. E. Hulme and the American Ezra Pound, in the early 1910s. Imagist poetic doctrine included the use of plain speech, the preference for free verse over closed forms, and above all the creation of the vivid, hard-edged image.

The first two of these tenets in particular helped to shape later modernism and have had a far-reaching impact on poetic practice in English. Shaped by Asian forms such as the haiku, the imagist poem tended to be brief and ephemeral, presenting a single striking image or metaphor (see "An Imagist Cluster" in NAEL). Pound soon dissociated himself from the movement, and the imagists-including the poets H. D., Richard Aldington, and John Gould Fletcher-continued to publish their annual anthology under the leadership of the American poet Amy Lowell.

Pound, meanwhile, went cn to become a literary proponent of vorticism, an English movement in the visual arts led by the painter and writer Wyndham Lewis. The vorticists championed energy and life over what they saw as the turpitude of European society and sought to tap into or create the concentration of energies they dubbed a "vortex." After having published only one issue of their now notorious journal Blast, the vorticists suddenly found their often violent rhetoric and their ambivalence about English national identity at odds with the real violence of World War I and the wartime climate of patriotism.

The second issue of Blast-published behind schedule and dubbed a "war number"-declared the vorticists' loyalty to England in the fight against German fascism on aesthetic grounds. It also announced the death in the trenches of one of the movement's leading lights, the French-born sculptor Henri Gaudier-Brzeska. This loss and the general dispersal of the vorticists mark a major turning point for English modernism.

As modernism developed, the flashy, aggressive polemics of Lewis and Pound were replaced by the more reasoned, essayistic criticism of Pound's friend and collaborator T. S. Eliot. Eliot's Waste Land and James Joyce's Ulysses were technically innovative and initially controversial (Ulysses was banned in the United States and Great Britain), but their eventual acceptance as literary landmarks helped to bring modernism into the canon of English literature. In the decades to come, the massive influence of Eliot as a critic would transform the image of modernism into what Eliot himself called classicism, a position deeply rooted in a sense of the literary past and emphasizing the impersonality of the work of art.

In the post-World War II period, modernism became the institutionally approved norm against which later poetic movements, from the "Movement" of Philip Larkin to avant-garde Language Poetry, reacted. Nonetheless, the influence of modernism, both on those artists who have repudiated it and on those who have followed its direction, was pervasive. Joyce, Eliot, Virginia Woolf, and other modernists provided compositional strategies still central to literature.

Writers as diverse as W. H. Auden, Samuel Beckett, Derek Walcott, and Salman Rushdie have all, in one way or another, continued to extend the discoveries of the modernist experiment-adapting modernist techniques to new political climates marked by the Cold War and its aftermath, as well as to the very different histories of formerly colonized nations. Like the early twentieth-century avant-garde in European art and music, meanwhile, literary modernism has continued to shape a sense of art as a form of cultural revolution that must break with established history, constantly pushing out the boundaries of artistic practice.

Easter 1916 to the Troubles

Europe's former colonies struggled often violently for political sovereignty as nation-states. Ireland, Britain's oldest former colony, was one of the first to fight for its independence in the first half of the twentieth century. In addition to the creation of a new government, Ireland's struggle for independence entailed creating new ideas about Irish national identity through literature and the arts. This Norton Online Topic explores how twentieth-century Irish writers attempted to re-imagine Ireland, particularly during two periods of crisis: in the aftermath of the Easter Rebellion in 1916 and the later outbreaks of sectarian violence from 1969 (known as the Troubles) in Northern Ireland.

The 1916 Easter Rising grew out of Irish political and cultural nationalism and the desire for political sovereignty in Ireland. The growing resentment over the British control of Ireland led a secret revolutionary group known as the Irish Republican Brotherhood (IRB) to plan to take over Dublin on Easter Sunday, April 23, 1916.

On the day after Easter, Monday, April 24, 1916, a group of Irish leaders (including Thomas Clarke, Padraic Pearse, Thomas MacDonagh, and James Connolly) and about 1,600 Irish rebels, both men and women, took over several buildings and streets in the center of Dublin. On the steps of the General Post Office in Dublin, Pearse issued a Proclamation of Ireland's independence from British rule, announcing the birth of the Republic of Ireland and the institution of a provisional government. Five days later, with much of Dublin's city-center in ruins and aflame, the leaders were forced to surrender to a much larger British military force. In the ensuing weeks, fifteen of the leaders of the Easter Rising were executed by firing squad. At the time of the Easter Rising many Irish people were skeptical of the rebels' efforts to force the British Empire from Ireland. But after the swift execution and mass imprisonment of the Irish rebels, the public became more fervently nationalist, opposing the British presence in Ireland. As a result, the leaders of the Rising became martyrs within the public imagination.

The Easter Rising challenged modern Irish writers to re-imagine the Irish nation and national identity. Irish writers criticized the tyranny of British colonialism and shared the hope for an independent Ireland. Yet they also depicted the dangers of Irish nationalism, including its connections with armed violence, with cultural exclusion and racism, and, especially, with the ethic of blood sacrifice. In different ways, both W. B. Yeats's poem "Easter, 1916" and Sean O'Casey's play The Plough and the Stars ask skeptical questions about a violent Irish nationalism, even as they imagine an Ireland free from colonial rule.

Many Irish writers have figured the Irish nation as a woman to be fought for, as in the Easter 1916 Proclamation: "Ireland, through us, summons her children to her flag and strikes for her freedom." Since the rise of feminism in the 1960s, contemporary Irish women writers such as Eavan Boland (NAEL) have attempted to revise this image of Ireland as woman-both to bear witness to real Irish women's oppression and to criticize how the long history of British colonialism has limited Irish conceptions of gender and nationality.

Though Ireland gained national independence in 1922, the island of Ireland is not politically united. The twenty-six counties that comprise most of the island form the Republic of Ireland; the largely Catholic Republic (called only "Ireland") is fully independent from British rule. The six counties forming Northern Ireland are still under British control, and they constitute a separate political entity. Northern Ireland is also religiously divided between a Roman Catholic minority and an Ulster Protestant majority, and Ulster Protestants have historically had more political and economic power than Northern Irish Catholics. The combination of political and economic inequality and religious differences between these two groups has contributed to the waves of political and sectarian violence, or Troubles, since the late 1960s. The Troubles began when civil rights marches by Northern Irish Catholics for equal housing, voting, and economic rights were forcibly broken up by the Northern Irish police, or Royal Ulster Constabulary. On Sunday, January 30, 1972, during a demonstration against the unlawful imprisonment of Catholics, British soldiers fatally shot thirteen unarmed demonstrators and wounded another fourteen. "Bloody Sunday" inflamed Northern Irish Catholics and led in the 1970s and '80s to increased armed conflict between Catholic and Protestant paramilitary groups, frequent bombings, the deployment of more British troops and tanks to the streets of Northern Ireland, and the illegal internment of Catholics suspected of paramilitary ties.

By the 1990s, however, political leaders from both sides (including Gerry Adams of Sinn Fein and John Hume of the Social Democratic and Labour Party) began a series of talks to end the conflict in Northern Ireland. With the help of other Northern Irish leaders, British Prime Minister Tony Blair, and U.S. President Bill Clinton, these talks culminated in the Good Friday Agreement on April 10, 1998. This document effectively gives Northern Irish people the power to implement and run their own government apart from Westminster, London. The following month, the people of Ireland and Northern Ireland overwhelmingly passed by referendum the Good Friday Agreement. Despite the passing of the Agreement and the IRA announcement of a ceasefire in 1994, the political climate in Northern Ireland remains tense.

Like earlier modern Irish writers, contemporary Northern Irish writers have also felt compelled to respond to the Troubles in order to re-imagine Northern Ireland. The frequency and intensity of the Troubles have placed new pressures and raised new questions for Northern Irish writers. How, for instance, can a Northern Irish writer illustrate the disturbing nature of political violence without sensationalizing it? Can literature effectively offer consolation in the face of such atrocities? How can national unity and inclusiveness be imagined amidst ongoing cultural, political, and religious divisions? In works that range from elegy to farce, these are among the questions grappled with by writers of different political and religious communities, including Seamus Heaney, Paul Muldoon, Michael Longley, Fiona Barr, and a London-born writer of Irish parentage, Martin McDonagh.

The bloody events of the 1916 Easter Rising and the Troubles in Northern Ireland, both historical outgrowths of British colonialism, have had a lasting impact on how Irish and Northern Irish writers imagine the nation. Irish writers such as Yeats, James Joyce, and O'Casey were among the century's earliest postcolonial subjects to forge, question, and critique the meaning of the Irish nation and national identity. Yeats and Joyce have influenced postcolonial writers from countries that gained independence later in the century, such as Salman Rushdie (India), Derek Walcott (St. Lucia), and Chinua Achebe (Nigeria). Contemporary Irish, Northern Irish, and Irish diaspora writers such as Heaney, Longley, Muldoon, Boland, Barr, and McDonagh continue to make sense of the still-present history of British colonialism, the fact and meaning of sectarian and political violence, and they sometimes even glimpse hope for peace and reconciliation.

5

The Landscape of Indian English Literature

Indian English literature rose as an interesting by-product of an eventful encounter in the late eighteenth century between a powerful Britain and a stagnant India. The first period of Indian English literature may be said to end in the 1850s before the Indian Revolt of 1857. During this period British rule in India was generally accepted by most Indians as a great boon divinely delivered.

The holocaust of the Revolt ushered in different ideas. After consulting a few books, the writer, however, doesn't claim a scholar or an expert to dwell on the summary of Indian English literature.

But according to FW Bain, India as a withered trunk suddenly shot out with foreign foliage. One form this foliage took was that of original writing in English by Indians, thus partially fulfilling Samuel Daniel's prophesy in the sixteenth century concerning the English language.

The first problem that confronts every historian of Indian English literature, it is said, is to define its nature and scope clearly.

The question has been made rather complicated owing to two factors: first, this body of writing has, from time to time, been designated variously as Indo-Anglian literature, Indian writing in English and Indo-English literature;

secondly, the failure to make clear-cut distinctions has also often led to confusion between categories such as Anglo-Indian literature, literature in the Indian languages translated into English and oriental composition in English by Indians.

There is an interpretation of the term "Indo-Anglian literature" as comprising the work of Indian writers in English and Indo-English literature as consisting of translations by Indians from Indian literature into English. John B Alphonso Karkala in his Indo-English literature in the nineteenth century, 1970 uses the term Indo-English literature to mean literature produced by Indians in English.

Broadly speaking, Indian English literature may be defined as literature written originally in English by authors, Indian by birth, ancestry or nationality. It is clear that neither Anglo-Indian literature nor literal translations by others can legitimately form part of this literature.

The former comprises the writings of British or western authors concerning India. Rudyard Kipling, F.W. Bain, Paul Scott, Sir Edwin Arnold, F.A. Steel and M.M. Kaye are well known to have written about India, but it is argued that their work obviously belongs to British literature.

Similarly, translations from the Indian languages into English cannot also form part of Indian English literature, except when they are creative translations by the authors themselves.

The Eurasians who form a small class of Indian society called Anglo-Indian claim English as their mother tongue, but with notable exceptions like Henry Derozio, Aubrey Menen and Ruskin Bond, it is now discovered that few of them had tried to express themselves creatively in English.

But even in their case, the Indian strain in them is bound to condition the nature of both their artistic sensibility and their way of expression. Since literature is not a science, there will be a no man's land in which all attempts at strict definition are in danger of getting lost in a haze. Thus, there are exceptional cases like Anand K Coomaraswamy and Ruth Prawer Jhabvala. The former, born of a Sri Lankan Tamil father and an English mother, was neither an Indian citizen nor did he live in India, and yet the entire orientation of his thought is so unmistakably Indian that it is impossible not to consider him an Indian English writer.

Jhabvala is virtually an international phenomenon who was born of Polish parents in Germany. She received her education in English, married an Indian, lived in India for more than twenty years, and had written in English. On becoming daughter-in-law of India, she showed such close familiarity and deep understanding of Indian social life that she has rightly found a place in the history of Indian English literature.

On the other hand, what has been known is that V.S. Naipaul's Indian ancestry is indisputable, but he is so much of an outsider when he writes about India and Indians and so much of an insider when he deals with Caribbean life and character, that there can be no two options on his rightful inclusion in the history of West Indian Writing.

Now, it is established that Indian English literature, thus defined is not part of English literature, any more than American literature can be said to be a branch of British literature. It is legitimately a part of Indian literature, since its differentia is the expression in it of an Indian ethos.

Its use of English as a medium may also give it a place in Commonwealth literature, but that is largely a political entity. In any case, this does not in the smallest measure affect the claim of Indian English literature to be primarily a part of Indian literature.

Another problem is that of choosing from among the various titles given to it from time to time-viz, Indo-Anglian literature, Indian Writing in English, Indo-English literature and Indian English literature.

While many are allergic to the expression "Indo-Anglian", some would prefer "Indo-English." Indo-Anglian is reasonably handy and-descriptive. But a major flaw in the term of Indo-Anglian as pointed out by Alphonso Karkala is that it would suggest relation between two countries (India and England) rather than a country and a language. Indo-Anglian is thus hardly an accurate term to designate this literature. At last, being puzzled, an enterprising London printer changed it to Indo-Anglican.

As regards one's fondness of English, one Kashiprasad Ghose (1809-73), ambitiously composed original verse in English by studying prosody and criticism on the advice of his British teacher. He failed to produce the one to be reckoned with, owing to sheer lack of English root.

The course of Indian English literature is an absorbing record of the steady march of the Indian writers in English from pitifulness to authentic literary expression. Far from remaining merely imitators of the British, Indian English writers struggled valiantly against prejudice, neglect and ridicule. And at their best, they had proved themselves to be proud heirs to the two equally rich worlds of the East and the West. Likewise, after some decades, the present writing in English will greatly contribute to the said literature.

Gracefully, a writer may be eulogized for his writing today, but later his writing may not be accepted for reason of flaws as we all depend on a foreign language. Occasionally, rather than all of the time some writers in India too can write even like the English themselves. But we can only write like any Indian.

How expressively and uniquely noted Khush-want Singh and Rajinder Puri write are sufficient to form part of Indian English literature, and they find it as a means to express their ideas on any given topics easier in English than in their respective native languages. One such can be called distinctive dialectical English, current in South-East Asia.

One's sure right choice of words and perfect control of sentence structure, which are essential in writing, is an uphill task -for an average writer, and all of us of such category.

Our method of expression, therefore, is a dialect to prove some day to be as distinctive and colourful as the Irish and the American or English of other South East Asian countries.

INTRODUCTION

Just a few centuries ago English was spoken by just five to seven million people on one, relatively small island, and the language consisted of dialects spoken by monolinguals. Today there are more non-native than native users of English, and English has become the linguistic key used for opening borders: it is a global medium with local identities and messages (Kachru 1996: 11,14). English has become a world language, spoken by at least 750 million people. It is more widely spoken and written than any other language, even Latin, has ever been. It can, indeed, be said to be the first truly global language. English is nowadays the dominant or official language in over 60 countries.

Kachru, for instance (1997:68-69), states the increase in the use of English in Asia as "overwhelming": at present, the estimated population using English in Asia adds up to 350 million. India is the third largest English-using population in the world, after the USA and the UK. Literatures in English are nowadays recognized as part of the national literatures, and English is also recognized in the over-all language policy of the nation.

The language has penetrated deeply in the society, which has, in its turn, resulted in several varieties of English in India. The development of those new varieties is connected with historical and social factors. The new Englishes have all their own contexts of function and usage, and they have also, in their turn, affected the native varieties of English.

Indian English is used mainly by Indians whose native language it is not. It is a minority language, but yet a language of national affairs, and its status is often called into question by, as Bailey puts it, "not only by foreigners with their ideas of proper English, but also by Indians who remain ambivalent about its distinctive features and uncertain about its future" (Bailey 1991: 145). In fact, many of transplanted kinds of English are so attuned to the idea of a foreign standard of propriety that their independence remains partial.

The emergence of these new varieties has raised questions concerning the power of English language, questions of identity and new pragmatics of the language in new, foreign surroundings. The spread of English across different cultures and languages has meant the diversification of English, which, in turn, raises questions about the standardization of English.

The purpose of this study will be to study language attitudes in India (especially attitudes towards English) and to analyze the use of languages in different domains (family, friendship, neighbourhood, transactions, education, government, employment). Additionally, the aim is also to find out about the informants' preference for the model of the variety of English in India.

The Spread of English Around the World – The New Englishes

In the following, I will use Kachru's model of new Englishes (in e.g. The New Englishes: 1-5). He has visualized the spread of English around the world as three concentric circles representing different ways in which the language has been acquired and is currently used.

The Inner Circle refers to the traditional historical and sociolinguistic bases of English in the areas where it is the primary language (native or first language; UK, Ireland, Canada, the USA, Australia, New Zealand). The Outer Circle comprises regions colonized by Britain; the spread of English in non-native settings, where the language has become part of the country's chief institutions, and plays an important "second language" role in a-multilingual setting (India, Singapore, Malawi). The Expanding Circle involves nations which recognize the importance of English as an international language, but they do not have the history of colonization, nor does English have any special status in their language policy. In these areas, English is primarily a foreign language.

The term "new Englishes" is used for the varieties which have developed in the Outer Circle, have been transplanted and, therefore, can also be called "diaspora varieties". In a historical and linguistic sense, these varieties are not new. They are called "new" because it is only recently that they have been linguistically, and literaturewise, recognized and institutionalized, although they have a long history of acculturation in geographical, cultural and linguistic contexts different from the English of the Inner Circle. There is a decline of competence from educated English to "broken" English (which is considerably mixed with local languages).

Kachru has discussed the power of English in many of his writings (e.g. Kachru 1986c). Bolinger (cited in Kachru 1986c: 121) has used a metaphor the loaded weapon to characterize language. According to Kachru, questions about language and power go beyond linguistics into history, sociology, attitude studies, politics and economic considerations. The power of language is intimately connected with societal power. It can be manifested by using persuasion, regulation, inducement or force to add a code to a speech community or by the suppression of a particular language variety and the elevation of another.

There are two hypotheses concerning language power: the intrinsic-power hypothesis and the acquired-power hypothesis. The first one claims that English would intrinsically possess certain linguistic characteristics which would make it a preferred language for international purposes (e.g. Jespersen 1905, quoted in Kachru 1986c). This position can, according to Kachru, to some seem similar to claims of racial superiority. The second hypothesis emphasizes the ways in which a language acquires power, and thus it is also easier to understand.

A fact is that English has spread as a result of exploitation and colonisation. It s notable that, especially in many ex-colonies of Britain, English is still the language of an exclusive social elite. Cheshire, for instance, has discussed this (Cheshire 1991: 6).

Kachru (1986c: 128-129) has given various reasons for which languages are used in a society. They can be used to expand the speech community, as a vehicle of cultural or religious enlightenment to deculturize people from their own tradition (to the "civilizing process" also belonged distancing from native cultures: the colonizers wanted to introduce European literature to the natives, at the same time remaining ignorant of their indigenous literatures), to gain economic advantage, to control domains of knowledge and information, and for deception. The following statement by Charles Grant clearly demonstrates the attitudes of the British Raj in India (1831-1832; quoted in Kachru 1986c: 128):

The Hindoos err, because they are ignorant and their errors have never fairly been laid before them. The communication of our light and knowledge to them would prove the best remedy for their disorders.

The most important reason for the success of English is, according to Kachru (1986c:129-132), naturally the historical role of England as a colonial power. In India, for example, the political power naturally attributed a power to the language of the Raj (called the linguistic elitism strategy), and it also became a symbol of political power. English came to be the language of the legal system, higher education, pan-regional administrative network, science and technology, trade and commerce - either because the indigenous languages were not equipped for these roles and English provided for a convenient vocabulary, or because the use of English was considered prestigious and powerful. English became gradually a major tool for acquiring knowledge in the sciences and the humanities. It has come to represent modernization and development, and, as a link language, it has acquired intranational roles over the years.

Linguistic power can be manifested by using one of the following power strategies: persuasion, regulation, inducement and force. Kachru (1986c:123-127) has listed as examples of linguistic power suppression of a particular language (variety) and the elevation of another. Strategies can include crude linguistic power (e.g. the imposition of Japanese on the Koreans and the Malays during World War II), indirect psychological pressure (e.g. claims of "Other-World" power) and pragmatic power.

Kachru (1987:222) lists also some other reasons for the dominance of English around the world: its propensity for acquiring new identities, its power of assimilation, its adaptability to "decolonization" as a language, its manifestation in a range of lects, and its provision of a flexible medium for literary and other types of creativity across languages and cultures.

The Parameters and Dimensions of the Power of English

At present, English dominates functional domains in the widest possible register range. Kachru (1986c: 130) has presented some parameters of the power of English (which can also be understood as individual motivations for learning the language): Demographic and numerical Unprecedented spread across cultures and languages; on practically every continent Functional Provides access to most important scientific, technological, and cross-cultural domains of knowledge and interaction Attitudinal Symbolizes - certainly to a large group across cultures - one or more of the following: neutrality, liberalism, status and progressivism Accessibility

Provides intranational accessibility in the Outer Circle and international mobility across regions (cf. "link language" and "complementary language") Pluricentricity has resulted in the nativization and acculturation of the language. These two are, then, responsible for the "assimilation" of English across cultures Material a tool for mobility, economic gains, and social status Parameters for the power of English/ individual motivations for learning English.

In the same country the English language can be characterized by different terms representing the power of the language: POSITIVE NEGATIVE National identity Anti-nationalism Literary renaissance Anti-native culture Cultural mirror (for native cultures) Materialism Modernization Westernization Liberalism Rootlesness Universalism Ethnocentrism Technology Permissiveness Science Divisiveness Mobility Alienation Access code. Terms representing the power of English.

Often the same term may be used both in a positive and in a negative sense, depending on who uses it. The bad effects of the increasing power of English have been conscious and unconscious lingocide and dislocation of native cultural traditions by introducing Westernization. English is often seen as a tool of economic exploitation and domination. On the other hand, the Outer Circle sees English also as a tool of national identity and political awakening (as in the independence struggle in India), a window on the world, and a link language (Kachru 1986c: 136).

According to Bailey, too, English involves both positive and negative cultural values: economic development yet exploitation, political and cultural ideas and institutions, enrichment of English but possibly this at the cost of indigenous languages, opportunities to communicate with readers around the world yet at the expense of one's own language (Bailey 1991: 165).

Cheshire (1991:6) points out that although the spread of English has often been associated with the death of indigenous languages in those countries to which it has been transplanted, in India this was not the case. In Saghal's (1991:300) view, too, the role of English in India has not been replacive: it has not driven out any of the indigenous languages. Rather, she claims, English has enriched Indian languages (as well as it has been enriched by them).

According to Kachru (1986c:137), the power bases of English have to be seen in both material terms and psychological terms. English is supported in the Outer Circle for cultural renaissance, spread of nationalism, pan-regional literary creativity and neutrality, and there is a strong emotional attachment to the language. The psychological factors are important also because they are vital for creating an identity.

Kachru (see e.g. Kachru 1986a:9) stresses the neutrality of English as one clear advantage of using it: English is free from any undesirable (e.g. ethnic or religious) connotations native languages may have. The pros of using English have wiped away the fact that it originally was the colonizer's language (Kachru 1986a: 9).

Domains of Control

Kachru (1986c:132-133) mentions four basic areas in which the power of English manifests itself: linguistic, literary, attitudinal and pedagogical. Linguistic control is reflected, for example, in the codification of a language, the attitudes toward linguistic innovation and lexicographical research. The literary aspect refers to the ethnocentric attitude toward literary creativity in the Outer Circle. The attitudinal aspect is involved in issues concerning the identities of individuals and speech communities.

Kachru, for instance, stresses the importance of attitudes when determining the power of a language: what one thinks the language will do for him or her and what others think of a person when he or she uses the language. The pedagogical aspect deals with teaching of English in global contexts (the concerns including the model and the methods for teaching of English, which are often commercially motivated and quite seldom consider the local needs of different countries).

Historical Overview: The Establishment of East India Company

In the following, I will briefly go through the story of British India. The information below is mainly from The New Encyclopaedia Britannica (NEB; 1974), Kachru (1982 and 1983), Bailey (1991). It was Vasco da Gama who, in 1498, came ashore at Calicut, and restored a link between Europe and the East. India was "a land of spices and of marvels" to European people. Portugal's control of the Indian Ocean lasted throughout the 16th century. The turning point came in the 1580s: in 1580 Portugal was annexed to Spain. Spain was not too interested in former interests of Portugal, and gradually the control of the East fell through their hands. The route to the East was opened to the Dutch and English. The Dutch were first ones to arrive in 1595. The Dutch objective was, plain and simply, the trade. They were not so interested in proselytizing people, or trying to expand their empire; they were monopolists rather than imperialists (NEB 392).

The document establishing the British contact with the Indian subcontinent was the Charter of December 31, 1600, granted by Queen Elizabeth I. It granted a monopoly on trade with India and the East to some merchants of London - the East India Company was formed (Kachru 1982:353). The company's objective was actually the spices of Indonesia, but because of Dutch opposition (e.g. massacre of Amboina in 1623), they decided to change plans and go to India instead. The English won victory of some Portuguese in India as well, and the Mughal court, which resented the Portuguese, granted the English the right to trade and to establish factories in return for becoming the virtual naval auxiliaries of the empire (NEB 393).

The English trade became more profitable than that of the Dutch, and the region gradually fell under British contact and domination. In 1818, the British Empire became the British Empire of India, instead of the British Empire in India. The diplomatic settlement remained in force until 1947 (401).

A question that has frequently been asked is: How was this sort of subjection of a whole subcontinent possible? Probably the answer lies in the innate divisiveness of Hindu society (class and caste divisions); for the Indians the neighbours were more unwelcome than outsiders; and the outsiders could actually help in defeating the neighbour. The outsiders were, in the end, accepted as masters; the Indians would rather be mastered by them than dominated by a rivaling family inside India (402).

The Three Phases of the Introduction of Bilingualism in English in India

According to Kachru, there have been three phases in the introduction of bilingualism in English in India. The first one of them, the missionary phase, was initiated around 1614 by Christian missionaries. The second phase, the demand from the South Asian public (in the eighteenth century) was considered to come about through local demand, as some scholars were of the opinion that the spread of English was the result of the demand and willingness of local people to learn the language. There were prominent spokesmen for English. Kachru mentions two of them, Raja Rammohan Roy (1772-1833) and Rajunath Hari Navalkar (fl.1770). Roy and Navalkar, among others, were persuading the officials of the East India Company to give instruction in English, rather than in Sanskrit or Arabic. They thought that English would open the way for people to find out about scientific developments of the West. Knowledge of Sanskrit, Persian, Arabic or of Indian vernaculars would not contribute to this goal (Kachru 1983: 67-68).

A letter of Raja Rammohun Roy addressed to Lord Amherst (1773-1857) from the year 1823 is often presented as evidence of local demand for English. Roy embraced European learning, and in his opinion, English provided Indians with "the key to all knowledge -- all the really useful knowledge which the world contains" (quoted in Bailey 1991: 136). In the letter Roy expresses his opinion that the available funds should be used for employing

> European gentlemen of talent and education to instruct the natives of India in mathematics, natural philosophy, chemistry, anatomy, and other useful sciences, which the natives of Europe have carried to a degree of perfection that has raised them above the inhabitants of other parts of the world. [quoted in Kachru 1983: 68]

Roy's letter has been claimed to be responsible for starting the Oriental-Anglicist controversy, the controversy over which educational policy would be suitable for India. The third phase, the Government policy, begun in 1765, when the East India Company's authority was stabilized (Kachru 1983: 21-22). English was established firmly as the medium of instruction and administration. The English language became popular, because it opened paths to employment and influence (NEB 1974: 406). English of the subject Indians became gradually a widespread means of communication.

During the governor generalship Lord William Bentinck in the early nineteenth century, India saw many social reforms. English became the language of record of government and higher courts, and government support was given to the cultivation of Western learning and science through the medium of English. In this he was supported by Lord Macaulay (ibid, 403).

Macaulay's Minute and the Beginnings of Bilingualism in English in India

Lord Macaulay was a central figure in the language debate over which language(s) should be used as the medium of education in India. The Orientalists were in the favour of use of classical languages of Indian tradition, such as Sanskrit, Persian and Arabic, which were not spoken as native languages. The Anglicists, on the other hand, supported English. Neither of these groups wanted to suppress the local vernaculars, mother tongues of the people. Both the groups agreed that education would be conducted in the vernacular during the first years of education. The Anglicist group included Charles Grant (1746-1823), Lord Moira (1754-1826) and T.B. Macaulay (1800-59); H.T. Prinsep (1792-1878) acted as the spokesman for the Orientalists" group (Kachru 1986a: 35).

The Anglicist group's views were expressed in the Minute of Macaulay, which is said to mark "the real beginnings of bilingualism in India" (McCrum et al. 1988: 325). According to the document, which had been prepared for the governor general William Bentinck, after listening to the argument of the two sides, a class should be formed in India, a group of people who would act as interpreters between the British and Indians, "a class of persons, Indians in blood and colour, but English in taste, in opinion, in morals and in intellect" (Bailey 1991: 138). Macaulay's proposal was a success; and the following year Lord Bentinck expressed his full support for the minute, declaring that the funds "administered on Public Instruction should be henceforth employed in imparting to the native population a knowledge of English literature and science through the medium of the English language" (ibid).

According to Bailey, in Macaulay's thinking Indian languages would be enriched by English, so that they could become vehicles for European scientific, historical and literary expression (ibid, 140). English gradually became the language of government, education, advancement, "a symbol of imperial rule and of self-improvement" (McCrum et al. 1988: 325).

Macaulay justified the imposition of British power on the country by simply arguing that although this policy in India might seem controversial and strange sometimes, it can be so, for the Empire is itself the strangest of all political anomalies...that we should govern a territory ten thousand miles from us, a territory larger and more populous than France, Spain, Italy and Germany put together...a territory inhabited by men differing from us in race, colour, language, manners, morals, religion; these are prodigies to which the world has seen nothing similar. Reason is confounded...General rules are useless where the whole is one vast exception. The Company is anomaly, but it is part of a system where everything is anomaly. It is strangest of all governments; but it is designed for the strangest of all Empires. [Bailey 1991: 137].

According to Kachru, the far-reaching Minute was highly controversial because of disagreement about whether it was correct to impose an alien language on Indians. The Orientalists expressed their disagreement in a note dated 15 February 1835, but they could not stop it from passing and had to give way (Kachru 1983: 68-69). On 7 March 1835, the Minute received a Seal of Approval from Lord William Bentinck (1774-1839), and an official resolution on Macaulay's resolution was passed. This resolution "formed the cornerstone of the implementation of a language policy in India and ultimately resulted in the diffusion of bilingualism in English" (68).

There are many sharing the view of Alastair Pennycook that in fact both Anglicism and Orientalism really worked together towards the same direction. He rejects the view that Orientalism was somehow a "good and innocent project that only had the rights of the colonized people at heart". He claims that, in reality, Orientalism was as much part of colonialism as was Anglicism (Pennycook 1994: 103). Although Orientalism is usually considered more sympathetic towards the local languages and cultures than Anglicism, it acknowledged the superiority of Western literature and learning, and it was a means to exercise social control over the people, and imposing of western ideas (Pennycook 1994: 102).

Pennycook claims, too, that although Macaulay is credited the most influential individual in the language question, the issue is more complex than simply Macaulay arriving in India, writing the Minute on education. and then heading off back to England with having English firmly transplanted in the colony. In his view, then, it is important to understand that Macaulay just articulated a position which had been discussed for a long time already (Pennycook 1994: 77). He goes on further to argue that the Indian bourgeoisie was demanding English-language education as much as the missionaries and educators (79), seeing knowledge of English as an essential tool in gaining social and economic prestige (76).

English becomes the Language of the Elite, Press and Administration

In the following years, English was established firmly as the medium of instruction and administration by the British Raj (1765-1947). Indian education was ever greater anglicized as the English language became rooted in an alien linguistic, cultural, administrative and educational setting. The first universities were established in India in 1857 (in Bombay, Calcutta and Madras). English became accepted as the language of the élite, of the administration, and of the pan-Indian press. English newspapers had an influential reading public. Indian literature in English was also developing (Kachru 1983: 69).

ENGLISH IN INDEPENDENT INDIA

India, after becoming independent in 1947, was left with a colonial language, in this case English, as the language of government. It was thought that the end of the British Raj would mean the slow but sure demise of the English language in South Asia. This, of course, has not happened. The penetration of English in these societies is greater that it has ever been (Kachru 1994: 542).

Nationalist imperative wanted that English continue to be used. Nationalist motivations were of the opinion that an indigenous Indian language should be adopted as the official language. Hindi seemed most qualified for that, since it had more native speakers than any other Indian language and was already widely used in interethnic communication (Fasold 1984: 24).

In addition, it was thought that linguistic unity was a prerequisite for political and national unity. Thus, Hindi was designated by the constitution as the language of communication between and within the states. It was to replace English within 15 years. The plan was that Hindi would be promoted so that it might express all parts of the "composite culture of India" (Spolsky 1978: 56).

There were, however, several problems with selecting Hindi, and since the protests were often violent (e.g. the riots in Tamil Nadu in May 1963, protesting against the imposition of Hindi), the government wanted to adapt a policy which would help to maintain the status quo. Firstly, Hindi is not evenly distributed throughout the country; e.g. in Tamil Nadu, in the south, only 0.0002 per cent of the people claimed knowledge of Hindi or Urdu, whereas in the northern states this figure can rise up to 96.7 per cent.

Secondly, it was thought that the speakers of other languages would be offended by its selection; other Indian languages, for example Tamil and Bengali, had as much right to be national languages as Hindi. The other Indian communities felt they would be professionally, politically and socially disadvantaged were Hindi given the central role.

Thirdly, Hindi was thought to need vocabulary development before it could be used efficiently as a language of government. In spite of these problems, Hindi was chosen as the national language in the constitution, and English was to be replaced by Hindi in fifteen years' time. However, due to the continuous opposition in the south, this replacement was not politically possible. In 1967 a law was passed which allowed the use of both Hindi and English for all official purposes - and that situation still exists (Fasold 1984: 24).

The controversy between Hindi, Urdu and Hindustani made the case for Hindi even worse. Support for Hindustani almost ended with independence; Hindi's supporters' enthusiasm was not, also, channeled in a constructive direction. As a result, English continues to be a language of both power and prestige (Kachru 1986a: 8).

THE POWER OF ENGLISH: THE CASE OF INDIA

The British were given a lot of political stature due to their political power, and they were required to adopt a pose that would fit their status. Language became a marker of the white man's power. Kachru quotes E. M. Forster in A Passage to India (Kachru 1986: 5):

> *"India likes gods. And Englishmen like posing as gods". The English language was part of the pose and power. Indians accepted it, too (ibid).*

English was used in India and elsewhere in the colonies as a tool of power to cultivate a group of people who identify with the cultural and other norms of the political elite (cf. Macaulay's Minute). European values were, naturally, considered somehow inherently better whereas the indigenous culture was often considered somehow barbaric. English was considered as a "road to the light", a tool of "civilization". The Europeans thought that they can bring emancipation to the souls; they considered this as their duty. They sincerely thought they would contribute to the well-being of the native people in the colonies, and their language was elevated into being almost divine.

English provided a medium for understanding technology and scientific development. Non-western intellectuals admired accomplishments of the west. European literature was made available in colonies. Macaulay shows his ignorance towards the native languages in India by saying (cited in Kachru 1986a: 7):

> *I have never found one amongst them (the Orientalists) who would deny that a single shelf of a good European library was worth the whole native literature of India and Arabia.*

In India, English gradually acquired socially and administratively the most dominant roles: the power and prestige of language was defined by the domains of language use. Ultimately the legal system, the national media and important professions were conducted in English (Kachru 1986a: 7). In the words of Kachru, skilled professional Indian became the symbol of Westernization and modernization. Raja Rammohan Roy was committed to the idea that the "European gentlemen of talent and education" should be appointed to instruct the natives of India. English came to be used by Indians, as well. (Kachru 1986a:7).

By the 1920s English had become the language of political discourse, intranational administration, and law, a language associated with liberal thinking. Even after the colonial period ended, English maintained its power over local languages.

English was eventually used against Englishmen, their roles and intentions as it became the language of resurgence of nationalism and political awakening: the medium, ironically, was the alien language. Mohandas K. Gandhi (1869-1948), for instance, although struggled to create consensus for an acceptable native variety as the national language, expressed his message to the elite in English.

Definition of the Concept of Multilingualism

Linguistic diversity -- multilingualism -- is, according to Mahapatra, found in most present-day nations (Mahapatra 1990: 1). In the Webster's Encyclopedic Unabridged

Dictionary of the English Language (1996: 940), a multilingual person is defined as one "able to speak more than two languages with approximately equal facility". Kachru describes the same phenomenon as the "linguistic behavior of the members of a speech community which alternately uses two, three or more languages depending on the situation and function". (Kachru 1986a: 159).

How Does Multilingualism Develop?

According to Fasold (1984: 9), there are four different kinds of historical patterns that can lead to societal multilingualism. These patterns are migration, imperialism, federation and border area multilingualism. In this context, I will concentrate on the pattern of imperialism.

The subtypes of imperialism are colonization, annexation, and economic imperialism. Typical of imperialist processes is that relatively few people from the controlling nationality take up residence in the new area. Former British, French, Spanish, Portuguese and Dutch colonies in Africa, Asia and South America can serve as examples (ibid, 10).

Although relatively few people come to live in the subjugated territories, the language becomes very important in the territory (ibid, 10). Spolsky, too, remarks that the larger the scale of colonization from the homeland is, the more secure place the conquerors' language will be in the new land, although even a small ruling group may be able to maintain their language, provided they have contact with the homeland. Often in this case, the conquered people will be forced to learn the language of the conquerors (Spolsky 1978: 24).

In annexation and colonization, the imperialist language is likely to be used in government and education; in economic imperialism, the imperialist language is necessary for international commerce and finance: a foreign language will become widely used because of the economic advantage associated with it (Fasold 1984: 10).

The Indian Case

A regional language has its geographical bounds defined within the state (Spolsky 1978: 26).

In addition to the designation of Hindi as an official language and fourteen others as national languages, each state can choose its own regional language for use in local government affairs and in education among the languages spoken in its territory. India's constitution guarantees the right of all citizens to communicate in their own language with any governmental agency (Bonvillain 1993: 304).

There are over 900 million people and more than one thousand languages in India; the area is thus one of the most diverse linguistic and cultural areas in the world. Thus, it comes as no surprise that there are many problems in classifying and labeling languages in India. One reason is that languages tend to fade into other ones, so that it is difficult to say which are different languages, or which are just dialects of one language (Fasold 1984: 22).

In 1971, it was estimated that the rate of bilingualism in India was 13%. 99% of English speakers are second-language speakers, whereas in many other languages there are no non-native speakers at all (although there are large numbers of native speakers) (Mahapatra 1990: 7).

Spolsky describes the situation on the Indian subcontinent as one highlighting the "multitude of problems facing a political unit that contains a great number of languages". He further points out that it comes as no surprise that India has some difficulty in setting up a language policy: the constitution, for example, avoids choosing a single official language (Spolsky 1978: 42-43).

D.P. Pattanayak describes Indian societal multilingualism as a non-conflicting type, in which different languages are allocated different functions. He describes mother tongue as the "expression of primary identity and of group solidarity". People are identified with certain linguistic, ethnic, religious or cultural groups through ones mother tongue. "Mother tongue anchors the child to culture", Pattanayak continues. In his view of multilingualism, it can be successful only if there is respect for multiplicity, "respect for the different", in a society (Pattanayak 1990: viii-xii).

Spolsky points out that although there are so many languages in India, most of the people do not know any other Indian language than their own. English is most widely spoken second language , followed by Hındi. English is more useful as a "lingua franca"; the usefulness of Hindi as a lingua franca is regionally limited (Spolsky 1978: 42).

National versus Official Languages

Following Platt, I would like to distinguish between national and official langages: national language -- a language that is considered representative of a nation or nationality. The term connotates of belonging to a nation, of ethnic and/ or cultural identity. Usually it is a local language spoken as native language by at least some of the population of a nation (Platt 1984: 19).

Official language -- language generally used for government administration and the Higher Courts of Law, in the media and as one of the languages of education, at least of secondary and higher education on a nationwide basis (ibid, 19).

Fifteen National Languages

In the early 1950s, a serious problem of linguistic and ethnic diversity was recognized by the Indian government. As a solution to the problem, states were established along linguistic lines, so that in all but two of India's eighteen states the majority spoke a common language (Bonvillain 1993: 303).

Officially, 15 national languages are recognized by the Indian government. In many cases the State boundaries have been drawn on linguistic lines. The acknowledged languages are: Assamese, Bengali, Gujarati, Hindi, Kannada, Kashmiri, Malayalam, Marathi, Oriya, Punjabi, Sanskrit, Sindhi, Tamil, Telegu and Urdu. India is divided linguistically into two major language families, the Indo-Aryan and the Dravidian languages (Indian Culture. 1998) (appendices 1 and 2). The most widely spoken national languages in India are (in addition to Hindi): Bengali (7,5%), Telugu (7,4%), Marathi (7,2%), Tamil (6,9%), Urdu (5,1%), Gujarati (4,2%), Malayalam (3,8%), Kannada (3,8%), Oriya (3,4%) (India 1996:18).

The Indic (or Indo-Aryan) languages are a branch of the Indo-European group of languages, and were the language of the central Asian peoples who invaded India. Most of Indian languages of the north belong to this group. The Dravidian languages, on the other hand (e.g. Tamil, Telugu, Malayalam) are native to south India (although they are influenced by Sanskrit and Hindi) (Culture on commercenetindia. 1998).

There is an ongoing fear that Indian languages will be ignored as English is becoming more and more popular in India. One should be cautious about this, since Mark Tully claims (Tully 1997:160) one can obtain a deeper knowledge of the culture only through the knowledge of the language (or one of the languages) of that culture. He quotes Robert Phillipson and Tove Skutnabb-Kangas (1996), according to whom the consequence of the current language policy is that many among the younger generations of Indians are being deprived of familiarity with their cultural heritage, and quite probably of an education that would enable them to contribute to the solution of Indian problems in the future.

Nowadays, however, something is being done to keep Indian native languages alive. Computer applications, for instance, are appearing in Indian languages, and training centres have been set up to teach them to people in Indian languages (The Bline on Indiaserver. 1997.). Motorola has also been reported to have launched pagers in three Indian languages (which was the first time a pager which can display messages in Indian languages has been launched). This means that people who do not know English very well are able to send or receive messages in their mother tongue (The Hindu on Indiaserver. 1997).

Hindi, the Official Language

Hindi descends directly from Sanskrit. More than 180 million people in India regard Hindi as their mother tongue. It belongs to the Indo-Aryan group of languages (Hindi. 1998). It is, according to the Article 343 (1) of the Constitution, the Official Language of the Union (India Constitution. 1998.)

The position of Hindi as the Official Language of the Union becomes problematic the souther in India one gets: while it is the predominant language in the north, in the south very few people speak it. The most ferocious opposition toward the adoption of Hindi comes from the south; along with the strongest support for the retention of English (Culture on Commercenetindia. 1998).

English in India – and Who Speaks English to Whom and When?

In terms of numbers of English speakers, the Indian subcontinent ranks third in the world, after the USA and UK. An estimated 4% of the Indian population use English; although the number might seem small, out of the total population that is about 35 million people (in 1994)(Crystal 1995:101). Although the number of speakers of English in India is somewhat limited (as compared to the total population), that small segment of the population controls domains that have professional prestige (Kachru 1986a: 8).

English is virtually the first language for many educated Indians, and for many, who speak more than one language, English is the second one. Indian speakers of English are primarily bi- or multilingual Indians who use English as a second language in contexts in which English is used among

Indians as a "link" or an "official" language. Only a minimal fraction of the English-using Indian population has any interaction with native speakers of English. According to Kachru's survey (the population of which was graduate faculty of English in the universities and colleges), only 65.64 percent had occasional interaction with native speakers of English; 11.79 percent had no interaction and 5.12 percent claimed to have daily interaction with native speakers of English (ibid, 110).

The Role of English in Indian Multilingual Setting

English serves two purposes. First, it provides a linguistic tool for the administrative cohesiveness of a country, and, secondly, it serves as a language of wider communication (Kachru 1986a: 8). English functions in the Indian socio-cultural context to perform roles relevant and appropriate to the social, educational and administrative network of India (Kachru 1986a: 111).

English is used in both public and personal domains and its functions "extend far beyond those normally associated with an outside language, including the instrumental, the regulative, the interpersonal and the innovative, self-expressive function" (Kachru 1986a: 37). As pointed out before, the role of English is not replacive: it overlaps with local languages in certain domains (Kandiah citing Sridhar, 1985;Shridhar and Shridhar, 1986; 1991: 273).

English as the Language of Administration and Press

English is not classified as one of the 15 national languages of India (NEB:286). Although Hindi is the Official Language of the Union; provision was made in the Constitution that English would be used in official work until 1965, after which Hindi would replace it. Because of the opposition of the Dravidian south against Hindi, the Indians decided to further extend the role of English as an additional language with Hindi to be used for purposes of the Union and in Parliament. English is now recognized as an associate official language, with Hindi the official language. It is recognized as the official language in four states (Manipur, Meghalaya, Nagaland, Tripura) and in eight Union territories.

Various political and nationalistic pressures continue to push for the choice of Hindi as a national language. However, it is hard to remove English from its place as a language of wider communication, lingua franca, especially among the educated elite, or to replace the regional languages in mass communication by Hindi.

Fasold (1984:139) suggests that English lacks the symbolic power required to be chosen as the sole official language in India, although it does have a high communicativity necessary for the successful function of a nationalist language.

English plays a dominant role in the media; it has been used as a medium for inter-state communication, the pan-Indian press and broadcasting both before and since India's independence. The impact of English is not only continuing but increasing.

The English press in India initiated serious journalism in the country. The number of English newspapers, journals and magazines is on the increase. According to Kachru (1986b:12), at present there are 3,582 Indian newspapers in English. English-language newspapers are published in practically all states of the Republic. Of a total of 19,144 newspapers registered in India in 1982, those in English accounted for 18.7 percent, whereas the newspapers in Hindi accounted for 27.8 percent.

Language Planning: English in Education

English is the state language of two states in eastern India, Meghalaya and Nagaland. It is the main medium of instruction at the postgraduate level, and it is taught as a second language at every stage of education in all states of India.

In India, as in other linguistically and culturally pluralistic societies, the position of English is determined by various political, cultural and social considerations. Kachru (1986b:20) sees primarily three questions which continue to be discussed. The first question concerns the position of English in early and in higher education. The second question is concerned with the roles of the regional language, Hindi and English. The third question deals with the model of English presented to Indian learners, and how that presentation can be made uniformly and effectively. The Government of India has primarily been concerned with the first two questions, which are directly related to language planning at both the national and state levels. There are, as yet, no acceptable answers to any of these questions (Kachru 1986b:20).

In the 1960s a bitter conflict considering the status of various languages in India arose from concerns of the southern states (in which Hindi is not widely spoken) that the use of Hindi in the government services would disadvantage them for employment in those areas. They thought, also, that it was unfair for them having to learn both Hindi and English, whereas native speakers of Hindi would only have to learn English.

Consequently, the Three Language Formula was developed for the educational load to be more fair, to promote national integration, and, to provide wider language choice in the school curriculum (Srivastava 1990: 43). According to the formula, people from non-Hindi areas study their regional language, Hindi, and English. Hindi speakers, on the other hand, study Hindi, English and another language. Baldridge quotes Kamal Sridhar (1989):

"The Three Language Formula is a compromise between the demands of the various pressure groups and has been hailed as a masterly - if imperfect - solution to a complicated problem. It seeks to accommodate the interests of group identity (mother tongues and regional languages), national pride and unity (Hindi), and administrative efficiency and technological progress (English)." (Baldridge 1996: 12).

Although the formula sounds fine in theory, Baldridge (ibid) states that the Three Language Formula has proved to be a failure in India as a whole, since it has not been followed in practice. Hindi states did not enforce the curriculum, and the anti-Hindi DMK government in Madras removed all teaching of Hindi from schools in Tamil Nadu.

Thus, in India, there is a great number of sociolinguistic pressures influencing the development of language education; Spolsky (1978: 55-64) has stated that the language policy of the school system is both a result of the pressures and a source of pressure itself. He, too, claims education to be the strongest weapon for enforcing language policy , listing the following pressures to have an effect on language planning in a society: family (attitudes at home), religion (if the maintenance of a language is based on a belief in a "holy tongue"), ethnicity, political pressures (aiming at establishing national unity; a language tradition is acknowledged as a powerful force within a nationalist movement), cultural pressures, economic pressures (which include commerce, advanced science and technology: the idea is that not all languages have modern technological vocabulary and it is more rational to adopt a language such as English for this purpose), the mass media (e.g., if there is no media in a particular language, there will be strong pressure to learn another language which is better provided), legal pressures (lack of the official language can often become the basis for discrimination), military pressure (desirability to use one common language) (Spolsky 1978: 53-63).

Mark Tully (1997:161-162) points out that the élitist status of English in India creates problems for the economic development because that means that the education of the mass of people will be ignored. He argues that the solution for the situation would be that the spread of English throughout India would be encouraged so that it would become a "genuine link language of the country, not just, as it is at present, the link language of the élite".

INDIAN ENGLISH LITERATURE

India is the third largest English book-producing country after the United States and the United Kingdom, and the largest number of books are published in English. Creative writing in English is considered an integral part of the literary traditions in South Asia. Indeed, according to the words of an Indian critic Iyengar three decades ago, quoted by Kachru, there seems to be an acceptance of Indian English literature as "one of the voices in which India speaks...it is a new voice, no doubt, but it is as much Indian as the others" (Kachru 1994:528-529). Sanyal claims, too, that Indian writing represents a new form of Indian culture. It has become assimilated and is today a dynamic element of the culture (Sanyal 1987: 7).

It can be said to be a challenge for the Indian novelist to write about his experiences in a language which has developed in a very different cultural setting; in a "foreign" language; how to create sense of reality and intensity of Indian life in the medium of English language (Sanyal 1987: 7). The integrity of the writers writing in English is often suspect in their own country, and in other English-speaking countries they are treated as marginal to the mainstream of English literature (Kachru 1986b:19). Indian English writers are sometimes accused of abandoning the national or regional language and writing in a western, "foreign", language; their commitment to the nation is considered suspect. Indian writing in English dates back to the 1830s, to Kashiprasad Ghosh, who is considered the first Indian poet writing in English. Sochee Chunder Dutt was the first writer of fiction. In the beginning, however, political writing was dominant (Kachru 1994: 530-531) (e.g. Rammohan Roy wrote about social reform and religion in the medium of English (Sanyal 1987:19).

Stylistic influence from the local languages seems to be a particular feature of much Indian literature in English; the local language structure is reflected as e.g. the literal translation of local idioms (Platt et. al: 1984: 181). According to Kachru, however, South Asian novelists have not only nativized the language in terms of stylistic features; they have also acculturated English in terms of the South Asian context (Kachru 1994: 530).

A view of the mother tongue being the primary medium of literary creativity is still generally held across cultures. Creativity in another tongue is often considered as a deviation from the norm. The native language is considered pure, it is treated as a norm. This causes difficulties for non-native writers of English: it is not rarely that they have to defend themselves writing in English (Kachru 1997:66-87). CUP.

The thematic range of literatures has been extended in India: in fact, Kachru points out that English has functioned "as the main agent for releasing the South Asian languages from the rigorous constraints of the classical literary traditions". English has created new experimentation in the field of Indian writing (Kachru 1994: 535-536). Kachru points out that the linguistic centre of English has shifted. This means that English no longer only represents the Judeo-Christian traditions and Western concepts of literary creativity. The ranges of English have expanded, as the varieties within a variety have been formed (Kachru 1986a: 130-131).

Nativization of Indian English

The process of nativization is due both to transfer from local language as well as to the new cultural environment and communicative needs (Saghal 1991: 300). Because of deep social penetration and the extended range of functions of English in diverse sociolinguistic contexts there are several varieties, localized registers and genres for articulating local social, cultural and religious identities (Kachru 1997:69).

Also, factors such as the absence of a native group. inadequate teaching and acquisitional limitations (e.g. lack of exposure and facilities, learning under compulsion) contribute to the process (Saghal 1991: 300).

Scholars (such as Kachru, Halverson, Verma, Mehrotra and Sridhar) have all concluded that the South Asian varieties of English are being nativized by acquiring new identities in new socio-cultural contexts. They have emerged as autonomous local varieties with their own set of rules that make it impossible to treat them simply as mistakes of deficient Englishes (Kandiah 1991: 275).

South Asian English has developed to a more distinctive level than in other countries where English is used as a second language (Crystal 1988: 258). English in India has evolved characteristic features at the phonological, lexical, syntactic and even at discourse level.

Initially, these innovations were rejected by purists, but they are becoming increasingly accepted: English is not anymore treated as a foreign language; it is part of the cultural identity of India. These innovations have led to some problems related to pedagogical standards, national and international intelligibility and typology (Saghal 1991: 303).

Is Diversification Decay?

The idea of corruption and barbarity of transplanted kinds of English became accepted by the end of the eighteenth century. The evaluation of different kinds of transplanted English is based on the fate of American English, the first transplanted variety to be despised. According to Bailey, attitudes toward transplanted varieties of English have taken many forms, from categorical denunciation of an entire national variety to niggling criticism of minute details of local usage...Received wisdom declares that transplanted English must be somehow different, and probably worse; the image, in short, anticipates the evidence.(Bailey 1991: 133).

Indians in their use of English have always been restrained in comparison to Americans, for instance. In India numerous British teachers and officials have been quick to censure all departures from the Standard British English forms. "Imperfections" in Indian English were held up to scorn (ibid, 142).

The Question of Standard English

A standard variety has undergone at least some degree of regularisation or codification, it is recognized as a prestigious variety or code by a community, and it is used for high functions alongside a diversity of low varieties (Holmes 1992:83). It provides a means of communication across areas with various different dialects. According to Saghal, a rather nebulous educated Indian English variety close to the native standard is favoured as a model for Indian English by the general consensus (Saghal 1991: 303).

According to Kachru, the spread of English and its intercultural uses raise questions concerning diversification, codification, identities, cross-cultural intelligibility and power and ideology. The ultimate danger could be decay or even loss of international intelligibility, some have argued (Kachru 1987:220-221). In the multilinguistic and culturally pluralistic context of India, the English language has developed its regional, social and occupational varieties: typically Indian registers of legal system, business, newspapers, creative writing (Kachru 1986a: 110).

The fact that English has acquired multiple identities and a broad spectrum of cross-cultural interactional contexts of use is, according to Kachru, "a purists' and pedagogues' nightmare and a variationists' blessing". As a consequence of the spread of English, there are "various semiotic systems, several linguistic conventions and numerous cultural traditions: English absorbs and unfolds meanings and values from diverse cultures" (Kachru 1987: 207-211). Kachru points out that the contexts of diversification of English are not just deficiencies, but that there are deeper sociological, linguistic and cultural reasons. The diversification often, then, is symbolic of "subtle sociolinguistic messages" (ibid, 218).

Crystal points out that while, on one hand, English-speaking communities are striving to nativize the language to reflect their own experiences, on the other hand many are of the view that a universally intelligible, more ore less standardized medium would be desirable (Crystal 1988: 261-262). Not the least because "British English is now, numerically speaking, a minority dialect, compared with American, or even Indian English" (ibid, 10).

Samuel Ahulu suggests that the concept of Standard English be redefined. According to his view, Standard English is usually associated with British and/or American English. English, however, as an international language, has developed, and continues to develop forms or features divergent from British and/or American English.

As arguments that any divergence from British or American English is an error appear unrealistic, Standard English, in Ahulu's view, should accommodate to the developments of new Englishes. The variability of non-native Englishes should, ideally, be seen as styles of speech or expression which makes a part of the speakers' repertoire; they should not be thought of as errors. English lacks standard codification which would reflect its international character adequately. Thus, one of the major problems with new Englishes appears to be the issue of codification (Ahulu 1997: 17-19),

The variation manifested in the use of English as an international language should be subsumed within the concept of "Standard English", and the divergent forms should be recognised as standard practice or styles of Standard English; styles of speech or expression to which speakers of English as an international language will be exposed, and which will constitute their repertoire.

Cheshire points out that sociolinguistic analyses can contribute to English language teaching issues by ensuring that descriptions of world varieties of English have a sounder empirical base. Current descriptions are all too often given as lists of assorted departures from southern British standard English or American standard English with no attempt at determining the extent to which the local linguistic features function as part of an autonomous system (1991:7).

Measurement Techniques-What is a Language Attitude?

Some language-attitudes studies are strictly limited to attitudes toward the language itself. However, most often the concept of language attitudes includes attitudes towards speakers of a particular language; if the definition is even further broadened, it can allow all kinds of behavior concerning language to be treated (e.g. attitudes toward language maintenance and planning efforts) (Fasold 1984: 148).

Attitudes are crucial in language growth or decay, restoration or destruction: the status and importance of a language in society and within an individual derives largely from adopted or learnt attitudes. An attitude is individual, but it has origins in collective behaviour. Attitude is something an individual has which defines or promotes certain behaviours. Although an attitude is a hypothetical psychological construct, it touches the reality of language life. Baker stresses the importance of attitudes in the discussion of bilingualism. Attitudes are learned predispositions, not inherited, and are likely to be relatively stable; they have a tendency to persist. However, attitudes are affected by experience; thus, attitude change is an important notion in bilingualism. Attitudes vary from favourability to unfavourability. Attitudes are complex constructs; e.g. there may be both positive and negative feelings attached to, e.g. a language situation (Baker 1988:112- 115).

According to Lambert (1967), attitudes consist of three components: the cognitive, affective and conative components (Dittmar 1976: 181). The-cognitive component refers to an individual's belief structure, the affective to emotional reactions and the conative component comprehends the tendency to behave in a certain way towards the attitude (Gardner 1985:).

The major dimensions along which views about languages can vary are social status and group solidarity. The distinction of standard/nonstandard reflects the relative social status or power of the groups of speakers, and the forces held responsible for vitality of a language can be contributed to the solidarity value of it. Another dimension, called ingroup solidarity or language loyalty, reflects the social pressures to maintain languages/language varieties, even one without social prestige (Edwards 1982:20)

Fishman and Agheyisi (1970) have suggested that there is a mentalist and behaviourist viewpoint to language attitudes. According to the mentalist view, attitudes are a "mental and neutral state of readiness which cannot be observed directly, but must be inferred from the subject's introspection". Difficulties arising from this viewpoint include the question that from what data can attitudes be derived, and in what way are they quantifiable.

According to behaviourism, attitudes are a dependent variable that can be statistically determined by observing actual behaviour in social situations. This also causes problems; it can be questioned whether attitudes can be defined entirely in terms of the observable data (Dittmar 1976: 181).

Fasold suggests that attitudes toward a language are often the reflection of attitudes towards members of various ethnic groups (Fasold 1984: 148): people's reactions to language varieties reveal much of their perception of the speakers of these varieties (Edwards 1982: 20).

Many studies have demonstrated that judgements of the quality and prestige of language varieties depend on a knowledge of the social connotations which they possess. Thus, for instance, the use of dialects and accents would be expressions of social preference, which reflect an awareness of the status and prestige accorded to the speakers of these varieties. A prestige standard form of a language has no inherent aesthetic or linguistic advantage over nonstandard varieties. The prestige is usually the product of culture-bound stereotypes passed on from one generation to the other (ibid., 21).

Le Page and Tabouret-Keller (1985) stress the importance of the nature of intergroup relations in the discussion of language attitudes and uses: they vary as the nature of intergroup relations changes. When relations change, status relationships, and therefore perceptions, attitudes and uses, change. Speakers select their code from a variety of socially marked models. Change takes place when the social values of the models change and the behaviour of the speech community also changes (ibid, 172).

When studying language attitudes, the concept of motives is important. Two basic motives are called instrumental and integrative motives. If L2 acquisition is considered as instrumental, the knowledge in a language is considered as a "passport to prestige and success". The speaker/learner considers the speaking/learning of English as functional (Ellis 1991: 117). On the other hand, if a learner wishes to identify with the target community; to learn the language and the culture of the speakers of that language in order to perhaps be able to become a member of the group, the motivation is called integrative. In generally, research has proved the integrative motivation to have been more beneficial for the learning of another language (Loveday 1982: 17-18). On the other hand, Gardner & Lambert, for instance, have found out that where the L2 functions as a second language (i.e. it is used widely in the society), instrumental motivation seems to be more effective. Moreover, motivation derived from a sense of academic or communicative success is more likely to motivate one to speak a foreign/second language (Ellis 1991: 118).

Measurement Techniques

There are three assessment techniques relevant to the study of language attitudes: content analysis of societal treatment, direct measurement and indirect measurement (Sebastian 1982: 7).

In the content analysis of societal treatment, language maintenance and shift are examined on the basis of analyses of laws and policies regarding language use in the public domain. An example of this type of language attitude study could be Fishman's (1966) Language Loyalty in the United States. These kind of studies provide the basis for descriptions of the standard language, as well as of language change (ibid, 7).

Another important method is the direct measurement technique, which observes language attitudes by the use of questionnaires (either in written form or in individual interviews). Frequently asked questions concern language evaluation, language preference, desirability and reasons for learning a particular language, evaluation of social groups who use a particular variety, self-reports concerning language use, desirability of bilingualism and bilingual education, and opinions concerning shifting or maintaining language policies. The method tends to focus upon beliefs (ibid, 7).

In a totally indirect method the subjects are not aware that it is their language attitudes that are being studied. Indirect language attitude techniques comprise speaker evaluation studies, such as matched-guise studies, in which hearers have to evaluate different varieties of a language spoken by the same speakers. Speaker evaluation studies form the basis of the socio-psychological perspective on language attitudes (ibid, 8).

Speech Repertoires in Multilingual Settings: Various Codes of a Community

Pandit (1979) has given an example of how a multilingual speaker might use the different codes in his repertoire. He describes an Indian businessman living in a suburb of Bombay. His mother tongue and home language is a dialect of Gujarati; in the market he uses a familiar variety of Marathi, the state language; at the railway station he speaks the pan-Indian lingua franca, Hindustani; the language of work is Kachi, the code of the spice trade; in the evening he will watch a film in Hindi or in English and listen to a cricket-match commentary on the radio in English. One can ask: what roles does each of these different languages and varieties perform in the community and the individual (ibid, 172-173)?

In a multilingual speech community a whole range of languages, or repertoire, is available to speakers, who choose to use some of them in their linguistic interaction to perform particular social roles. Repertoire applies at two different levels to both the community and the individual. A speaker does not usually control the whole range of the codes of a community's repertoire continuum but only a number of these (Hamers & Blanc 1989: 172-173).

Diglossia

The various codes in a multilingual speech community usually fulfill complementary functions. They are used differentially according to the interlocutor, domain, topic and role, and the choice of one rather than the other involves an act of identity. on the part of the speaker. Diglossia is at hand if different varieties or languages co-occur throughout a speech community, each with a distinct range of social functions in complementary distribution (Hamers and Blanc 1989: 173-174).

Ferguson first introduced the term diglossia in 1959 to refer to a relationship between varieties of the same language, but nowadays the term covers also relationships between different languages used in a society (ibid, 33-35). The variant reserved for informal uses within a speech community, the low variety, enjoys less social prestige: it is the language of informal interactions (such as ones family life).

The high variety, in its turn, is used in formal and outgroup situations (Sebastian 1982: 8).

The low variety is typically acquired at home as a mother tongue, the high variety, on the other hand, is learned later, normally at school, never at home. It is a language of institutions outside the home (Hamers & Blanc 1982: 34).

Fishman distinguished in 1971 between a high and low language, where the high language corresponds to status, high culture, strong aspirations toward upward social mobility, whereas the low language is more associated with solidarity, comradeship and intimacy by its speakers (Carranza 1982: 64).

Carranza has come to the conclusion that the level of prestige which languages/language varieties enjoy is influenced by two factors: social structure and cultural value systems: the social structure is an important determinant of how a language is regarded by members of the society. Cultural values, on the other hand, are important especially in the case of a less prestigious language for it to be maintained: it must be associated with positive values with which its speakers can identify themselves (ibid).

Domain Analysis

Joshua Fishman has introduced domain analysis which describes the use of languages in various institutional contexts in a multilingual society. Fishman suggests that one language is more likely to be appropriate in some specific contexts than another (Fasold 1984: 183):

Proper usage indicates that only one of the theoretically co-available languages or varieties will be chosen by particular classes or interlocutors on particular kinds of occasions to discuss particular kinds of topics. (Fishman 1972: 15).

Domains are defined in terms of institutional contexts or socio-ecological co-occurrences. They attempt to designate the major clusters of interaction situations that occur in particular multilingual settings. Domains enable us to understand that language choice and topic...are...related to widespread socio-cultural norms and expectations (Fishman 1972: 19).

According to Fishman, there is no invariant set of domains applicable to all multilingual settings, as language behavior reflects the socio-cultural patterning. Domains can thus be defined intuitively, theoretically or empirically. They, too, can differ in terms of socio-psychological and societal-institutional level. Socio-psychological analysis distinguishes intimate, informal, formal and intergroup domains. These domains can then be identified with domains at the societal-institutional level (such as home, school, etc.): which coincide with which activities (ibid, 19-20).

Barker claims (ibid, 29) that domains are as real as the very social institutions of a speech community and they show a marked paralleling with such major institutions. (ibid, 22).

In a research of the Puerto Rican community in New York (in 1971), Fishman, Cooper and Ma arrived at a list of five domains: family, friendship, religion, employment and education (Romaine 1995: 30). Anju Saghal, on the other hand, in her study on language use in India, described the language use in India in the three domains of Family, Friendship and Institution (Saghal 1991: 299).

Görlach (1991: 29) points out that in countries in which English is a native language, societies have used English for various functions, whereas in countries, such as India, in which English has been a second language, a foreign language, it has been restricted to the domains of administration, law and parts of education, and the media, some forms of literature, othe:· uses of language being reserved to the mother tongue.

Bayer describes as a deciding factor for the development of different status and functions of languages a hierarchy of identities which can be found in all multilingual societies: identities are stressed differing degrees of attachment, primary attachment being stressed to one identity. Languages are allocated specific roles and they are used in different contexts: the use of the mother tongue, for instance, is generally restricted to the home and in-group interaction, whereas the dominant language of the environment is the language of administration, education and mass communication. Thus language acts as a "token of cultural identity of individuals and groups" (Bayer 1990: 101).

Bonvillain states, too, that one language is usually having greater prestige than others in a society. Factors such as the social status of native speakers and economic, political and social contexts of contact contribute to this (Bonvillain 1993: 303). Bailey (1991: 117) quotes Matthews (1908) who claims that the success of the spread of a language and its general acceptance depend very little upon the qualities of the language, but is very much dependent on the qualities of the race that has it as a mother tongue, and on the position the race holds in the society.

Methodology

Hypothesis

My hypothesis is that English and one's mother tongue are used in different domains and for different purposes in India. The status of English in India is high among the élite by which it is used mostly in the formal domains (such as education, government and employment); more informal domains (such as the family, friendship and neighbourhood) are reserved for the mother tongue. Still, the use of English as a medium for creative self-expression is also on the increase; and English has become nativized in the Indian environment.

According to my hypothesis, instrumental motivation can be mentioned as the most important kind of motivation for the use of English in India. Hindi has more cultural symbolic value than English: English is spoken because it is useful to a person, or even, in a sense, obligatory to know to advance, while Hindi is in the cultural sense closer to people and easier to be identified with.

I assume, too, that even though English is acquiring new identities in new cultural contexts, such as in India (which in itself should be a natural phenomenon), often the new Englishes are considered as deviations of the standard British or American English norm, and Indian people, too, are quite ambivalent about their variety of the language.

Thus, I think that to my question about the suitable norm for the English in India, many people will answer: RP (Received Pronunciation: BBC English; Standard English in Britain) or General American English.

A Description of the Study

The study was conducted with the help of internet and e-mail. The group of informants was collected by announcing at home pages of Indian universities for people interested in taking part in the study about Indian multilingualism. The surveys were e-mailed to the informants, who filled it in and e-mailed it back to me. This method of collecting the data worked smoothly: e-mail was a fast way to correspond with the informants.

The informants were asked to fill in a survey about multilingualism in India. It was not specified that the attitudes towards the use of English were being studied. The first part of the survey included statements related to domains such as family, friendship, neighborhood, transactions, education, government and employment. The informants' duty was to fill in the language he most often uses for each occasion. The aim was to do a domain analysis of the use of English in India to find out which language(s) does an Indian person use in which situations.

The second part of the study comprised of 35 statements related to attitudes towards English and other languages of India. The third part of the was related to the model of English: the respondents had to give their opinion as to which model of English would suit India best.

Domain analysis and a study of language attitudes are strongly interlinked: the attitudes, which develop in a society during a course of time can determine the domains in which a particular language is used in a society. They determine the place a language holds in a society. By including a domain analysis in the study, it is possible to get a better, and probably a more realistic idea of the language situation in India. Consequently, domain analysis is an effective method to find out about the use of different languages in different domains of life.

The third part of the study, the question about the model for Indian English is also connected with attitudes: it shows the preference for either the domestic Indian variety, or the "foreign" one (such as RP or American English).

With the three separate parts I wanted to ensure that (the three parts, although separate, are still very closely connected) it would be harder for people to try to give "politically correct" answers (or answers which an informant might think would be expected to be given by him) because there is a bigger possibility that they will be noticed in other parts of the study.

In my opinion, also, the inclusion of such a big number of questions (the number of which no informant actually complained about) made the study more reliable. I think that had I had a smaller number of questions, the treatment of the topic would have been considerably more narrow.

The Informants

The total number of informants was thirty, which, in my opinion, proved to be an adequate number. Only two of the informants are female, all the others are male.

One of the reasons to the small number of female informants may be that most of the universities where the informants are studying/have studied are institutions of technology (28 had studied/were currently studying technical subjects, such as engineering and computer sciences), and these institutions most probably are male-dominated; thus there is simply a greater possibility of finding male informants. One informant was pursuing her PhD studies in psychology and one has a Master's degree in Philosophy. All the informants have either Bachelor's, Master's or PhD degree (11 Bachelors', 17 Masters', 2 PhDs').

The informants come from nine different states in India. This made the study more interesting but, on the other hand, one cannot draw too far-reaching conclusions, for instance, about the attitudes of people who live in Maharastra on the basis of just two informants. That is, also, one reason why I have not concentrated so much on the states where the informants come from. Nine of them are from Andhra Pradesh, seven from Tamil Nadu, six from West Bengal, two from Kerala and another two from Maharastra. There is, too, one informant from each of the following states: Uttar Pradesh, Haryana and Rajasthan.

In India, the state where one comes from is important, for some of the states are more pro-English or pro-Hindi,or pro-regional language than others. Traditionally, the opposition of Hindi has been the most fervent in the south (such as in Tamil Nadu, for instance).

One reason to this may be that Hindi belongs to a different language group than the Dravidian languages which are native to the south of India, and it is thought of as unfair to have such an unfamiliar language as an official language.

Sometimes, however, the use of Hindi is opposed simply because people do not want to appoint any special role to Hindi. They do not see why Hindi would be more special than any other language.

The mother tongues of the informants vary; mostly following the states' borders (which is not surprising, for, in India, states are divided along linguistic lines). Only three people out of the thirty informants reported as having Hindi as their mother tongue (the informants from Rajasthan, Haryana and Uttar Pradesh). Thus, in my study, about 10 percent had Hindi as their mother tongue: in the whole of India the percentage is, however, 20 percent (180 million). The other informants speak the following languages:

- Andhra Pradesh: Telugu
- Tamil Nadu: Tamil (plus one Marathi, one Telugu)
- West Bengal: Bengali
- Kerala: Malayalam
- Maharastra: Telugu, Marathi
- Jammu and Kashmir: Kashmiri

Telugu is thus spoken by the majority (37%), Bengali comes next (20%), Tamil follows with 17%, Hindi 10%, Malayalam and Marathi (10% both) and Kashmiri (3%).

All the informants speak at least three languages (English included); some claim to speak even up to six languages. One informant reports that he writes only in English, another one that she only speaks her mother tongue, but does not write in it.

One informant claims she has spoken English since she learnt to speak, so it is almost like a mother tongue for her. 19 informants report that they started to learn English when they were between two to six years old (in kindergarten/at school). The rest of the people do not mention any specific age (only saying, for instance, that they learnt English at school or "very young"). One says he started learning English when he was eight. The majority of the people have had their education in the medium of English (most of them since kindergarten).

Attitude Survey

Domain Analysis

The survey included statements related to domains such as family, friendship, neighborhood, transactions, education, government and employment. The informants' duty was to fill in the language he/she most often uses for each occasion (grading the frequency of use from one to four, four indicating the highest frequency). The aim was to analyze the use of English in India in different domains.

The domains used in the study could be divided into formal and informal domains: education, employment and government are formal; family, friendship, neighborhood and transactions more informal domains.

The Family Domain

Although some informants seem to be quite polyglots, even in the family domain (such as Ker1, who reported the use of English and mother tongue just as common, Tamil1, Mah1, and few others), all in all, mother tongue was, as could be expected, the most common language used at home (for 87% of the informants). English was the second most common reported language (English 3%, En/L1 10%). It was, perhaps surprisingly, most popular (17%) when "discussing a personal matter/problem", although even then L1 was far more popular, with 79%. Discussions with family members at dinner are usually carried out in the mother tongue (90%).

Among West Bengalis, L1 was reserved, almost exclusively, for the family domain. Tamils, on the other hand, mentioned English most often (even though as a secondary option after the L1) thus, here, too, we can see the preference of the people of Tamil Nadu to English, rather than Hindi. Hindi is mentioned only once in groups other than for which it is a mother tongue, when "commenting on a -TV program which is in your mother tongue/Hindi". Probably then, too, the reason was that one of the options given for the medium of the TV program was Hindi; perhaps it feels natural to comment on a TV program in the same language as it is in. It was interesting to note, however, that the use of Hindi did not increase (in general) even though it was the medium of a TV program: mother tongue was also then the most popular option. Hindi was mentioned as an option in very few papers.

Hindi does not seem to be very popular among Tamils. The reason to this is fairly obvious, since Hindi has traditionally not been very popular in the south; Hindi is not one of the languages spoken in the area. Tamils, in general, support the use of English. Their reasons for favouring English have been explained earlier on in the study.

Bengalis are not too keen supporters of Hindi, either. They are very proud of their own language; many think that it would have the same right as Hindi has to be the official language of the country (it is surprising, however, that Hindi is reported as the second most common language used at home by a West Bengali (perhaps, for instance, one of the family members of the informant speaks Hindi as his/her mother tongue)). The Bengalis were supporting English for the same reason during the Anglicist-Orientalist controversy in the beginning of the 19th century.

Friendship Domain

In this domain, the responses are divided more evenly between different languages than in the family domain, and many, too, reported use of several different languages in the same situation. English was clearly quite popular (41% of all the situations). If you include the answers in which English was mentioned together with Hindi or L1, the percentage will be even higher (65%). As a comparison, L1 was used 27% of the time, and Hindi 5 % of the time. Hindi does not seem to work as a lingua franca, or a link language equivalent of English, in India.

Over half of all personal letters are written in English (62%). People are also introduced to each other most often in English (L1 29%, Hindi:6%). People who have not met before, too, prefer English as the common language of conversation (40%; L1 33%, Hindi 6%).

Personal problems are not talked about in English (21%), but usually in L1 (31%). On the other hand, many informants report several different languages; combinations such as L1/E (17%) and L1/E/H (14%) are quite common. Maybe this is due to the fact that many have friends and acquaintances with a different language from them (considering how many different languages there are in India).

General topics are usually conversed in English (33%), after which come L1 (27%) and E/L1 (17%). Hindi is not popular here, either. 11.1.3 9.1.3 Neighbourhood In 67% of the cases, English is reported as the most commonly used language when conversing with neighbours. Hindi and E/H (both 13%) come next, followed by L1 and regional language (both 3%).

In case the mother tongues of the neighbours differ, English serves as the link language most of the time (67%). Hindi and H/E are reported second most common languages (13% both). If, however, the mother tongues of the neighbours are same, only one informant claims to resort to English, others report that they would use it together with Hindi (3%) or L1 (7%).

Transactions

9.L1 and Hindi are most commonly used languages of transaction in this study. This is not unexpected, for many common Indian people do not speak English much at all (in India English is, as mentioned earlier, the language of the élite and the educated).

The informants reported that they most often use L1 when in shops, at the railway station etc. (29%). Hindi comes next (25%), after which English (18%).

In the market place L1 is more clearly the most commonly used language (with 50%; Hindi 18%). L1/H/E and regional language both 7%. If combinations such as L1/H/E, L1/E and E/H are counted together, English is used at the market place 20% of the time.

Education

In education, English is the most common medium (87% of all the situations). At school, friends who spoke the same language usually talked in L1 (45%), although English comes next (25%), and Hindi third (14%). English was considered the best medium of communication in the instances in which the languages of the parties in question differed (75%; Hindi 14%).

Government

English dominates in the domain of government, both when it comes to writing letters (93% are written in English) and also as a general language of the domain (70%; Hindi 7%). But, when meeting government officials, there is more division: English is still the most common language (37%), but L1 is also used quite often (23%), as well as Hindi (10%) and a regional language (10%).

Employment

As well as job interviews are without exception carried out in English (100%), so are also business letters written in English. If one's and one's boss's languages differ, the common language will most often (97%) be English. E/H comes second (3%).

When it comes to talking to one's colleagues who come from different parts of India, 67% of the time one would resort to English (Hindi 17%, E/H 17%, H/L1/E 3%).

Attitude Survey

There were 35 questions related to attitudes towards different languages of India. I also wanted to include questions related to languages other than English to have a wider perspective of the position and status of English in India. The informants were asked to grade the statements from one to four, depending on how much one agrees/disagrees with a given statement.

The attitudes of Indian informants towards the use of English (and other languages) are studied from mainly two different perspectives:

1. affective/integrative dimension
2. pragmatic/instrumental dimension

I have also reserved one perspective for (3) the attitudes towards Hindi and other native languages (although those attitudes will be commented upon in other dimensions, as well. There is, too, a fourth dimension; other findings of the study (under which those attitudes have been placed which could not appropriately be included anywhere else).

Affective/Integrative Dimension

Statement 3 ("I like speaking English"), 10 ("I identify myself with British and the Angloamerican culture") and 14 ("English provides a range of aesthetic experiences in literature") are related to affective/integrative dimension.

(1=strongly disagrees, 2=disagrees, 3=agrees, 4=strongly agrees with the statement.)

Statement	1	2	3	4
"I like speaking English."	1	5	10	14

80% of the informants like speaking English; 20% report not to. Those 20% seem to consider speaking English not as a matter of option or willingness; it is just plain reality. The informants do not identify themselves with British and Anglo-American culture (83%); only one reports that he/she identifies him/herself strongly with the culture, and 13% said that they somewhat identified themselves with it. Indian values seem to be still important to the informants; 73% of the informants do not identify themselves with western values (only two people say they identify themselves with western values).

Statement	1	2	3	4
"I identify myself with British and Angloamerican culture."	18	7	4	1

However, English does provide a range of aesthetic experiences in literature for over half (53%) of the informants; for 47% it does not (with 7% strongly disagreeing).

Statement	1	2	3	4
"English provides a range of aesthetic experiences in literature"	2	12	10	6

Pragmatic/Instrumental Dimension

Speaking English is considered an advantage by 93% of the informants (with 60% strongly agree). The informants strongly disagreeing with the statement included one person with Hindi as his/her mother tongue and one ardent supporter of Bengali.

Statement	1	2	3	4
"Speaking English is an advantage"	--	2	10	18

Statements number 11 and 12 had to do with the role of English with employment opportunities. Most of the people admitted (93%) that it is useful to know English when looking for a job. Only two people strongly disagreed with the statement.

Statement	1	2	3	4
"English offers advantages in seeking good job opportunities."	2	--	6	22

People are, too, fairly convinced that without the knowledge of English their job opportunities would be relatively limited; 76% thinks that without the knowledge of English they could not get a job at all (53% strongly agreeing). However, still 23% of the informants, almost one fourth, disagreed with the statement (13% strongly). One interesting ambivalence must be noted: some informants, claiming that English is not needed when looking for a job, reported, however, in the domain analysis very frequent use of English in the domain of employment. Thus, it can be concluded that the informants perhaps wanted to answer to these questions in the way which, for instance, show loyalty towards a certain language, or in the way the situation ideally (in his view) would look like.

Statement	1	2	3	4
"Without the knowledge of English I could not get a job."	4	3	7	16

87% of the informants think of English as one way of securing one's chances to get a good job (although, as one informant put it, "It depends on what kind of job"). Hindi is, in general, too, perceived as "less useful to know than English" (57%). 41% disagree with this, though. One informant did not give his/her answer to this question at all.

Statement	1	2	3	4
"Hindi is less useful to know than English."	5	7	10	7

The great majority (97%) of the informants think that even if they did not know Hindi, they still would get a job. Only one informant claimed that he/she could not get a job without the knowledge of Hindi (one informant did not answer in the question).

Statement	1	2	3	4
"Without the knowledge of Hindi I could not get a job."	15	13	--	1

The informants seem to support the role of English as an associate official language, for 62% of them say that "to be admitted to a public post, one should be able to speak English". One informant did not give his/her answer.

Statement	1	2	3	4
"To be admitted to a public post, one should be able to speak English."	--	11	9	9

Most (94%) of the informants think all children should learn English at school (however, some acknowledged the illusion of that statement:"Wish, but I don't think it's possible"). Only two people disagree with the statement. Also, English would be chosen as the medium of instruction in the majority of cases (93%).

Only 24% (10% strongly agreeing) think that children resent having to learn English (67% of the people strongly agreeing come from West Bengal). Two informants did not answer this question.

Statement	1	2	3	4
"Most children resent having to learn English."	11	11	3	3

Attitudes towards Hindi and Other Native Languages

The informants would prefer using their mother tongue in most situations, whenever possible (83%; 53% strongly agreeing). 16% disagree with the statement, however (maybe because they use different languages according to the situation and the people they are with).

Statement	1	2	3	4
"I prefer using my mother tongue in most situations, whenever possible."	1	4	9	16

Hindi was not quite as popular: only 10% of the informants (all of whom actually speak Hindi as their L1) would like to speak Hindi whenever possible. 67% disagreed with the statement (17% strongly). Most (72%) of the people who disagreed with the statement come from either Tamil Nadu of West Bengal. One informant argued:"Hindi is someone else's regional language, it's not mine. Why should I use it? Why is Hindi special? Why not Bengali, or Tamil, or Malayalam, or any of the wonderful Indian languages?"

Statement	1	2	3	4
"I prefer using Hindi in all situations, whenever possible."	5	15	7	3

The maintenance of Hindi is perceived as important for the development of India in 33% of the responses. 64% disagrees with the statement (27% strongly). Three of the four informants who strongly agreed with the statement speak Hindi as their mother tongue; one person who also strongly agreed comes from Jammu and Kashmir. Perhaps as one reason for her ardent support for Hindi (his/her mother tongue is Kashmir) could be given that she would quite clearly like to be identified with the Hindi-speaking rather than with the Urdu-speaking population (and the culture) in the area. Language is, after all, an important marker of identity.

Statement	1	2	3	4
"I think it's important to maintain Hindi to enable India to develop."	8	11	7	4

It can be mentioned, too, that, quite surprisingly, two Tamils and one West Bengali also agreed that Hindi is indeed important for the development of India. One who disagreed with the statement wrote:"You should not bias a multicultural, multiethnic country by favouring one native language over the other. It leads to domination of other regions by one region".

44% of the informants think that they owe it to their forefathers to preserve Hindi, whereas 55% disagree with the statement (with remarks such as "Well I believe in the survival of the fittest" and India is a multilingual country and each region has its own predominant linguistic loyalties". One Bengali wrote:"I owe it to my forefathers to preserve

BENGALI. A person whose mother tongue is Hindi owes it to HIS forefathers to preserve his language!"). Again, the ones who strongly agree are the ones mentioned in connection with the previous statement. One person did not give his answer to this question.

Statement	1	2	3	4
"We owe it to our forefathers to preserve Hindi."	8	11	7	4

People do feel that they owe it to their forefathers to try to preserve the mother tongue of their people: 83% agrees with the statement (55% strongly). 17% disagree on this one; one comment was quite straightforward:"If most people can communicate in a language then I don't think other languages need to be preserved as antique items". One person did not give his view of the matter.

Statement	1	2	3	4
"We owe it to our forefathers to try to preserve the mother tongue of our people."	2	3	8	16

The statement "I strongly identify myself with my mother tongue and the group that speaks it" is maybe thc most important one for this section. 72% claims identification with their mother tongue and the group that speaks it. Still, 21% of the informants claim they do not identify with the mother tongue at all. Most identified themselves more with the mother tongue and the group that speaks it than British and Anglo-American culture; only two informants claimed the opposite. Two informants claimed no identification with neither.

Statement	1	2	3	4
"I strongly identify myself with my mother tongue and the group that speaks it."	6	2	11	10

A little over half of the informants (60%) thought that creative writing can be done in a foreign language; the language does not matter, as long as the person is a skilled writer: "It depends on personal skills" and "You can be comfortable with many languages, it depends on the individual". Still, 40% of the people are of the opinion that creative writing should preferably be done in one's mother tongue, 17% were strongly agreeing (one informant wrote: "I feel so as I can not express my feelings as I want in English".)

Statement	1	2	3	4
"I think it is better for an Indian person to write creative writing (e.g. books, poems) in his/her mother tongue, rather than in English. In English, it seems so artificial."	3	15	7	5

In most of the informants' views (70%), the use of Hindi should be encouraged throughout India. One informant stated further: "At least till higher literacy rate is obtained". (Yet, the same informant would like to educate his child rather in the medium of English because of "globalization".)

Statement	1	2	3	4
"I think the use of Hindi should really be encouraged throughout India as a whole."	5	4	13	8

A little more than half of the informants (60%) would like to see Hindi as the official language of India also in the future.

Statement	1	2	3	4
"Hindi should always remain as the official language of India."	4	8	9	9

Most (67%) of the informants feel proud to speak the language and consider it a big part of their culture and identity (although 13% of them strongly disagreed with the statement: one informant added:"I assume "our" implies North India" and one Bengali commented:"It is a regional language. It is no greater or less than BENGALI". One person from Tamil Nadu explained the linguistic situation in the south as follows: "Hindi is not at all prevalent in the Southern states, especially Tamil Nadu...so in the Southern states, English is more often the common language if people of different languages meet").

Statement	1	2	3	4
"I feel proud to say I can speak Hindi: it is such ā big part of our culture, heritage and identity. I could almost say, it symbolizes those."	6	4	11	9

A little more than half of the informants disagreed with the statement "by speaking Hindi I show commitment to my country" (one added "and I show commitment to my soul"). Two people did not answer.

Statement	1	2	3	4
"By speaking Hindi I show commitment to my country."	7	9	8	4

Hindi is clearly associated with Indian culture: most (74%) of the informants think they would miss out on many enjoyable parts of the culture, such as folk music and literature, without the knowledge of Hindi. It is surprising that one of the informants who disagreed with the statement speaks Hindi as his/her mother tongue! All informants of the Andhra Pradesh group agreed with the statement, all the other Hindi-speakers, as well as the person from Jammu and Kashmir agree (as expected), almost all (75%) informants from Kerala and Maharastra groups agree (with Mah2 strongly disagreeing), in the Tamil group 57% agree with the statement. The West Bengalis most strongly disagree with the statement (with 67%; of which 75% strongly disagreeing).

Statement	1	2	3	4
"Without the knowledge of Hindi, I would miss out on many rewarding and enjoyable parts of culture, such as folk music and indigenous literature."	5	3	11	11

Other Findings

The clear majority of the informants considers speaking both Hindi and English an advantage. Although both the languages are thus considered important, they are important in different domains and for different purposes.

Statement	1	2	3	4
Speaking both Hindi and English is an advantage."	1	--	9	20

English is considered important to India as a whole. Only 10% disagreed somewhat with the statement (two Tamils and one West Bengali).

Statement	1	2	3	4
"English is important to India as a whole."	--	3	14	13

Most informants do not feel the need for more TV and radio programs available in English. 44% of the informants, however, would like to have more broadcasting in English.

Statement	1	2	3	4
"There should be more TV and radio programs available in English."	--	17	8	5

The majority (80%) would like to see English always on public signs, notices and adverts, although, as one informant adds:"along with regional languages".

Statement	1	2	3	4
"English should be used on public signs, notices and adverts, always."	2	4	15	9

According to the majority of the informants (63%), English carries higher status than Hindi in India.

Statement	1	2	3	4
"The status of Hindi is higher than that of English in India."	7	12	8	3

English is perceived, on the whole, advantageous to the country. As much as 93% think this way, with the exception of one informant from Tamil Nadu and another from West Bengal.

Statement	1	2	3	4
"On the whole, I can say that English has been and continues to be an advantage to India."	2	--	13	15

English, on the other hand, in the informants' opinion (74%), does not make up a significant part of the country's history and identity: only 23% (3% strongly) think it does. Two informants did not give their answers.

Statement	1	2	3	4
"English makes up a significant part of our history and identity."	11	11	5	1

The belief that Indian people most often use English with other Indians is also confirmed in the study. One third uses English most often with foreigners. One person did not answer to this question.

Statement	1	2	3	4
"When I use English, it is most often with native speakers or foreigners, not with Indian people."	5	15	7	2

THE MODEL FOR ENGLISH IN INDIA-THE INFORMANTS' VIEWS

At the end of the survey, there were additional questions dealing with the preferred model for Indian English. The informants had to state the model of English they aim for, and which, in their opinion, would best be suited for India.

Earlier on in the study Saghal stated that educated Indian English variety close to the native standard would be favoured as a model for Indian English by the general consensus (Saghal 1991: 303). In this study it turned out, however, that in fact the majority of the informants (70%) felt that RP (Received Pronunciation: BBC English; Standard English in Britain) would serve as the best model for Indian English, 10 % thought General American English would be better, and 17% preferred the Indian variety of English.

The reason to the result may be that most of the informants do not seem to acknowledge their own, Indian, variety of English, but automatically assume that the model has to come from outside; people somehow feel compelled to refer to an outside variety. Crystal thus seemed to be right in pointing out that when, on one hand, the English-speaking communities do acknowledge a language should reflect their own experiences, on the other hand many are of the view that there should be one, universally intelligible, more or less standardized medium (Crystal 1988: 261-262). In the following, a sample of answers will be presented.

The informants gave reasons for the preference of RP as follows:

"The English in India has a British background... Standard English in India has strong influence on Indian English and I think that is best for India."

"Why not follow the standards set by, say, Oxford, to have uniformity? We are still taught colonial English at school and a good lot of us still prefer J.R.R. Tolkien to Jeffrey Archer

But, also some people supported the Indian variety:

"I would think that the Indian kind of English with a generous use of Indian slangs thrown in is the one that is mostly used and I don"t see any problem in continuing it....formal written English has also been Indianized to a large extent and I would prefer it that way."

"For a general Indian, I think Indian variety of English is best suited since it is understood properly by a huge number".

"Indian English - cause locals more comfortavle with it. Also leads to better creativity and self-expression..."

Supporters of General American English argued that:

"I guess till a decade ago, people wanted to follow British English. But you know, after this software boom, and the opportunities in the USA for Indian professionals,

this changed the situation and now the younger generation aims at General American English...I think American English suits us well."

In support of uniformity (and an international standard) in English around the world some of the informants argued:

"I think RP would be a reference which everyone can follow. Otherwise different states and regions in India would develop different usages, which may not be desirable....the basic language structure shouldn't be changed irreversibly."

"All of us cannot speak with the same accent but I think there should be uniformity as far as spelling of words is concerned...we should definitely give importance to spelling, grammar and the likes which I think forms the basis of a language. I think British English should be the role model."

..."though there may be local versions of English there should be a definite and fixed form of English to be followed for formal and inter-nation exchanges wherever possible."

Some people claimed they had both RP and the Indianized variety as the model, depending on the situation:

"I'd consider RP as my model in all official, business transactions, but everywhere else the Indian variety goes...most people stick to RP for official work and the Indian variety for informal conversation."

"One should adopt the King's English which can be well understood throughout the world. At the same time Indian English works extremely well within the country."

In the support of variation in a language:

..."it is natural that language develops. But it would be nice if there was a body to standardize it the world over (so that we don't have some people speaking one version and the others some other version). Again, pride, cultural influences and some other things make it impossible to

force one version on others. My personal opinion is that, as long as you can get your message across effectively, it does not matter what version you use (I presume languages were developed for the soul purpose of communication and expression".

"there is so much of variation that it's quite difficult to make a generalized statement which can qualify as fair"

"Non-native Englishes are NOT deviant...They add richness to the original language, help it to grow, and are VERY NATURAL - this is NOT my mother tongue. My mother tongue WILL dominate."

"Well...if anybody has any problem with coping up with so many accents of English...they probably don"t approve of their ancestors who sailed thousands of miles across the globe spreading the language in the first place!

"I don't think RP has any relevance anymore as far as the growth and acceptance of the language is concerned. The richness and fun that diversity brings along is tremendous!"

"I like the little different English versions which could be more close to the culture than one standard. But I don't like them to be too different which makes life tough for new comer".

..."in this dynamic world, a language gets richer by absorbing different words from different languages to describe a phenomenon more convincingly...there should not be a snobbish restriction on the variation of English."

The idea of correctness of a variety over others was also expressed:

"I can understand English customed to India quite well but I think that it would be preferable for us to use the correct phonetics and grammar, which I think the awareness of is growing".

"BBC English is easy and... taught in schools in India... I personally feel a language should be taught in purest form... it is better to follow single English."

"...the English which the new generation speaks has American slangs and they want to follow the Western culture. This was not the case during our fathers' college days (say 60's) wherein they learnt the RP correctly and had a better English."

Some people also expressed in their view that Indian English is somehow deviant:

"With the increased exposure to the international media I'm sure some accent corrections will take place..."

"I would prefer the Indian variety...Though the English in the BBC would be of a more standard and orthodox type still I think it would be difficult to get the accent. Indians have been good in vocabulary and grammar (as good as the British sometimes), the only difference being that all good writers might not be so good in spoken English and even if they are good they may not follow the accent exactly."

One explained the nature of English in India:

"Here we express only ideas in English, not emotions. Our English here is more for ideas and official communication than for expressing our feeling."

CONCLUSION

According to the present study, different languages are definitely being allocated different roles in India; languages are used differently according to the domain in question. I was especially interested in the role of English, but as languages can not exist in a vacuum, also the uses of other languages in the society have to be taken into account.

English in India has, indeed, come far from its original uses in the colonial times when it was mostly used as the language of the government. Nowadays, English has spread into many new domains, also the more personal ones, such as the family and friendship. English has, also, acquired new functions, including the self-expressive or innovative function.

Today, in fact, it is hard, almost impossible to think of English as it is used in India only simply as another foreign language.

English in India is a diglossically high language. The reasons for this lie in the colonial times when the power was attributed to English, the language of the Raj. From then on, English became a symbol of political power, the position of which it holds, still: English, today, represents the scientific knowledge, modernization and development.

The use of English clearly increases in the more formal domains. Also, the more formal the situation is, the bigger the number of languages possible for each occasion.

In the domains of education, government and employment it is, without doubt, the most preferred medium. It is, however, making its way to more informal domains, as well: about 40% of the informants claim to speak English with friends, and people get introduced to each other most often in English.

Over half of all personal letters, too, are written in English. In the neighborhood domain English is the most preferred option when people's languages differ.

Thus, the usefulness of Hindi as a lingua franca seems to be regionally limited, as Spolsky has claimed (Spolsky 1978: 43)). In the domains of education, government and employment English shows itself, without doubt, as the most preferred medium.

In the domain of transactions, L1 is used more often than English at both the market place and in shops and at the railway station. This is quite natural when one is reminded that English is, really, a language of the educated: quite possibly the people selling goods and food in the market place do not often know a word of English.

Attitudes about a language are important, for they more or less determine its place in the multilingualism of a country.

English has traditionally been the language of the government and other domains with prestige, and still today it carries more prestige than Hindi in India and it is, too, considered important and an advantage to the country as a whole.

People's motives for supporting English are mostly instrumental: the results of the study reveal that English is perceived as a useful language to know mostly because of job opportunities: English is considered necessary would one want to have a job. On the other hand, Hindi is not perceived important when it comes to getting a job: only one informant claimed he/she could not get a job without the knowledge of Hindi.

The informants, too, support the role of English as an associate official language, for 62% of them require a person to be able to speak English to be admitted to a public post. Education is an important proof of the status of a language in a society, and if this is true, in the case of English its status seems quite secure: over 90% of the informants are of the opinion that all children should learn English at school.

Whereas English was considered important to India in most of the responses (90%), Hindi is perceived important for the development of the country only in 33% of them.

The informants strongly identified themselves with their mother tongue and the group that speaks it; this is important for the maintenance of the native languages of the country: especially in the case of varieties with less official acknowledgement group solidarity becomes very important. The maintenance of a group's language makes one part of it.

Integrative motivation seems to be very important for maintaining Hindi as the official language of India. It is, also, beneficial for the maintenance of a language to be associated with positive cultural values; especially when a less prestigious language is in question. Although, as mentioned earlier, English is clearly perceived as a more useful language to know, people on the other hand can identify themselves more easily with Hindi (only 17% said they identified themselves with British and Anglo-American culture, whereas about 67% of the informants feel proud to speak the language and consider it a big part of their culture and identity).

Most of the informants would like the use of Hindi to be encouraged in India, as well as they would like to see it as the official language also in future. Most of them thought, too, that they would miss out on many enjoyable parts of culture could they not speak Hindi.

Although Spolsky has claimed that people rarely know any other language other than their own, this was clearly not the case in my study: people reported, on average, four different languages.

The usefulness of Hindi as a lingua franca, however, appeared to be regionally limited, as in some areas few people know it or they dislike speaking it. Many people do not see any reason why Hindi would be any better as an official language than their mother tongue.

Indian English has definitely emerged as a variety of its own in the eyes of the Indian people themselves. Although many acknowledged RP (Received Pronunciation: BBC English; Standard English in Britain) as the best model for Indians to strive for, almost as many supported variety in a language arguing that because of linguistic and cultural reasons, Indian English is naturally different from, say, the British standard variety of English.

Some people, though, expressed their view of Indian variety as somehow "deviant" by talking about corrections which should take place in the variety, and also by comparing Indian English to the more standard and orthodox type of standard variety of English as used in Britain.

People, indeed, seem to be somewhat ambivalent about Indian English and its features. Some people would even divide the use of English so that RP would be reserved for more formal uses, whereas "Indian English" (whatever one understands with it) is considered suitable for, as one informant puts it, "informal conversation".

As we can see from the results of the study, English has become more nativized in the Indian environment: it seems that English now belongs to India's linguistic repertoire in a very natural way. English, however, is still clearly a language of "ideas, not of emotions", as one informant put it.

6

The Cambridge History of English and American Literature

ANGLO-INDIAN LITERATURE

Early Historians

On the analogy of the literature of the great British self-governing dominions, Anglo-Indian literature should, logically, be the territorial English literature of British India. But the degree to which the ever-changing English community that guards and administers India differs from the settled inhabitants of Canada or Australia is, at the same time, an explanation of the main peculiarities of that literature and, also, the measure of the difficulty which confronts any attempt to define it.

Anglo-Indian literature, as regards the greater part of it, is the literature of a comparatively small body of Englishmen who, during the working part of their lives, become residents in a country so different in every respect from their own that they seldom take root in its soil. On the contrary, they strive to remain English in thought and aspiration. By occasional periods of residence in England, they keep themselves in intimate touch with English life and culture: throughout the period of their life in India they are subject to the influence of two civilisations, but they never lose their bias towards that of England, which, in most cases, ultimately reabsorbs them.

Anglo-Indian literature, therefore, is, for the most part, merely English literature strongly marked by Indian local colour. It has been published, to a great extent, in England, owing partly to lack of facilities in India, and, partly, to the fact that the Anglo-Indian writer must, as a rule, make his appeal mainly to the public in England and only secondarily to the English community in India. The actual writing has often been done in England during furlough or after retirement, because that is precisely the time when the Anglo-Indian has leisure for literary work. The years of retirement are also specially fertile for another reason, since not until he leaves India has the official complete freedom from those bonds of discipline which, in India, have always hampered the free expression of opinion. Thus, Anglo-Indian literature is based in origin, spirit and influences upon two separate countries at one and the same time.

That this condition of affairs has prevailed in the past does not necessarily imply that it must continue. The future of the English language in India is a question of great moment to English literature. As a collateral, though not by any means inevitable, result of the establishment of the British Indian empire, English has become the language of government and a common medium of literary expression throughout a vast sub-continent containing 300,000,000 inhabitants. At the time when the empire was founded on the ruins of the Mogul dominion, the Persian language performed that double task, and it might have continued to do so had Englishmen preferred to orientalise themselves rather than to anglicise those among whom they lived.

But, in addition to the natural disinclination of the Englishman to steep himself in orientalism, the introduction of English law and English learning carried with it, as an almost necessary corollary, the adoption of English as the language of universities and of the highest courts of justice. Hence, it followed that English became a medium of literary expression for the educated Indian. His writings in our language, together with those of the domiciled community of European or mixed origin, constitute a strictly territorial English literature, and may be-regarded as that part of Anglo-Indian literature which is most potential of development in the future; but, in the past, they have, naturally, attracted little notice in comparison with the writings of the English immigrant population.

Father Thomas Stephens, who went to Goa in 1579, was the first Englishman to settle in India, and Anglo-Indian literature began with his letters, of no extrinsic value, to his father, which have been preserved by Purchas. Master Ralph Fitch, merchant of London, travelled in India and the east from 1583 to 1591, and his lively description of his adventures, preserved by Hakluyt and Purchas, was of the utmost value to those who sought to promote an English East India company.

For a hundred years after the East India company received its charter, Anglo-Indian literature consisted solely of books of travel. Of the large number of writings of this class, a few may find mention here.

Sir Thomas Roe, the gallant Stewart diplomat who was the ambassador of James I at the court of "the Great Mogoar, King of the Orientall Indyes, of Condahy, of Chismer, and of Corason," wrote a very readable journal narrating his life at the court of Jahangir. Edward Terry, his chaplain, wrote a Relation of a Voyage to the Easterne India, full of interesting observation, and including an account of his meeting with the "Odcombian legstretcher," Thomas Coryate 1 whom Roe also mentions.

William Bruton's Newes from the East Indies relates how the English obtained their first footing in Orissa in 1632, and is a fine piece of vigorous narrative English. William Methold, who was in India at the same time, tells in his Relations of the Kingdome of Golconda, preserved by Purchas, of his experiences in south India; while John Fryer, who belongs to the latter half of the seventeenth century, and had an interview with Aurangzib, throws a good deal of light on the contemporary politics of western India in his New Account of East India and Persia. These English writers of travel tales are far less famous than their brilliant French contemporaries of the seventeenth century, Bernier and Tavernier; but their naïveté, in the face of the many novel things they saw, combined with the delightful seventeenth-century narrative style in which they wrote, gives their writings a distinction which Anglo-Indian literature of this kind has never recaptured.

The greater part of the eighteenth century, until near the close of the governorship of Warren Hastings, was, in a literary sense, all but uneventful. It was a period of anarchy and war in India. The beginning of the century saw the English mere traders struggling for a foothold in India; its closing decades saw them sovereigns of vast territories. Alexander Hamilton, who was in the east from 1688 to 1723, wrote A New Account of the East Indies, but his book, though comprehensive, is rather rambling and commonplace. Between his date and 1780 there are only a few names which call for comment. Pre-eminent among them was that of Robert Orme.

Born in India in 1728, he returned to the land of his birth as a "writer" in 1743, and there, during the course of a successful official career, in which he was closely connected with many of the events afterwards discussed in his books, he gathered the knowledge which enabled him to become one of the greatest of Anglo-Indian historians. 2 His History of the Military Transactions of the British Nation in Indostan is the prose epic of the early military achievements of our race in India. An indefatigable, rather than a brilliant, writer, Orme remains a mine in which all subsequent historians must quarry. In his Historical Fragments of the Mogul Empire, of the Morattoes and of the English concerns in Indostan from the year 1659, the conscientious and unwearied narrator of contemporary events became the industrious investigator of past history, though it is by his first book that Orme's name chiefly lives.

Alexander Dow, who died at Bhagalpur in 1779, not only translated histories from the Persian, but wrote two tragedies, Zingis and Sethona, which were produced at Drury lane. His authorship of these plays, which were oriental in setting, was challenged by Baker in his Biographia Dramatica, "for he is said by those who know him well to be utterly unqualified for the production of learning or of fancy, either in prose or verse."

Others who may be mentioned are John Zephaniah Holwell, a survivor of the Black Hole, who wrote on historical and other subjects after his retirement in 1760, including a Narrative of the deplorable deaths of the English gentlemen who were suffocated in the Black Hole, which was included in his India Tracts.

Charles Hamilton, who wrote a history of those Rohilla Afghans whose expulsion from Rohilcand brought much odium upon Warren Hastings; James Rennell, the father of Indian geography, who wrote after his retirement in 1777; and William Bolts and Henry Verelst, whose quarrels in India resulted in the production of polemical history by them both.

The closing years of Warren Hasting's Indian career saw the real birth of English literature and literary studies in India. Hicky's Bengal Gazette, the first newspaper of modern India, was founded at Calcutta by James Augustus Hicky in 1780. It was a scurrilous production, but a sign of life. James Forbes left India in 1784, carrying with him the collected materials which he afterwards published as his Oriental Memoirs. The appointment, in 1783, of Sir William Jones as judge of the supreme court was an event of high importance in the history of the relations between east and west, as was also his foundation of the Asiatic society of Bengal.

He is remembered primarily as the earliest English Sanskrit scholar; but, in the domain of Anglo-Indian letters, he takes rank not only by his translation of Kalidasa's Sakuntala, but, also, as the first Anglo-Indian poet. He had written verse before he came to India; while in India, he addressed the gods of Indian mythology in a series of hymns which, if not of the highest order of poetry, are yet aflame with enthusiasm and knowledge. Inferior to Jones as an orientalist, but superior as a poet, was John Leyden, that "lamp too early quenched," as Sir Walter Scott put it. He lived in the east from 1803 to 1811, and, though he, too, is remembered chiefly as an orientalist, he is to be noted as the first of that long line of writers who expressed in verse the common feelings of Englishmen in "the land of regrets." His poetry is a simple expression of the emotions which all Anglo-Indians experience at some time-pride in the military achievements of our race, loathing at the darker aspects of Indian superstition and the exile's longing for home. His Ode to an Indian Gold Coin deserves a place in every Anglo-Indian anthology of verse as an expression of this last emotion.

The closing years of the eighteenth century, and the first two decades of the nineteenth, were marked by other signs of literary advance. Hugh Boyd, who, by some, was alleged to be Junius, was in India from 1781 to 1794, and made some attempt, in essays on literary and moral subjects in local journals which he conducted, to keep alive the flame of English literary culture in his adopted country. In 1789, the quaint translation into English of Ghulam Hussein Khan's Siyar-ul-Muta'akhkhirin by the Franco-Turk Raymond, alias Haji Mustapha, was published in Calcutta. The intrinsic interest of this contemporary history of India, combined with the oriental phraseology and the Gallicisms with which the translation abounds, renders Raymond's book one of the most curious pieces of literature among Anglo-Indian writings.

Meanwhile, Henry Thomas Colebrooke made a name for himself as the leading Sanskrit scholar of the day; James

Tod was carrying on those researches in Rajputana which he ultimately gave to the world in the classic Annals and Antiquities of Rajasthan, a work fuller of romance than most epics; Mark Wilks, in the south of India, was both helping to make history and amassing the materials for writing it, which he eventually published as his impartially and critically written Historical Sketches of the South of India. Sir John Malcolm, who, also, took part in many of the events which he described, followed with his Political History of India in 1811, and, subsequently, with his History of Persia, his Central India and other works, including a volume of poems; while Francis Buchanan-Hamilton wrote on scientific and historical subjects, including An Account of the Kingdom of Nipal. As belonging to this period, too, may be mentioned Eliza Fay's Original Letters from Calcutta, descriptive of her travels from England to Calcutta, and the anonymous Hartly House, described as a novel, though, in form, a series of letters written by a lady and descriptive of life in Calcutta towards the close of the eighteenth century. Finally, Mary Martha Sherwood, the children's writer, was in India during this period and her Little Henry and his Bearer was the gift which she gave to Anglo-Indian children in memory of the child she had lost.

The thirty or forty years which preceded the mutiny were full of events of the greatest moment for the future of the English language in India. Macaulay was in India from 1834 to 1838, and his minute on education resulted in the definite adoption by lord Bentinck's government of the English language as the basis of all higher education in India. Ram Mohan Roy, the Bengali reformer, had advocated in English writing this and other reforms, the style of which Jeremy Bentham compared favourably with that of James Mill. David Hare, a Calcutta watchmaker, gave him strong support, and eventually in 1816 the Hindu college was founded at Calcutta for the instruction of Indians in English; and the decision of the government of India, in 1835, that its educational subsidies should promote mainly the study of European literature and science, found its natural sequel in the foundation, in 1857, during the very crisis of the mutiny, of universities in which English was to be the medium of instruction at Calcutta, Madras and Bombay. The government of India had set out to give its subjects, so far as might be, an English mind.

As a result of this policy, there is, in modern British India, a steady and increasing output of English literature written by Indians. But, as is only natural, so drastic an innovation as the complete changing of a people's literary language could not bear immediate results of value, and not only has the bulk of Anglo-Indian literature continued to be written by Englishmen, but, for a very long time, it remained doubtful whether Indians, could so completely become Englishmen in mind and thought as to add, except in the rarest and most exceptional cases, anything of lasting value to the roll of English literature.

While this remarkable change was beginning in India, Anglo-Indian writers were not idle. Heber, Bishop of Calcutta, claims attention here rather by his Narrative of a Journey from Calcutta to Bombay than by his few Anglo-Indian poems; Henry Louis Vivian Derozio, most famous of those of our Indian fellow-men who are neither exclusively European nor Indian but share the blood of both, put all the pathos and passion of his own sensitive nature into his metrical tale The Fakeer of Jungheera; Henry Meredith Parker is remembered not only as an actor and musician but as a poet, essayist and story-teller.

Among his productions was an Indian mythological narrative poem called The Draught of Immortality and two clever volumes of miscellaneous prose and verse entitled Bole Ponjis (The Punch bowl). Major David Lester Richardson, of the Bengal army, abandoned military life and devoted himself to education and literature. He takes rank among Anglo-Indian writers mainly as a literary critic, though he also wrote poetry and history. The titles of his books, such as Literary Leaves, Literary Chit-Chat, Literary Recreations, are an index of the general trend of his mind, and suggest that he was probably happier in his work at the Hindu college, to which, by Macaulay's influence, he was appointed in 1836 as professor of English literature, than he had been in his previous career. Henry Whitelock Torrens, who was secretary of the Asiatic society from 1840 to 1846, was a clever essayist as well as a journalist and scholar, and his scattered papers were deservedly collected and published at Calcutta in 1854. Sir Richard Francis Burton was in India during this period, but his fame cannot be said to be specially Anglo-Indian.

Of the historians during the period, James Grant Duff and Mountstuart Elphinstone are pre-eminent. Grant Duff's History of the Mahrattas (1826) and Elphinstone's History of India (1841) are two of the classics of Indian history. The romantic interest of the former book, the accurate though uninspiring conciseness of the second, and the pioneering ability shown by both in the untilled regions which they surveyed, gave these books a standing which they still hold, despite the advance of knowledge since they appeared. Other historians were Horace Hayman Wilson, the Sanskrit scholar, who continued and edited James Mill's History of British India; John Briggs, the translator of Ferishta's Muhammedan Power in India; Sir Henry Miers Elliot, the unwearied student of the history of Mussulman India, whose History of India as told by its own Historians was edited after his death by John Dowson; and Sir John Kaye, prominent in the history of Anglo-Indian letters as the founder, in 1844, of The Calcutta Review, to which he frequently contributed. He also, long after his departure from India, wrote Indian history voluminously, his History of the Sepoy War in India being his best known work.

7

The Metaphysical Poets

SAMUEL JOHNSON (1709-1784.)

The criticism of the 'metaphysical poets' occurs in the Life of Cowley, published as one of the _Lives of the Poets_ in 1780. The name 'metaphysical poetry' was first devised by Dryden, in his _Essay of Dramatic Poesy_. It was revived by Johnson, and is now generally accepted by historians of English literature. It is used by Johnson, as it was used by Dryden, to express the love of remote analogies, which was a mark of the poetry of Donne and those who wrote more or less after the manner of Donne. But it has a deeper meaning than was probably intended by its inventors. It is no unapt term to indicate the vein of weighty thought and brooding imagination which runs like a thread of gold through all the finer work of these poets. Johnson did no harm in calling attention to the extravagance of much of the imagery beloved by the lyric poets of the Stuart period. But it is unpardonable that he should have had no eye for the nobler and subtler qualities of their genius, and equally unpardonable that he should have drawn no distinction between three men so incomparable in degree and kind of power as Cleveland, Cowley, and Donne. Some remarks on the place of the metaphysical poets in English literature will be found in the Introduction.

Cowley, like other poets who have written with narrow views, and, instead of tracing intellectual pleasure to its natural sources in the mind of man, paid their court to temporary prejudices, has been at one time too much praised, and too much neglected at another.

Wit, like all other things subject by their nature to the choice of man, has its changes and fashions, and at different times takes different forms. About the beginning of the seventeenth century appeared a race of writers that may be termed the metaphysical poets; of whom, in a criticism on the works of Cowley, it is not improper to give some account.

The metaphysical poets were men of learning, and to show their learning was their whole endeavour; but, unluckily resolving to show it in rhyme, instead of writing poetry, they only wrote verses, and very often such verses as stood the trial of the finger better than of the ear; for the modulation was so imperfect, that they were only found to be verses by counting the syllables.

If the father of criticism has rightly denominated poetry, _an imitative art_, these writers will, without great wrong, lose their right to the name of poets; for they cannot be said to have imitated anything; they neither copied nature nor life; neither painted the forms of matter, nor represented the operations of intellect.

Those, however, who deny them to be poets, allow them to be wits. Dryden confesses of himself and his contemporaries that they fall below Donne in wit, but maintains that they surpass him in poetry.

If wit be well described by Pope, as being "that which has been often thought, but was never before so well expressed", they certainly never attained, nor ever sought it; for they endeavoured to be singular in their thoughts, and were careless of their diction. But Pope's account of wit is undoubtedly erroneous: he depresses it below its natural dignity, and reduces it from strength of thought to happiness of language.

If by a more noble and more adequate conception that be considered as wit which is at once natural and new, that which, though not obvious, is, upon its first production, acknowledged to be just; if it be that which he that never found it wonders how he missed; to wit of this kind the metaphysical poets have seldom risen. Their thoughts are often new, but seldom natural; they are not obvious, but neither are they just; and the reader, far from wondering that he missed them, wonders more frequently by what perverseness of industry they were ever found.

But wit, abstracted from its effects upon the hearer, may be more rigorously and philosophically considered as a kind of _discordia concors_; a combination of dissimilar images, or discovery of occult resemblances in things apparently unlike. Of wit, thus defined, they have more than enough. The most heterogeneous ideas are yoked by violence together; nature and art are ransacked for illustrations, comparisons, and allusions; their learning instructs, and their subtlety surprises; but the reader commonly thinks his improvement dearly bought, and, though he sometimes admires, is seldom pleased.

From this account of their compositions it will be readily inferred that they were not successful in representing or moving the affections.

As they were wholly employed on something unexpected and surprising, they had no regard to that uniformity of sentiment which enables us to conceive and to excite the pains and the pleasure of other minds: they never inquired what, on any occasion, they should have said or done; but wrote rather as beholders than partakers of human nature; as Beings looking upon good and evil, impassive and at leisure; as Epicurean deities making remarks on the actions of men and the vicissitudes of life without interest and without emotion. Their courtship was void of fondness, and their lamentation of sorrow. Their wish was only to say what they hoped had never been said before.

Nor was the sublime more within their reach than the pathetic; for they never attempted that comprehension and expanse of thought which at once fills the whole mind, and of which the first effect is sudden astonishment, and the second rational admiration. Sublimity is produced by aggregation, and littleness by dispersion. Great thoughts are always general, and consist in positions not limited by exceptions, and in descriptions not descending to minuteness. It is with great propriety that subtlety, which in its original import means exility of particles, is taken in its metaphorical meaning for nicety of distinction.

Those writers who lay on the watch for novelty could have little hope of greatness; for great things cannot have escaped former observation. Their attempts were always analytic; they broke every image into fragments: and could no more represent, by their slender conceits and laboured particularities, the prospects of nature or the scenes of life, than he who dissects a sunbeam with a prism can exhibit the wide effulgence of a summer noon.

What they wanted, however, of the sublime, they endeavoured to supply by hyperbole; their amplification had no limits; they left not only reason but fancy behind them; and produced combinations of confused magnificence that not only could not be credited, but could not be imagined.

Yet great labour, directed by great abilities, is never wholly lost: if they frequently threw away their wit upon false conceits, they likewise sometimes struck out unexpected truth: if their conceits were far-fetched, they were often worth the carriage. To write on their plan, it was at least necessary to read and think. No man could be born a metaphysical poet, nor assume the dignity of a writer, by descriptions copied from descriptions, by imitations borrowed from imitations, by traditional imagery and hereditary similes, by readiness of rhyme and volubility of syllables.

In perusing the works of this race of authors, the mind is exercised either by recollection or inquiry; either something already learned is to be retrieved, or something new is to be examined. If their greatness seldom elevates, their acuteness often surprises; if the imagination is not always gratified, at least the powers of reflection and comparison are employed; and in the mass of materials which ingenious absurdity has thrown together, genuine wit and useful knowledge may be sometimes found, buried perhaps in grossness of expression, but useful to those who know their value; and such as, when they are expanded to perspicuity and polished to elegance, may give lustre to works which have more propriety though less copiousness of sentiment.

This kind of writing, which was, I believe, borrowed from Marino [Footnote: As Marino's chief poem, _L'Adone_, was not published till 1623, and as most of Donne's poems must have been written earlier, this is very unlikely. Besides, the resemblance is more apparent than real. Metaphysical poetry was a native product. See Introduction.] and his followers, had been recommended by the example of Donne, a man of very extensive and various knowledge; and by Jonson, whose manner resembled that of Donne more in the ruggedness of his lines than in the cast of his sentiments.

When their reputation was high, they had undoubtedly more imitators than time has left behind. Their immediate successors, of whom any remembrance can be said to remain, were Suckling, Waller, Denham, Cowley, Cleveland, and Milton. Denham and Waller sought another way to fame, by improving the harmony of our numbers. Milton tried the metaphysic style only in his lines upon Hobson the Carrier. Cowley adopted it, and excelled his predecessors, having as much sentiment and more music. Suckling neither improved versification, nor abounded in conceits. The fashionable style remained chiefly with Cowley; Suckling could not reach it, and Milton disdained it.

Critical remarks are not easily understood without examples, and I have therefore collected instances of the modes of writing by which this species of poets, for poets they were called by themselves and their admirers, was eminently distinguished.

As the aūthors of this race were perhaps more desirous of being admired than understood, they sometimes drew their conceits from recesses of learning not very much frequented by common readers of poetry. Thus Cowley on _Knowledge_:

The sacred tree midst the fair orchard grew;

The phoenix Truth did on it rest.

And built his perfum'd nest,

That right Porphyrian tree which did true logick shew.

Each leaf did learned notions give,

And th' apples were demonstrative:

So clear their colour and divine,

The very shade they cast did other lights outshine.

On Anacreon continuing a lover in his old age:

Love was with thy life entwin'd,

Close as heat with fire is join'd,

A powerful brand prescrib'd the date

Of thine, like Meleager's fate.

The antiperistasis of age

More enflam'd thy amorous rage.

In the following verses we have an allusion to a Rabbinical opinion concerning Manna:

Variety I ask not: give me one

To live perpetually upon.

The person Love does to us fit,

Like manna, has the taste of all in it.

Thus Donne shows his medicinal knowledge in some encomiastic verses:

In everything there naturally grows

A Balsamum to keep it fresh and new,

If't were not injur'd by extrinsique blows;

Your youth and beauty are this balm in you.

But you, of learning and religion,

And virtue and such ingredients, have made

A mithridate, whose operation

Keeps off, or cures what can be done or said.

Though the following lines of Donne, on the last night of the year, have something in them too scholastic, they are not inelegant:

This twilight of two years, not past nor next,

Some emblem is of me, or I of this,

Who, meteor-like, of stuff and form perplext,

Whose what and where, in disputation is,

If I should call me any thing, should miss.

I sum the years and me, and find me not

Debtor to th' old, nor creditor to th' new,

That cannot say, my thanks I have forgot,

Nor trust I this with hopes: and yet scarce true

This bravery is, since these times shew'd me you.

--_Donne_.

Yet more abstruse and profound is Donne's reflection upon Man as a Microcosm:

If men be worlds, there is in every one

Something to answer in some proportion

All the world's riches: and in good men, this

Virtue, our form's form, and our soul's soul is.

Of thoughts so far-fetched as to be not only unexpected but unnatural, all their books are full.

TO A LADY, WHO WROTE POESIES FOR RINGS

They, who above do various circles find,
Say, like a ring th' aquator heaven does bind.
When heaven shall be adorn'd by thee,
(Which then more heaven than 't is, will be)
'T is thou must write the poesy there,
For it wanteth one as yet,
Though the sun pass through 't twice a year,
The sun, which is esteem'd the god of wit.
--_Cowley_.

The difficulties which have been raised about identity in philosophy are by Cowley, with still more perplexity, applied to Love:

Five years ago (says story) I lov'd you,
For which you call me most inconstant now;
Pardon me, madam, you mistake the man;
For I am not the same that I was then;
No flesh is now the same't was then in me,
And that my mind is chang'd yourself may see.
The same thoughts to retain still, and intents,
Were more inconstant far; for accidents
Must of all things most strangely inconstant prove,
If from one subject they t' another move:
My members then, the father members were
From whence these take their birth, which now are here.
If then this body love what th' other did,
'T were incest, which by nature is forbid.

The love of different women is, in geographical poetry, compared to travels, through different countries:

Hast thou not found each woman's breast

(The land where thou hast travelled)

Either by savages possest,

Or wild, and uninhabited?

What joy could'st take, or what repose,

In countries so uncIviliz'd as those?

Lust, the scorching dog-star, here

Rages with immoderate heat;

Whilst Pride, the rugged Northern Bear,

In others makes the cold too great.

And when these are temperate known,

The soil's all barren sand, or rocky stone.

--_Cowley_.

A lover, burnt up by his affections, is compared to Egypt:

The fate of Egypt I sustain,

And never feel the dew of rain.

From clouds which in the head appear;

But all my too much moisture owe

To overflowings of the heart below.

--_Cowley_.

The lover supposes his lady acquainted with the ancient laws of augury and rites of sacrifice:

And yet this death of mine, I fear,

Will ominous to her appear:

When found in every other part,

Her sacrifice is found without an heart.

For the last tempest of my death

Shall sigh out that too, with my breath.

That the chaos was harmonized, has been recited of old; but whence the different sounds arose remained for a modern to discover:

Th' ungovern'd parts no correspondence knew,

And artless war from thwarting motions grew;

Till they to number and fixt rules were brought.

Water and air he for the Tenor chose.

Earth made the Base, the Treble flame arose.

--_Cowley._

The tears of lovers are always of great poetical account, but Donne has extended them into worlds. If the lines are not easily understood, they may be read again:

On a round ball

A workman, that hath copies by, can lay

An Europe, Afric, and an Asia,

And quickly make that, which was nothing, all.

So doth each tear,

Which thee doth wear,

A globe, yea world, by that impression grow,

Till thy tears mixt with mine do overflow

This world, by waters sent from thee my heaven dissolved so.

On reading the following lines, the reader may perhaps cry out, "Confusion worse confounded":

Here lies a she sun, and a he moon here,

She gives the best light to his sphere,

Or each is both, and all, and so

They unto one another nothing owe.

--_Donne._

Who but Donne would have thought that a good man is a telescope?

Though God be our true glass, through which we see
All, since the being of all things is He,
Yet are the trunks, which do to us derive
Things, in proportion fit, by perspective
Deeds of good men; for by their living here,
Virtues, indeed remote, seem to be near.

Who would imagine it possible that in a very few lines so many remote ideas could be brought together?

Since't is my doom, Love's undershrieve,
Why this reprieve?
Why doth my She Advowson fly
Incumbency?
To sell thyself dost thou intend
By candle's end,
And hold the contrast thus in doubt,
Life's taper out?
Think but how soon the market fails,
Your sex lives faster than the males;
As if to measure age's span,
The sober Julian were th' account of man,
Whilst you live by the fleet Gregorian.
--_Cleveland_.

Of enormous and disgusting hyperboles, these may be examples:

By every wind, that comes this way,
Send me at least a sigh or two,
Such and so many I'll repay
As shall themselves make winds to get to you.
--_Cowley_.

In tears I'll waste these eyes,
By Love so vainly fed;
So lust of old the Deluge punished.
--_Cowley_.

All arm'd in brass the richest dress of war,
(A dismal glorious sight) he shone afar.
The sun himself started with sudden fright,
To see his beams return so dismal bright.
--_Cowley_.

An universal consternation:

His bloody eyes he hurls round, his sharp paws
Tear up the ground; then runs he wild about,
Lashing his angry tail and roaring out.
Beasts creep into their dens, and tremble there;
Trees, though no wind is stirring, shake with fear;
Silence and horror fill the place around:
Echo itself dares scarce repeat the sound.
--_Cowley_.

Their fictions were often violent and unnatural.

OF HIS MISTRESS BATHING

The fish around her crowded, as they do
To the false light that treacherous fishers shew,
And all with as much ease might taken be,
As she at first took me:
For ne'er did light so clear
Among the waves appear,
Though every night the sun himself set there.
--_Cowley_.

The poetical effect of a lover's name upon glass:

My name engrav'd herein
Doth contribute my firmness to this glass;
Which, ever since that charm, hath been
As hard as that which grav'd it was.

--_Donne_.

Their conceits were sometimes slight and trifling.

ON AN INCONSTANT WOMAN

He enjoys thy calmy sunshine now,
And no breath stirring hears,
In the clear heaven of thy brow,
No smallest cloud appears.
He sees thee gentle, fair and gay,
And trusts the faithless April of thy May.

--_Cowley_.

Upon a paper written with the juice of lemon, and read by the fire:

Nothing yet in thee is seen:
But when a genial heat warms thee within,
A new-born wood of various lines there grows;
Here buds an L, and there a B,
Here sprouts a V, and there a T,
And all the flourishing letters stand in rows.

--_Cowley_.

As they sought only for novelty, they did not much inquire whether their allusions were to things high or low, elegant or gross; whether they compared the little to the great, or the great to the little.

PHYSICK AND CHIRURGERY FOR A LOVER

Gently, ah gently, madam, touch
The wound, which you yourself have made;
That pain must needs be very much,
Which makes me of your hand afraid.
Cordials of pity give me now,
For I too weak for purgings grow.
--_Cowley_.

THE WORLD AND A CLOCK

Mahol, th' inferior world's fantastic face,
Through all the turns of matter's maze did trace;
Great Nature's well-set clock in pieces took;
On all the springs and smallest wheels did look
Of life and motion; and with equal art
Made up again the whole of every part.
--_Cowley_.

A coal-pit has not often found its poet; but, that it may not want its due honour, Cleveland has paralleled it with the sun:

The moderate value of our guiltless ore
Makes no man atheist, and no woman whore;
Yet why should hallow'd vestals' sacred shrine
Deserve more honour than a flaming mine?
These pregnant wombs of heat would fitter be
Than a few embers, for a deity.
Had he our pits, the Persian would admire
No sun, but warm's devotion at our fire:
He'd leave the trotting whipster, and prefer
Our profound Vulcan 'bove that waggoner.

For wants he heat or light? or would have store
Of both? 'tis here: and what can suns give more?
Nay, what's the sun but, in a different name,
A coal-pit rampant, or a mine on flame!
Then let this truth reciprocally run
The sun's heaven's coalery, and coals our sun.

DEATH, A VOYAGE

No family
E'er rigg'd a soul for heaven's discovery,
With whom more venturers might boldly dare
Venture their stakes, with him in joy to share.
--_Donne_.

Their thoughts and expressions were sometimes grossly absurd, and such as no figures or licence can reconcile to the understanding.

A LOVER NEITHER DEAD NOR ALIVE

Then down I laid my head,
Down on cold earth; and for a while was dead,
And my freed soul to a strange somewhere fled:
Ah, sottish soul, said I,
When back to its cage again I saw it fly:
Fool to resume her broken chain!
And row her galley here again!
Fool, to that body to return
Where it condemn'd and destin'd is to burn!
Once dead, how can it be,
Death should a thing so pleasant seem to thee,
That thou should'st come to live it o'er again in me?
--_Cowley_.

A LOVER'S HEART A HAND GRENADO

Wo to her stubborn heart, if once mine come
Into the self-same room,
'T will tear and blow up all within,
Like a grenado shot into a magazin.
Then shall Love keep the ashes, and torn parts,
Of both our broken hearts:
Shall out of both one new one make;
From hers th' allay; from mine, the metal take.
--_Cowley_.

THE POETICAL PROPAGATION OF LIGHT

The Prince's favour is diffus'd o'er all,
From which all fortunes, names, and natures fall;
Then from those wombs of stars, the Bride's bright eyes,
At every glance a constellation flies,
And sows the court with stars, and doth prevent
In light and power, the all-ey'd firmament:
First her eye kindles other ladies' eyes,
Then from their beams their jewels' lustres rise;
And from their jewels torches do take fire,
And all is warmth, and light, and good desire.
--_Donne_.

They were in very little care to clothe their notions with elegance of dress, and therefore miss the notice and the praise which are often gained by those who think less, but are more diligent to adorn their thoughts.

That a mistress beloved is fairer in idea than in reality is by Cowley thus expressed:

Thou in my fancy dost much higher stand,
Than woman can be plac'd by Nature's hand;

And I must needs, I'm sure, a loser be,
To change thee, as thou 'rt there, for very thee.

That prayer and labour should co-operate are thus taught by Donne:

In none but us, are such mixt engines found,
As hands of double office: for the ground
We till with them; and them to heaven we raise;
Who prayerless labours, or without this, prays,
Doth but one half, that's none.

By the same author, a common topic, the danger of procrastination, is thus illustrated:

--That which I should have begun
In my youth's morning, now late must be done;
And I, as giddy travellers must do,
Which stray or sleep all day, and having lost
Light and strength, dark and tir'd must then ride post.

All that Man has to do is to live and die; the sum of humanity is comprehended by Donne in the following lines:

Think in how poor a prison thou didst lie;
After, enabled but to suck and cry.
Think, when't was grown to most, 't was a poor inn,
A province pack'd up in two yards of skin,
And that usurp'd, or threaten'd with a rage
Of sicknesses, or their true mother, age.
But think that death hath now enfranchis'd thee;
Thou hast thy expansion now, and liberty;
Think, that a rusty piece discharg'd is flown
In pieces, and the bullet is his own,
And freely flies; this to thy soul allow,
Think thy shell broke, think thy soul hatched but now.

They were sometimes indelicate and disgusting. Cowley thus apostrophizes beauty:

--Thou tyrant, which leav'st no man free!

Thou subtle thief, from whom nought safe can be!

Thou murderer, which hast kill'd, and devil, which would'st damn me.

Thus he addresses his mistress:

Thou who, in many a propriety,

So truly art the sun to me.

Add one more likeness, which I'm sure you can,

And let me and my sun beget a man.

Thus he represents the meditations of a lover:

Though in thy thoughts scarce any tracts have been

So much as of original sin,

Such charms thy beauty wears as might

Desires in dying confest saints excite.

Thou with strange adultery

Dost in each breast a brothel keep;

Awake, all men do lust for thee,

And some enjoy thee when they sleep.

The true taste of tears:

Hither with crystal vials, lovers, come,

And take my tears, which are Love's wine,

And try your mistress' tears at home;

For all are false, that taste not just like mine.

--_Donne_.

This is yet more indelicate:

As the sweet sweat of roses in a still

As that which from chaf'd musk-cat's pores doth trill,

As th' almighty balm of th' early East,

Such are the sweet drops of my mistress' breast.

And on her neck her skin such lustre sets,

They seem no sweat-drops, but pearl coronets:

Rank sweaty froth thy mistress' brow defiles.

--_Donne_.

Their expressions sometimes raise horror, when they intend perhaps to be pathetic:

As men in hell are from diseases free,

So from all other ills am I.

Free from their known formality:

But all pains eminently lie in thee.

--_Cowley_.

They were not always strictly curious, whether the opinions from which they drew their illustrations were true; it was enough that they were popular. Bacon remarks that some falsehoods are continued by tradition, because they supply commodious allusions.

It gave a piteous groan, and so it broke;

In vain it something would have spoke:

The love within too strong for't was,

Like poison put into a Venice-glass.

--_Cowley_.

In forming descriptions, they looked out, not for images, but for conceits. Night has been a common subject, which poets have contended to adorn. Dryden's Night is well known; Donne's is as follows:

Thou seest me here at midnight, now all rest:

Time's dead low-water; when all minds divest

To-morrow's business, when the labourers have

Such rest in bed, that their last church-yard grave,

Subject to change, will scarce be a type of this;
Now when the client, whose last hearing is
To-morrow, sleeps; when the condemned man,
Who when he opens his eyes, must shut them then
Again by death, although sad watch he keep,
Doth practise dying by a little sleep,
Thou at this midnight seest me.

It must be, however, confessed of these writers that if they are upon common subjects often unnecessarily and unpoetically subtle, yet where scholastic speculation can be properly admitted, their copiousness and acuteness may justly be admired. What Cowley has written upon Hope shows an unequalled fertility of invention:

Hope, whose weak being ruin'd is,
Alike if it succeed, and if it miss;
Whom good or ill does equally confound,
And both the horns of Fate's dilemma wound.
Vain shadow, which dost vanish quite,
Both at full noon and perfect night!
The stars have not a possibility
Of blessing thee;
If things then from their end we happy call,
'T is hope is the most hopeless thing of all.
Hope, thou bold taster of delight,
Who, whilst thou shouldst but taste, devour'st it quite!
Thou bring'st us an estate, yet leav'st us poor,
By clogging it with legacies before!
The joys, which we entire should wed,
Come deflower'd virgins to our bed;
Good fortune without gain imported be,

Such mighty customs paid to thee:
For joy, like wine, kept close does better taste;
If it take air before, its spirits waste.

To the following comparison of a man that travels and his wife that stays at home, with a pair of compasses, it may be doubted whether absurdity or ingenuity has the better claim:

Our two souls therefore, which are one,
Though I must go, endure not yet
A breach, but an expansion,
Like gold to airy thinness beat.
If they be two, they are two so
As stiff twin-compasses are two,
Thy soul, the fixt foot, makes no show
To move, but doth, if th' other do.
And though it in the centre sit,
Yet when the other far doth roam,
It leans, and hearkens after it,
And grows erect, as that comes home.
Such wilt thou be to me, who must
Like th' other foot, obliquely run.
Thy firmness makes my circle just,
And makes me end where I begun._
--Donne._

In all these examples it is apparent that whatever is improper or vicious is produced by a voluntary deviation from nature in pursuit of something new and strange, and that the writers fail to give delight by their desire of exciting admiration.

Bibliography

Allen, Ernst: *The English Novel: a Short Critical History*, London: Phoenix House, 1954.

Amitav Ghosh's: *The Shadow Lines: Critical Essays*, New Delhi, Atlantic, 2002.

Arthur Miller: *As a Critic of Drama*, New Delhi, Anmol, 2004.

Authors, Texts, Issues: *Essays on Indian Literature*, Delhi, Pencraft International, 2003.

Ayoni and Other Stories: *A Collection of Telugu Short Stories*, New Delhi, Stree Katha, 2001.

Ball, M. J. : *Phonetics: The Science of Speech*, London, Arnold. 1999.

Bennett, J. A. W.: *Middle English Literature*, Oxford, Clarendon Press, 1986.

Bentley, Eades: *The Jacobean and Caroline Stage*, Oxford, Clarendon Press, 1941.

Beyond Borders: *An Anthology of SAARC Poetry*, Noida, Rainbow, 2002.

Bhattacharyya, Nath: *Indian Religious Historiography*, New Delhi, Munshiram Manoharlal Publishers, 1996.

Brown, J. M.: *Ireland in Fiction; a Guide to Irish Novels, Tales, Romances, and Folk-lore*, London: Maunsel, 1919.

Bush, Douglas: *English Literature in the Earlier Seventeenth Century, 1600-1660*, Oxford, Clarendon Press, 1962.

Cahalan, M.: *The Irish Novel: a Critical History*, Boston, Twayne Publishers, 1988.

Caidin, Martin: *The Tigers are Burning*, NY, Hawthorn Books, 1974.

Cavanagh, John: *British Theatre: a Bibliography, 1901 to 1985*, Hampshire, Motley, 1989.

Chambers, Kerchever: *English Literature at the Close of the Middle Ages*, New York: Oxford University Press, 1947.

Classe, A.: *The Rhythm of English Prose*, Oxford, Blackwell, 1939.

Couper-Kuhlen, E.: *An Introduction to English Prosody*, London, Edward Arnold, 1986.

Courthope, John: *A History of English Poetry*, London, MacMillan and Co., 1903.

Crystal, D.: *Prosodic Systems and Intonation in English*, Cambridge, Cambridge University Press, 1969.

Davis, Brian L. : *Uniforms and Insignia of the Luftwaffe*, London, Arms and Armor, 1999.

Davis, Gwenn: *Drama by Women to 1900: a Bibliography of American and British Writers*, London, Mansell, 1992.

Derek, Albert: *Old English and Middle English Poetry*, London, Routledge & K. Paul, 1977.

Dobree, Bonamy: *English Literature in the Early Eighteenth Century, 1700-1740*, Oxford, Clarendon Press, 1959.

Edmund Spenser: *A Critical Study*, New Delhi, Anmol Pub., 2005.

Edmund, Kerchever: *English Literature at the Close of the Middle Ages*, New York: Oxford University Press, 1947.

Ferrence, G.: *Deadly Fashion: the Rise and Fall of Cigarette Smoking in North America*, New York, Garland, 1989.

Francis, Russell: *The Scottish Novel: from Smollett to Spark*, Cambridge, Harvard University Press, 1978.

Gerald, Eades: *The Jacobean and Caroline Stage*, Oxford, Clarendon Press, 1941.

Halliday, M. A. K.: *Intonation and Grammar in British English*, The Hague, Mouton, 1967.

Harivansh R.B.: *In the Afternoon of Time: An Autobiography*, New Delhi, Penguin, 2001.

Hart, Russell: *The Scottish Novel: from Smollett to Spark*, Cambridge, Harvard University Press, 1978.

Hogan, Robert Goode: *The Modern Irish Drama: a Documentary History*, NJ: Humanities Press, 1975.

Jack, Ian Robert James: *English Literature, 1815-1832*, Oxford, Clarendon Press, 1963.

James Baldwin: *Protest and Beyond: A Study of Afro-American Fiction*, New Delhi, Rajat Pub., 2005.

James, Ernest: *Principles of Textual Criticism*, San Marino, Huntington Library, 1972.

James, Runcieman: *English Literature of the Late Seventeenth Century*, New York, Oxford University Press, 1969.

Jhumpa Lahiri: *The Master Storyteller: A Critical Response to Interpreter of Maladies*, New Delhi, KPH, 2002.

Knowles, G.: *Patterns of Spoken English: An Introduction to English Phonetics*, London, Longman, 1987.

Laver, J.: *Principles of Phonetics*, Cambridge, Cambridge University Press, 1994.

Logan, P.: *The Later Jacobean and Caroline Dramatists*, Lincoln, University of Nebraska Press, 1978.

Matricardi, Paolo: *Complete Book of World War II Combat Aircraft*, NY, Military Press, 1988

Naipaul, V.S. : *A House for Mr. Biswas: With an Introduction by Ian Buruma*, New Delhi, Penguin, 1992.

Nath, Narendra: *Indian Religious Historiography*, New Delhi, Munshiram Manoharlal Publishers, 1996.

Neil Bissoondath: *Indo-Caribbean-Canadian Diaspora*, New Delhi, Rawat, 2005.

Nicoll, Allardyce: *A History of English Drama, 1660-1900*, Cambridge, University Press, 1952-65.

Perkins, David: *A History of Modern Poetry*, Cambridge, Belknap Press of Harvard University Press, 1976.

Philip Roth: *A Novelist in Crisis*, New Delhi, Classical Publishing, 2001.

Pierre, Turner: *Uniforms and Insignia of the Luftwaffe*, London, Arms and Armor, 1999.

Rahilly, J.: *Phonetics: The Science of Speech*, London, Arnold, 1999.

Raja Rao: *The Fictionist*, Delhi, B.R. Publishing, 2003.

Robert, Lewis: *The Black Corps*, Madison, University of Wisconsin Press, 1983.

Rogers, H.: *The Sounds of Language: An Introduction to Phonetics*, Harlow, Longman, 2000.

Royle, Trevor: *The Macmillan Companion to Scottish Literature*, London, MacMillan Reference Books, 1983.

Salzman, Paul: *English Prose Fiction, 1558-1700: a Critical History*, Oxford, Clarendon Press, 1985.

Seidlhofer, B.: *Pronunciation, Oxford*, Oxford University Press, 1994.

Stevenson, Lionel: *Victorian Fiction: a Guide to Research*, Cambridge, Harvard University Press, 1966.

Sutherland, John: *The Stanford Companion to Victorian Fiction*, Stanford, Stanford University Press, 1989.

Terence, P.: *The Later Jacobean and Caroline Dramatists*, Lincoln, University of Nebraska Press, 1978.

Underhill, A.: *Sound Foundations*, London, Heineman, 1994.

Vann, J. Don: *Victorian Novels in Serial*, New York, Modern Language Association of America, 1985.

Vikram Seth: *Multiple Locations, Multiple Affiliation*, New Delhi, Rawat, 2001.

Wearing, J. P.: *The London Stage, 1890-1899: a Calendar of Plays and Players*, NJ, Scarecrow Press, 1976.

Wickham, Glynne William Gladstone: *Early English Stages, 1300 to 1660*, London, Routledge and Paul; 1959.

William Blake: *A Critical Study*, New Delhi, Anmol, 2005.

William, John: *A History of English Poetry*, London, MacMillan and Co., 1903.

Yeats, W.B. : *Poetry and Plays*, New Delhi, Atlantic, 2002.

INDEX

❑❑❑